WHAT'S
RIGHT
WITH YOU

Debunking Dysfunction and Changing Your Life

BARRY DUNCAN, PSY.D.
Author of *The Heroic Client*

Health Communications, Inc.
Deerfield Beach, Florida

www.hcibooks.com

Library of Congress Cataloging-in-Publication Data

Duncan, Barry L.
    What's right with you : debunking dysfunction and changing your life /
Barry Duncan.
        p. cm.
    Includes bibliographical references.
    ISBN 0-7573-0254-8
    1. Client-centered psychotherapy. 2. Resilience (Personality trait) 3. Self-help
techniques. 4. Self-esteem. 5. Self-actualization (Psychology). I. Title.

    RC481.D863 2005
    616.89'14—dc22

                                                                2005040243

©2005 Barry Duncan
ISBN 0-7573-0254-8

Publisher: Health Communications, Inc.
            3201 S.W. 15th Street
            Deerfield Beach, FL 33442–8190

R-06-12

Cover design by Larissa Hise Henoch
Inside book design by Dawn Von Strolley Grove

Dedicated to the memory of

Lee Duncan

who taught me about
heroism and resilience

Contents

Acknowledgments

I remain indebted to my clients, who continue to teach me to do good work by depending on what's right with them. I would also like to pay tribute to my mentors from the Wright State University School of Professional Psychology: Scott Fraser, Steve McConnell and Russ Bent, not only for their selfless teaching and guidance but also for planting the seeds that grew into this book. I am particularly thankful to the following folks who read drafts of the book and gave me feedback: Roger Ferguson, Nick Drury, John Rose, Dan Smith, Gerard Medicis, Leonard Bohanon, Scott Williams, William Chase, and especially Jo McDermott and Brian DeSantis. I owe an incalculable debt to my friend and colleague Jacqueline Sparks, who tirelessly read draft after draft and whose perspective greatly enhanced the message of this book, as well as just about everything else. I am also grateful to Bill Wiggin, webmaster of www.heartandsoulofchange.com, and to all my colleagues at the Heart and Soul of Change Project, too many names to mention, for the inspiration to try to make a difference. I owe more than I can say to my best friend, Joe Rock, whose inimitable wit and unswerving support has never failed to give me just what I need. My family also deserves special mention— sons, Jesse (a Marine like his grandfather) and Matt (my favorite hockey player)—for their continued tolerance of my idealistic pursuits, and my mom and sisters—Doris Duncan, Linda Meyer and Sandra Blair—for always being there. A special thanks to Mary Susan Haynes, Bob Bohanske, and George Braucht for teaching me about recovery and peer support and for applying the ideas in this book to the training of peer support specialists. George and Neil Kaltenecker founded the Certified Addiction Recovery Empowerment Specialist (CARES) Academy under the auspices of the Georgia Council on Substance Abuse. The 40 hour CARES Academy trains people in recovery to deliver peer recovery support service. I feel especially indebted to HCI for enabling my passion for this material to become manifest and to Elisabeth Rinaldi for her invariable cheerfulness and hard work. Finally, I would like to thank Peter Lorenz for encouraging me to write the book I always wanted to write.

Preface

The spirit of self-help is the root of all genuine growth in the individual; and, exhibited in the lives of many, it constitutes the true source of national vigor and strength.

Samuel Smiles[1]

My dad, Lee Duncan, fled the hopeless poverty of an Appalachian hillside and an emerging violent confrontation with his stepfather (that he later resolved) by joining the Army at the ripe age of fifteen. A year later, he was at Pearl Harbor when it was bombed in 1941. His frightened mother wrote the commander of the base informing him that my father was not yet of age, and he was honorably discharged. Less than a year later, Dad reenlisted in the Marines and was quickly off to the South Pacific. Subsequently, he fought on Saipan during the bloody banzai charge and was on Iwo Jima when the raising of the flag was forever captured as a symbol of our freedom.

Lee Duncan received citations for his courage under fire. But my dad never bragged about his heroism—I had to pry these stories out of him and did not learn of some of them until he lay dying on a hospital bed. Like many of the Greatest Generation, he was only doing his job, and gladly. Dad was always careful not to glorify war and made it a point to bring to my attention the horror inherent in young people sacrificing their lives. Right after the war, he and his new bride, Doris, my mom, headed north for Ohio to find work in the factories. They worked like dogs but were frequently laid off and had to return to Kentucky to keep from starving. But they didn't give up. Finally, they gained enough seniority to maintain employment. They bought a house and realized the American dream.

Years later, Dad took a supervisor position at the factory and was promoted to shift foreman. He worked under several bosses until finally, when he was close to the early retirement he dreamed of, a new manager took over his department. They didn't get along—at all. Their conflicts escalated and, unfortunately, Dad was not political or strategic in his interactions with the new manager. Probably sealing Dad's fate, the plant manager, who thought that Dad walked on water because of his high production, was transferred. The new department manager fired my dad.

He was devastated. As with most men of his era, his identity was wrapped up in his job. But things got worse. Dad started having chest pains that resulted in an emergency admission for bypass surgery. While a commonplace procedure today (although not much easier), in 1977 it was relatively new and scary. My dad was fifty-two years old and faced a very uncertain future: no job and questionable health. He felt terribly wronged, betrayed and defeated, and he became very depressed.

My dad's response to adversity left a huge impression on me. Lee Duncan was no superman, and he was not perfect, but he certainly was heroic. In light of his war record, he may have been heroic in the traditional sense of the word, but he was also heroic as a human being. In truth, there was a lot right about him.

As soon as he was medically cleared, he went back to work in the factory, in a different department but the same factory that had turned its back on his thirty-plus years of dedicated service. Although he had been fired from his management position, he was permitted to return to the factory as a laborer. Most people saw this as the ultimate humiliation and totally unfathomable.

I asked him how he did it, how he faced that day of going back. Dad thought for a while and, in characteristic fashion, said there is no shame in working for a living, no matter what the job entailed. And then he said that it was the only way he could be who he was—that staying debilitated by his heart condition or discouraged by his firing was just not him. When he looked back on his life and the things he had faced, from a harsh stepfather, abject poverty, the tragedy of war and moving from the hills with nothing but his sixth-grade education to working three jobs to feed his family, he concluded that if he could handle those situations, he could handle this one—that within him was all he needed to answer this call to face adversity.

And he did with grace and dignity—so much so that he was once again promoted to supervisor in the new department. My mother, with her unwavering support and tenacious belief in her husband, was integral to my father's resilience, as she has been to mine at many different points in my life. Dad worked as a supervisor until he realized another of his dreams—retiring to Florida and fishing every day.

As a young man, with the lessons learned from my parents in hand, I began my training to become a psychologist. I was soon disheartened to discover that the mental health field was utterly obsessed with viewing people as mental invalids. In fact, I learned that the defining question that eclipsed all others was "What's wrong with you?" But it was more than a guiding question; it seemed to be the field's very mission to hunt down pathology—often hidden in such a way that only an expert could find it—lurking everywhere, waiting to strike its hapless prey like a monster in a bad horror movie. This view of people as damaged goods, hopeless victims of past trauma or their own biochemistry, just didn't fit my experience.

Over the years, I was delighted to discover that this pervasive attitude didn't fit scientific research about change either. Change, in truth, is far more about what's right with the people attempting it—their strengths, resources, ideas and relational support—than the labels they are branded with or even the methods the therapist uses. This information resonated with my experience, and I finally found a home in helping clients harness their abilities to solve life struggles, as well as doing my best to influence the mental health field to abandon the self-serving view of people as sick, fragile and incompetent. My efforts (along with those of my colleagues at the Heart and Soul of Change Project have spawned a worldwide "Heroic Client" movement based on the desire to give clients a voice in their own treatment and applying the bottom line of over fifty years of research about change.

And that bottom line—you are the engine of change. Change happens by marshaling your inherent abilities, *what's right with you,* to address the situation at hand; in the drama of change, you are the hero or heroine. This book translates this central finding and others from scientific research into easy, practical steps to make meaningful changes in your life.

What's Right with You also makes "outcome management"— a revolutionary innovation that is taking the world of psychotherapy, peer recovery support and other change facilitation services by storm—available to you so that you can create the best possible chance for personal transformation. Those of you in recovery and looking to help others in their journey will find the approach and tools in this book useful in your role as a recovery coach. My colleagues and I have been pioneers in this sea change in mental health, and this book brings this exciting new development, via practical tools, to you. This book not only provides many options to address your concerns, but also shows you how to measure your change and switch plans quickly when the provided assessment tool reveals no benefit.

Although I am convinced that you have the innate ability to make significant changes in your life, this book is not a replacement for therapy if you are thinking about suicide or if violence or its threat are a part of your day in any way. Please consult a mental health professional and know that there are endless possibilities for safety and relief.

It is my hope that this book inspires you to bring out your best to overcome life challenges—that you ask not "What's wrong with me?" but rather "What's right with me?" to solve the problems that concern you the most and become the person you were made to be.

Barry Duncan, Psy.D.
Jensen Beach, Florida

I

You Have Always
Had the Power

Those who wish to sing always find a song.
—Swedish proverb

This book is about change. Maybe you've tried to change before and have not had the success you hoped for. Maybe someone has told you it can't be done or achieving it will be, at best, an arduous and lifetime task. Or maybe you've been told that, if change does happen, it will be small and ultimately less than what you desire. This book will not try to convince you to be "realistic" or to settle for a glass that's half full. Nor will it detail your dysfunction, find your faults or identify what you are missing as a human being—this is not another book about what's wrong with you. Instead, it is about the plain fact that change is an inevitable part of existence and that what's right with you plays the biggest role in making change happen. How do I know this? As a clinical psychologist for over twenty years, I have witnessed countless acts of change from ordinary folks of all ages, shapes, sizes, stripes and flavors. I have seen people riddled with self-loathing, battling alcohol or drugs, struggling with intolerable marriages, terrorized by inexplicable voices, oppressed by their children's problems, traumatized by past or current life circumstances and tormented by unwanted thoughts. But no matter how troubled they were, no matter how distressing their situations, no matter how hopeless they felt, most found within themselves exactly what was needed to move forward in their lives—not fixed or cured, but no longer reading their life story from the section entitled "Future Dismal, Prospects Bleak." And so can you. By recruiting your natural human resiliency, the possibility of a better future can be first imagined and then actualized.

Innumerable times I have seen people triumph over adversity and turn tragedy into the dogged pursuit of a better life. These folks had no superpowers; they took no magic potions. Nor had they embarked on pilgrimages to receive wisdom from the masters or acquired a mythic sword to slay the fire-breathing dragon of disaster and destitution that had become their lives. In truth, they possessed nothing that you do not already have.

In my practice with thousands of people facing the worst of human dilemmas, I have consistently observed momentous change by everyday people. How did they accomplish these seemingly miraculous transformations? They found the reservoir of their own resources, immersed themselves in this natural pool of strengths and emerged with all they needed to resolve the challenge before them. They discovered what was *right* with them.

Consider the heroic story of Erica, a woman in her midthirties who came into therapy searching for an identity that she believed she had lost. All her life, Erica had wanted to be a police officer. As a teenager, she rode with state troopers, and as a young woman, she became the first female to graduate from the police academy. Erica lived her dream as an officer for several years, until a drunk driver plunged her into a coma that lasted two years. In a triumph of biomedicine, an experimental drug revived her, although she was left with some limitations and periodic seizures that made it impossible to work as a police officer. Without this identity she had devoted her life to achieving, she was no longer certain who she was.

Erica explained that she felt at a dead end in her life. Having recovered enough to go back to work of some kind, she could not even imagine a backup dream now that her career in police work seemed over. To complicate matters, Erica was also wrestling with the idea of being "disabled," a word she despised.

She recognized that she had some limitations and could not perform the strenuous duties she had once dispatched with ease. Still, the word stuck in her craw. As we explored her experiences on the path to recovery, I found myself amazed by her courage, resilience and wisdom. Here was a woman who had it all and lost it, who defied others' expectations of what she could and could not do many times—early on, when she became the first female graduate of the academy; later, when she unexpectedly came out of a coma; and now, despite her problems with seizures, she was fighting the expectations of her "disabled" label. She knew there was much more to her than any description of her disability could begin to capture. I knew it, too, as would anyone who spent any time getting to know her. I told Erica that one of the things I liked most about her was her refusal to accept her disability—it was a sure sign of her strength and not a resistance to accepting her limitations, as others had suggested.

As we discussed her incredible determinism, Erica told me that it had occurred to her that she might pursue a career teaching police officers. That pronouncement was a crucial step in Erica's journey toward reclaiming her life. She did not end up as a training officer, but she was able to reestablish her relationship with the work she loved by becoming a dispatcher. This satisfied Erica's itch for reconnecting with police work, which, for her, was a key to a meaningful life.

I don't mention my experience with Erica as an example of a therapeutic miracle—in fact, just the reverse. I offered Erica no irresistibly insightful pronouncements, no magic pills or silver bullet cures, just a supportive relationship that showcased her talents and fortitude. As it turns out, fifty years of research from psychotherapy about the factors that contribute to change confirm my experience with Erica; five decades of scientific studies indicate that the client is actually the single most potent factor, contributing an impressive *40 percent* of how change occurs.[2] In fact, the total matrix of who they are—their strengths and resources, their social supports, even fortuitous events that weave in and out of their lives—matters more than anything physicians or therapists might do. These factors might include persistence, openness, faith, optimism, a supportive grandmother, membership in a religious community, or a sense of personal responsibility, or in Erica's case, a refusal to accept her disability—all operative factors in a person's life *before* he or she enters therapy. They also include interactions between inner strengths and happenstance or luck, such as a new job, a marriage or a crisis successfully negotiated.

The idea that the individual's innate abilities are the central feature of any change endeavor may be surprising to you. Typically, when therapy is portrayed to nontherapists, it is easy to form the impression that it operates with technological precision. In movies and television melodramas, psychiatrists, psychologists and other mental health professionals sit high in the psychological saddle, displaying almost divine wisdom. After a gut-wrenching encounter with his or her internal demons, the patient is frequently shown departing the doctor's office irrevocably changed. It is almost as though he or she went in as a Saturn and left as a Lexus. Let's face it: this is inspirational entertainment at its best.

Contrary to popular myth, however, people do not leave therapists' offices with anything they did not already possess in some way. In truth, therapists and doctors are like the apprentice monks in one ancient Zen story who are seeking enlightenment and counseled to observe strict silence. Upon hearing this, the first young monk responds impetuously, "Then I shall not say a word." The second monk then chastises the first, saying, "Ha, you have already spoken." "Both of you are stupid," the third monk remarks and then asks, "Why did you talk?" In a proud voice, the fourth monk concludes, "I am the only one who has not said anything!"

Proponents of the various treatments are not unlike these four apprentice monks competing to show their unique grasp of the truth. All are eager to demonstrate their special insight into the mysteries of the human mind and the superiority of their remedies. Yet while the number of therapy models has proliferated, mushrooming from sixty to more than four hundred since the mid-1960s, decades of clinical research have not found any one theory, model, method or package of techniques to be reliably better than any other. No particular therapeutic school can claim superiority—not Freudian or cognitive-behavioral or medication or you name the latest from the therapeutic boutique of treatments. In fact, mountains of clinical studies indicate that the different therapy models and medications work about equally well.[3] The competition among treatments amounts to little more than the competition among aspirin, Advil and Tylenol. All of them relieve pain and work better than no treatment at all. None stands head and shoulders above the rest.

So what does this mean? It simply means that *your* ability to change transcends any differences among the different approaches. The methods work about equally well because people in distress capitalize on what each therapeutic model provides to address their problems—people take what is offered and make the best of it. They are active participants hunting for a more satisfying life and will use whatever lies before them to inspire positive change. *Change is far more about the person than the treatment.*

If people, not the methods, are really the kings and queens of change, then self-help material should be as useful as seeing a therapist or taking a drug. And it is. Large-scale studies have found that self-help treatments, such as self-help books, are as effective as therapy or medication for a wide range of problems. People seek out the resources they need to make the changes they desire. This research makes clear that the most influential contributor to change is YOU—not the therapy, not the method, not the helper, not the medicine.[4]

Consider a Gallup poll of one thousand Americans that revealed that 90 percent had overcome a significant health, emotional, addiction or lifestyle problem in the recent past. Human beings have remarkable resilience and recuperative abilities and triumph over the adversity of life with amazing regularity. While some individuals are helped by sharing their abusive histories with therapists or by taking drugs, many, many more overcome their horrendous pasts or other life struggles without treatment. In truth, change is a naturally occurring by-product of human experience.

> **CHECKPOINT:** What you bring to the table of change is most important—the main course regardless of the style or type of cuisine. If the treatment method was the pièce de résistance, then uniform results across different approaches and self-help would not be the norm, and people could not change on their own. Clinical research points to the inevitable conclusion that the engine of change is you.

The Pie of Change

The person who says it cannot be done should not interrupt the person who is doing it.

Chinese proverb

Figure 1.1 on page 8 depicts what research says about the percentage contribution of four factors to change.[5] Think of change as your favorite pie. You are the filling. The main ingredient to any pie is the filling, be it chocolate, custard, rhubarb or lemon. There is little point to the pie without it. Eating a pie without filling is like trying to change without your active involvement, without your resources, abilities and ideas. This book will show you how to rally these inherent strengths—what's right with you—to stand against and defeat the problems that concern you the most.

Relational support, accounting for 30 percent of how change occurs, is the crust or container for the filling. A supportive relationship accommodates you comfortably while allowing your resources to take center stage. The crust provides the container that allows the filling to be appreciated. Therapy provides a supportive context for change, but so can the important people in your life. If you desire a companion in your quest for something

FIGURE 1.1 The Pie of Change

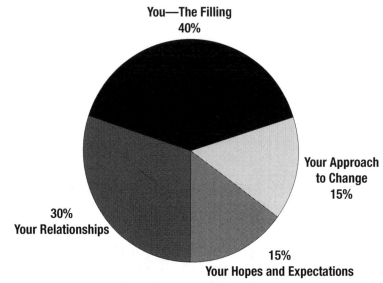

You—The Filling
40%

**Your Approach
to Change
15%**

30%
Your Relationships

15%
Your Hopes and Expectations

better, this book will demonstrate how you can recruit a "change partner" to encourage your progress toward your final destination.

The pie's mouthwatering visual presentation, enticing aroma and aroused hopes for culinary delight illustrate *expectancy*—a factor that contributes about 15 percent to change. Starting any change endeavor tantalizes you with visions of a delicious future, offering a healthy helping of hope to a sometimes distasteful present. *What's Right with You* builds on your hopes and expectations by helping you develop a plan that resonates with your own ideas and fits your sensibilities about how you can change.

Finally, the actual *approach* that is used to address a given concern covers only about 15 percent of how change happens and is best understood as the meringue on the pie. The meringue enhances the appearance of the pie and embellishes its taste but cannot stand well on its own, lest it run and lose its shape and definition. Without the rest of pie to give it form and substance, the meringue is nothing but fluff. The approach provides the means to an end and focuses your efforts, but it is meaningless without the benefit of your resources and ideas and active application. And the approach is certainly nothing but fluff if it doesn't deliver results—if it does not help you reach your goals. To ensure that the methods you choose for your change plan really get you where you want to go, this book will help you monitor your progress with a research-tested tool so that you know sooner rather than later if your strategy is working—and if not, practical suggestions for immediate modifications will get you back on track.

The secret is out! For you to change, you likely do not need to find a guru or learn any complex theory of human behavior or take any magic pills. Like Dorothy in *The Wizard of Oz*, you have always had the power to get back to Kansas. Research shows us that change in therapy does not come about from the special powers or authority of any particular physician or therapist. There are no sages or miracle cures. *Change principally results from empowering your preexisting abilities and restoring hope.*

Although my own experience in my family and decades of research have convinced me that the individual is most responsible for any changes that occur, an irrepressible sixteen-year-old named Tamara taught me the same lesson many years ago. To help make ends meet when I was working on my doctorate, I worked in a residential treatment center for troubled adolescents. During a period when the psychiatrist was on vacation and the center director was unable to cover for him, Tamara was admitted to the center. I was assigned her case and saw her every day in therapy, as well as in the group sessions I conducted. Tamara was like many of the kids, abused in all ways imaginable (and some ways you wouldn't want to imagine), drop-kicked from one foster home to another, with periodic suicide attempts and trips to hospitals and runaway shelters. In spite of all that, she was a pure delight—creative, funny and hopeful for a future far different than her childhood. The therapy went great, we hit it off famously, and Tamara settled in and started attending high school for the first time in many months.

Three weeks after her arrival, the psychiatrist returned and prescribed an antidepressant and lithium for Tamara. I was surprised by her reaction. Tamara adamantly opposed taking the medication—she said she had been down that road before. But her voice went unheard. I protested to the psychiatrist, citing evidence of how well she was doing, but to no avail. I was only a mental health grunt and a student to boot. I argued that forcing meds on Tamara could be harmful, but he did not listen. And it was.

Tamara soon ran away and went on a three-day binge of alcohol and drugs. A carload of men picked her up hitchhiking and ended the ride with a gang rape. Adding insult to injury, Tamara was forcefully injected with sedatives when the police brought her back to the center. When Tamara described this experience, she saw the horror on my face and reassured me that she had suffered far worse indignities than being forcefully tranquilized. It was little solace for either of us.

Tamara persisted in her ardent protests against the medication. I encouraged her to talk to the center director. Rather than listening, however, the director admonished her for resisting her treatment. Energized by Tamara's tenacity, I decided to investigate and spent the rest of the week in the medical school library. In contrast to what I had been told, little was known about how the drugs actually worked or what caused so-called mental illnesses. Furthermore, I was shocked to find that there was no scientific support, not one study, for prescribing these medications to children—let alone multiple drugs. Finally, and perhaps most appalling, the very helpfulness of medication was suspect—success rates were often barely better than sugar pills.

What did I get when I confronted the psychiatrist with these facts? Fired. Remarkably, Tamara transcended these experiences. She later wrote me and thanked me for supporting her voice in her own treatment. At age nineteen and on her own—away from the foster homes and residential centers—Tamara was a self-supporting new mother who also was attending the local community college part-time in preparation to become a counselor.

Tamara gave me hope. My experience with her taught me about the abuses of the mental health system and inspired me to spend much of my professional career fighting to include clients in all decisions that affect their well-being.[6] But perhaps more important, she taught me something about people and life: the resilience of the human spirit is infinite. Tamara came back from the most horrific of circumstances, and so could others—*so can you.*

Diseases, Disorders, Dysfunctions, Deficits, Disabilities—The Killer Ds

When money speaks, the truth keeps silent.
                              Russian proverb

This is not, however, the message that is delivered or embraced in American culture or increasingly across the world. Instead we are subjected to a 24/7 bombardment of misinformation that tells us we are not resourceful, strong or heroic, but rather that we are sick and getting sicker, victims of past or current trauma, or, even more pronounced of late, helplessly falling prey to our own biochemistry—the focus is overwhelmingly on what's wrong with us. According to the president's New Freedom Commission of Mental Health (2003), many people in the United States, including children, have signs and symptoms of a mental illness or substance abuse disorder, yet not all of those suffering are receiving appropriate treatment. Higher and higher rates of mental disorders (up to one-third of Americans, some say) continue to be reported in studies in the bible of mental illness, the *Diagnostic and Statistical Manual of Mental Disorders (DSM)* of the American Psychiatric Association.

The question, of course, is why? Some blame the rising divorce rate, others the decline of the traditional family; some emphasize the stress and trauma associated with modern life; still others fault the lack of services for those at risk. Another possibility is simply the rising number of diagnosable conditions. Consider that the *DSM* has itself experienced a dramatic growth in size over the last several decades. The sheer number of categories jumped from sixty-six in the first edition (1952) to well over three hundred in its current rendition. Apparently we are sick and getting sicker by the minute. Renowned psychiatrist Jerome Frank's ironic observation is being borne out—psychotherapy may be the only treatment that creates the illness it treats!

Furthermore, the number of mental health professionals has increased by an astounding 275 percent in the last two decades. Considering these two facts together—the rabbitlike proliferation of mental disorders and the exponential growth of therapists—has led some to cynically argue that the *DSM* transforms ordinary reactions to life stress into billable pathology to feed the voracious appetite of an ever-increasing supply of mental health practitioners.

In truth, we have all been caught in the undertow of a growing industry. It is a crusade that is warping what we think about ourselves, our relationships, our parents and our children. It is the D Industry, those forces that seek to diagnose us with disorders, diseases, deficits, dysfunctions, disabilities—the Killer Ds—or otherwise diminish our innate propensities to help ourselves. To illustrate the success of this industry, if drug treatments for mental "disorders" were books, they would be runaway bestsellers. In 2003, more than 150 million prescriptions were written for antidepressants, and more than $14 billion was spent on them. Twenty million prescriptions were written for Ritalin, surpassing the amount spent for antibiotics! These numbers seem even more astronomical when compared to the measly prescription rates of other countries—the United States is apparently, by far, the most demented nation in the world.

Hardly a day goes by without some mental health mogul pontificating on the sorry state of America's mental health. The key to the problem, we are told, is to educate people about the nature of mental illness and to destigmatize seeking therapeutic help. Hence, the country is now replete with offers for "free mental health checkups" like National Depression Day or National Anxiety Day. (I keep waiting for National I'm Mad at My Spouse Day and National I Don't Want to Go to Work Day.) The sheer number of these programs leaves one wondering who the real beneficiaries are of such efforts to "get out the sick." The fact that these endeavors are largely funded by drug companies and sponsored by mental health professional organizations should be telling.

The perpetual D information machine has cultivated a curious change in the way we view problems. Unhappiness is no longer thought to be shaped by such diverse forces as a sedentary, lonely or impoverished life; the loss of love, health or community; "learned helplessness" or feelings of powerlessness arising from unsatisfying work or an abusive relationship. Its resolution no longer requires anyone to do something different, get meaningful support from others, or for communities to address conditions or injustices that breed fear or despair. No, problems in living—our own and perhaps especially our children's—are now publicly defined as illnesses, treatable—thank heaven—by the miracle drugs and other treatments administered by experts.

Here's the surefire formula to service the needs of the pharmaceutical companies and ever-increasing supply of mental health professionals:

1. Take every challenge and struggle of human existence and turn it into a medical disorder, heretofore grossly neglected but now requiring treatment on a large scale.
2. Teach the public that is okay to have the disorder; it is not their fault. They are merely victims of trauma, bad genetics or a chemical imbalance.
3. Advertise the disorder with experts and testimonials; flood the public with television ads showing happy, attractive people living the most fulfilling lives—after they've received treatment.
4. Make sure the public knows that the problem will not go away on its own, that the suffering, dysfunctional individual must get treatment from experts.

This endless deluge of negative propaganda has unfortunately encouraged us to acquire a special D Detector.[7] This is not something you can buy at Radio Shack. This device is embedded deep in your psyche, implanted by the continual message that there is something wrong with you. When operating, it constrains its owner to scan self, marriage, family and friendships continuously for blips or signs of imperfection and trouble.

What's more, once a bogey or bandit appears on the screen, the Klaxon must be sounded, and treatment of one form or another scrambled to intercept the threat. We have become subjects of the D Empire, enforcing its doctrine on ourselves and each other, ever vigilant for signs and symptoms of mental illness.

Of course there is nothing wrong with being on the lookout for trouble or wanting to address problems in a proactive way, but when repeatedly exposed to this psychological witch hunt, an unspoken attitude is cultivated which says that, as people, we're all basically flawed, broken, incomplete, scarred or sick. Tragically, this pernicious perspective ultimately disempowers our innate abilities, choking and smothering more hopeful ways of understanding our problems, our endeavors to change or to help our loved ones.

And, of course, there is nothing wrong with seeking help! People do benefit from talking to a therapist or taking medication. However, you may have noticed that neither drugs nor therapy have ended the generation gap, made economic hardship any less real, or kept people from getting angry and feeling hurt. Therapy has not reduced the divorce rate in this country. Nor have drugs appreciably increased life satisfaction for the American public. The rates of depression have not changed for thirty years. Suicide rates, despite the millions taking antidepressants, have not reduced. Overall, the industry promises us much more than it can deliver and at a high cost—the belief that there is something wrong with us.

> **CHECKPOINT:** Approaching problems in life with the assumption that we are sick, flawed or broken, predisposes us to failure. Flying in the face of scientific research about change, such a perspective allows scant access to other, more hopeful ways of addressing problems, making invisible our own natural propensities for growth. *In truth, change is inevitable and decidedly human and primarily comes through the mobilization of one's strengths and abilities.*

Therefore, right now, it is time to jettison your D Detector! To symbolize your movement from the D mentality and your commitment to embrace what is naturally good and strong about you:

1. Find an old electronic device such an unused cell phone, broken answering machine, etc.
2. Label the device the "D Detector."
3. Spread out a garbage bag on the floor of your garage or driveway and place the D Detector on the bag.

4. Take a hammer and smash the device into a million pieces.

5. Wrap up what's left of the D Detector and throw it away; the trash gets picked up tomorrow. . . .

Lions of Change: About This Book

Until lions have their historians, tales of hunting will always glorify the hunter.

African proverb

This African proverb speaks to my intentions in this book. Building on the recognition that you are the real lion of change, you will become the historian of your own "hunt" for growth. You will draw upon your courage and cunning to overcome the problems that concern you the most.

Here is what we know from fifty years of research about change:

- Change does not come about from the special powers of any particular physician or therapist or therapeutic method; there are no gurus or miracle cures.
- Change happens when you use your inherent strengths and resources and are supported by relationships that take your innate goodness as a given.
- Change happens when you create a plan that is tailored to your ideas and therefore inspires the hope necessary for action.

Applying this research, the map for the first steps of your journey is charted in chapter 2. It demonstrates not only how to shed self-doubt but also how to enlist your heroic self—what's right with you—to support your efforts for meaningful change.

Chapter 3 discusses the importance of having someone in your corner to encourage you and offers guidelines about how to recruit a "change partner" as a companion in your travels to transformation. Addressing an oft ignored but critical factor, chapter 4 helps you learn *your own view of how change happens,* a crucial point in selecting the plan that will inspire hope and benefit you the most. Chapters 5 and 6 present two radically different problem-solving strategies that apply your strengths and abilities to create solutions to life challenges. Although providing numerous suggestions, more important is that these chapters give you the inside scoop on how to solve problems in the same way that therapists are taught. So rather than just giving you the bread, chapters 5 and 6 demonstrate how to cultivate the soil and grow the wheat. Chapter 7 brings it all together and shows you how to track your progress so that you know earlier rather than later whether your change plan is working—and how to use that information to adjust your methods for the best possible chance of success. It also describes how to continue to reap the benefits of the gains you have made, as well as numerous options about what to do if your plan isn't working. Each chapter ends with a short story that illustrates its main points and an exercise/summary of specific steps that will help you integrate the material. Tackle this book in a way that makes sense for you—after reading chapter 2, feel free to sequence the subsequent chapters to fit your particular circumstances. You may also want to journal your reactions to the exercises and your experiences with this book.

Ruby Slippers

If you want good service, serve yourself!
Spanish proverb

The Wizard of Oz is L. Frank Baum's wonderful story about life and the resolution of human problems.[8] The familiar tale involves four characters who each perceive something missing in their lives, that something is wrong with them. Each believes that a wizard is necessary to help them find completeness. The first, the Scarecrow, sorrowfully exclaims, "Oh, I'm a failure, because I haven't got a brain!" The Tin Man laments, " . . . that I could be kind-a-human, if I only had a heart." The Cowardly Lion whines, "My life has been simply unbearable . . . if I only had the nerve." Finally, there is Dorothy, who simply wants to return home to Uncle Henry and Auntie Em.

In time, despite calamity and distance, they arrive at the Emerald City and are finally granted an audience with the Great Oz. Impressively framed by fire and smoke, and after sufficiently scaring the pitiful crew, he proclaims in a thunderous voice: "The beneficent Oz has every intention of granting your requests! But, you must prove yourselves worthy by performing a small task. Bring me the broomstick of the Wicked Witch of the West . . . and I'll grant your requests. Now go!"

Disappointed, the four friends depart on the journey prescribed by the Great and Powerful Oz. Against all odds, the four heroically persevere against the Wicked Witch of the West and return with the broomstick. Despite their accomplishment, the mighty Oz is reluctant to grant their wishes. While the wizard tries to stall, Toto pulls aside a curtain and shows him up as a humbug. The humbled wizard quickly recovers and grants boons to the Scarecrow, Lion and Tin Man. Using ingenious salesmanship, he awards the Scarecrow a diploma—a doctorate in thinkology—to substitute for a brain. To the Cowardly Lion goes a "Triple Cross" for valor, signifying his courage. And finally, the Tin Man receives a testimonial and a watch that looks and sounds like a human heart.

The wizard also agrees to fly Dorothy back to Kansas. Yet, when Dorothy jumps out to retrieve Toto, his balloon unexpectedly takes off. Just when things look their worst, Glinda, the beautiful Good Witch of the North, suddenly appears and says, "You don't need to be helped any longer. You've always had the power to go back to Kansas." Dorothy wonders aloud, "I *have?*"

The Scarecrow and Tin Man ask Dorothy what she has discovered on her journey. Dorothy thoughtfully responds, "Well, I . . . I think that it . . . wasn't just enough to want to see Uncle Henry and Auntie Em . . . and it's that if I ever go looking for my heart's desire again, I won't look any farther than my own backyard; because if it isn't there, I never really lost it to begin with!"

Glinda, nodding and smiling, "That's all it is. . . . she had to find out for herself. Now those magic slippers will take you home in two seconds!"

This magical account of Dorothy and her friends provides a compelling metaphor for the struggle for change. Does change happen as a result of wizards, humbugs or witches? The Great and Powerful Oz, as the expert faced with overwhelming problems (whoever heard of a scarecrow wanting to think, a tin man wanting feelings, a lion needing courage or a girl wanting to return to an unheard-of place?), did what many professional helpers are trained to do. He prescribed a protracted journey (a particular technique or medication) to acquire something *he* thought they needed. For their part, Dorothy and her companions were so focused on seizing the Wicked Witch's broomstick that they did not see how wise and heroically they acted in accomplishing the task.

After his embarrassing exposure, the humbug cleverly addresses the requests of the Scarecrow, Tin Man and Lion, granting each something tangible. While these awards are not exactly what each expects, they are genuinely pleased to receive validation of their experiences and desires for completeness. But as the old America song goes, *"Oz never did give nothing to the Tin Man, that he didn't, didn't already have."*[9]

Dorothy's experience was significantly different—neither wizard nor humbug was of any service to her. But Glinda was. Glinda helped Dorothy find her own meaning about her perilous quest to Oz—her journey of change—and to *rely on her own resources* to return home, to reach her destination. This book adopts Glinda's way of helping. *What's Right with You* encourages you to find your own meanings at this important time in your life and shows you how to discover your inherent resiliency and abilities to solve life challenges. Although this book will not provide you with a magic wand or enable you to travel in a bubble, it will help you steadfastly know that you always walk into tough life circumstances with (or even on, in Dorothy's case) all you need—to not only prevail over adversity but also to transform yourself into the person you were made to become.

CHAPTER ONE BOTTOM LINE
Challenge the Killer Ds

Exercise One: You Have Always Had the Power

You may find it helpful to start a journal of your experiences with the exercises in this book. Consider the following questions:

1. How has the D Detector diverted attention from the kind of human being you are and would like to become? Ditch the D Detector like a blind date with a born-to-lose tattoo!

2. What are the traits, qualities and characteristics that describe you when you are at your very best? What were you doing when these aspects became apparent to you?

3. What kind of person do these aspects describe? Or what kind of person do these aspects show an aspiration toward?

4. What are the traits, qualities and characteristics that others would describe in you when you are at your very best? What were you doing when they noticed these aspects in you?

5. What kind of person do these aspects describe? Or what kind of person do these aspects show an aspiration toward?

6. Who was the first person to tell you that he or she noticed the best of you in action? What were you doing when this person noticed these aspects?

7. Who was the last person to tell you that he or she noticed the best of you in action? What were you doing when this person noticed these aspects?

8. When I am at my very best, I am _____.

9. Now that you are aware of yourself when you are at your very best, is there a difference between you at your very best and how you or others tend to see you? Read on.

2

Discovering the Hero Within

*It is easier to discover a deficiency
in individuals, in states, and
in Providence, than to see
their real import and value.*

—Hegel

There is an old story about two apprentice Zen monks who are discussing their respective masters while cleaning their temple. The first novice proudly tells his companion about the many miracles that he has seen his famous master perform. "I have watched," the young novice says, "as my master has turned an entire village to the Buddha, has made rain fall from the sky and has moved a mountain so that he could pass."

The other novice listens attentively and then demonstrates his deeper understanding by responding, "My master also does many miraculous things. When he is hungry, he eats. When he is thirsty, he drinks. When he is tired, he sleeps."

Like the first monk, many of us have become too enamored of "miracles" touted by the masters. We so badly want to believe that some expert has *the* answer for us. You don't have to watch TV for long to witness the amazing transformations of those suffering souls in drug ads or to behold the incredible weight loss achieved through this diet or with that exercise equipment. Thousands of clients and decades of research about change, however, have taught me to discard the claims of the gurus and snake oil salesmen, and instead honor these straightforward steps to achieve meaningful personal growth:

1. Acknowledge where we are.
2. Validate ourselves as human beings.
3. Tell our heroic stories, those that showcase our competencies and highlight our strengths.

These simple but magical acts are the eating, drinking and sleeping of making real changes in your life.

Acknowledge Where You Are: The Progress Rating Scale

So teach us to number our days, that we may apply our hearts unto wisdom.

Psalms 90:12

Discovering the hero within and enlisting your resources to make important changes in your life, like all journeys, begins with the first step: acknowledging where you are right now. View it as if you are looking at a map or direction board at the mall and finding the "you are here" spot. This must happen first, even before you identify where you are going or the pathways to get there.

Acknowledging where you are right now serves several important functions. Appraising your current circumstance allows you to get in touch with your thoughts and feelings about your particular situation in life. Embracing your place in the present simultaneously allows you to validate where you have been and reflect on where you are going.

The intersection of time, space and circumstance that you inhabit right now provides an anchor, a point of comparison that not only will help you identify goals but also allows you to assess whether you are progressing in your change efforts. Why is this important? Because we know that, regardless of the approach taken, *the general way that change occurs is highly predictable.*

Contrary to popular belief, studies of how people change in therapy have consistently found that it occurs earlier rather than later—most change occurs quickly. Many have found that at least 60 percent of clients coming to their first sessions report improvement in the presenting problems since the appointments were made—before therapy begins. Further, up to 35 percent of people in therapy make the changes they desire in the first few sessions, often before any actual treatment gets under way! Taking the first step often jump-starts the change process and activates the natural inclination toward growth. These same findings also show that as time in treatment increases, more and more effort is required to achieve even minor improvements.[10]

Importantly, the twin findings that (1) change happens earlier rather than later, and (2) there is a course of diminishing returns over time, make clear that efforts that result in little or no change (or a worsening of problems) *early* in the process are probably doomed to failure. In fact, early improvement—specifically, your experience of meaningful change within a few weeks—is one of the best predictors of your continued change and benefit. Researchers have found that when no improvement occurs by the sixth visit to a therapist, the client is not likely to improve over the entire course of therapy, *unless the approach to treatment is changed.* This doesn't mean people should abandon their therapists or current methods of change at the drop of a hat or if they are not immediately "cured." Rather it only suggests that, as a general rule, if change is going to happen, you will likely feel *some* relief from your concerns in relatively short order.

To capitalize on the research about how people change and to simplify the process of acknowledging where you are, my colleagues and I developed a fast and easy way to track progress, and you will be using a version of it to monitor the effectiveness of your efforts to improve your life. This so-called outcome measure has been scientifically tested and validated; it is widely used to track therapeutic progress in a variety of mental health settings. It is called the Outcome Rating Scale (ORS). The specific items on the ORS were adapted from the three areas of life functioning deemed appropriate by research about change. Specifically, the ORS addresses the realms of individual, relational and social well-being. Changes in these three areas are widely considered to be valid indicators of personal benefit.[11]

Make copies of the ORS on page 29 for future use. Think of how you have been doing in each of these areas of life and place a mark on each line accordingly, with low estimates of each dimension represented to the left and high to the right.

Start with the **Individual** domain and think about how you are doing *personally.* This line would be the place to indicate struggles with depression, anxiety, weight loss, sleeplessness or any distress that you alone experience and would like to change. Rating your status on this line also allows you to recognize when you are doing just fine on the personal side of things.

Next, consider how you are doing in the **Interpersonal** realm of life. How do you feel about your closest relationships? Are they going well, or is this the area that most reflects your distress about your life and where you want to focus your change efforts? If your relationships are great with your children but not so good with your spouse, mark the line to reflect your distress about your marriage. If all is fine in the family department, then indicate as such with your mark on the line, and move on to the social aspects of your life.

The **Social** domain is where you think about how you are doing in areas outside of your closest relationships. How are you doing in school or work (including work inside the home), and how are your friendships beyond the family? Are you satisfied with the roles you have chosen for your life? If you are not pleased with your occupation or role in life, or feel as if you are isolated without friends, this would be the line to indicate such experiences; this is also the place to show that these broader social parts of your life are going well.

Finally, the **Overall** domain asks you to take a big-picture look at your life and mark where you see yourself in general. Step back, take a look and indicate on this line your appraisal of your life in total.

The three areas, plus the overall rating, are measured on four lines that are ten centimeters each. For each line there is a possible score of ten, with the four lines adding up to a possible score of forty. Your score is simply the sum of your marks, to the nearest centimeter, on each of the four lines. A scoring template is provided, along with instructions, on the reverse side of the ORS. Take the template or a centimeter ruler and measure your marks on each line and then add them up.

The ORS is simply a benchmark to understand where you are right now. It allows you to become aware of how your life is going and in what areas you might consider making changes. A total score of twenty-five is what is called the clinical cutoff. This is the score that usually differentiates those who are experiencing enough distress to seek help from a therapist from those who are not. Or said another way, the score of twenty-five tends to separate those who are looking for something different in their lives from people who are content, to a large degree, with the way things are—not perfect, but acceptable. When used in clinical practice, the average score of persons seeking therapy is about nineteen. If you scored over twenty-five, clinically speaking, you're doing fine, which doesn't mean you're not in the market for change. Once you have completed the ORS and scored your responses, you'll know where you are *right now.* Take this initial score and plot it on the graph found in chapter 7 (page 185). This will allow you to monitor the effects of any change plan that you implement. Instructions for using the graph in chapter 7 are on page 186.

We will return to your score on the ORS at the conclusion of this chapter and throughout the rest of the book. Information you glean about your progress from the ORS will be central to your success in building a better life.

Validate Your Experience

The very greatest things—great thoughts, discoveries, inventions—have usually been nurtured in hardship, often pondered over in sorrow, and at length established with difficulty.

—Samuel Smiles

Now that you have acknowledged where you are and established a starting point for comparison on the ORS, it is time to validate your experience—to simply value yourself as a human being doing his or her best through the trials and tribulations of

OUTCOME RATING SCALE (ORS)

Name _____

Score _____ Date: _____

Looking back over the last week, including today, rate how well you have been doing in the following areas of your life (marks to the left represent low levels and marks to the right indicate high levels).

Individual
(Personal well-being)

|_____|

Interpersonal
(Family, close relationships)

|_____|

Social
(Work, school, friendships)

|_____|

Overall
(General sense of well-being)

|_____|

Directions and Scoring of the ORS

```
[ⁱᵘⁱⁱⁱⁱⁱⁱⁱⁱⁱⁱⁱⁱⁱⁱⁱⁱⁱⁱⁱⁱⁱⁱⁱⁱⁱⁱⁱⁱⁱⁱⁱⁱⁱⁱⁱⁱⁱⁱⁱⁱⁱⁱⁱⁱⁱⁱⁱⁱⁱⁱⁱⁱ]
 0     1     2     3     4     5     6     7     8     9    10
```

- Make copies of the ORS for future use.
- Think of how you have been doing in the past week in each of the areas listed on the ORS. On one copy of the ORS, place a mark on each line accordingly, with low estimates of each dimension represented to the left and high to the right.
- The three areas, plus an overall rating, are measured on four ten-centimeter lines. The four ten-centimeter lines add to a possible total score of forty.
- Your score is simply the total of the nearest centimeter marked on each of the four lines.
- With the above template or a centimeter ruler, measure your mark on each line and add them up.
- A total score of twenty-five is the clinical cutoff, which differentiates those who are experiencing enough distress to want change or to seek professional help from those who are not.
- The average score of persons seeking therapy is about nineteen, although up to one-fourth of those who enter therapy have scores over the clinical cutoff.

this sometimes unfair and tumultuous life. Many of us might believe we already do this, but often we do not validate ourselves in the face of adversity. *Validation* occurs when you accept your feelings and behaviors as completely understandable and can legitimize how you feel and what you have done. Validation happens when you can say, "No wonder I feel this way, given a, b and c," or "No wonder I did that, given a, b and c."

I know this is a very different way to approach things. People are usually dissuaded from validating themselves because they are admonished to "take responsibility for your actions" and "don't make excuses." Validating your experience does not diminish your contribution to the problem, nor does it seek to provide an easy excuse for your actions. Rather, it strives for a broader understanding of your circumstances, an outside-of-the-forest perspective that focuses on the absolute validity of your feelings and the positive intent of your behavior. Validation empowers you to find new ways of looking at your life so you may move on and take proactive steps to make the changes you desire.

On the flip side, *invalidation* demoralizes you and inserts self-doubt and self-loathing—significant obstacles for change and a surefire recipe for hopelessness. Nevertheless, most of us have learned, only too well, two forms of invalidating messages to pummel ourselves with during troubling times:

- messages that *contradict* or *dismiss* our feelings
- messages that *blame* us for life's inevitable pitfalls

The first type of invalidating message we receive from others or ourselves contradicts or dismisses our feelings. As an example, consider how you feel when the doctor snaps the latex glove and says "relax" as you peer up from the table. The contradiction between the message (relax) and how you feel (nervous) is so great that it keeps you stuck where you are and perhaps even exacerbates your anxiety. When you validate yourself as a human being, then you can move forward. When you tell yourself you have good reason to be anxious about the procedure the doctor intends to perform, you can move on to dealing with the discomfort of the situation and getting on with the rest of the day. *As a general rule, your feelings are valid—period.* The idea here is that if you are experiencing a particular emotion, you have good (valid) reasons to feel that way, even if others don't quite get it.

Consider Carrie, who is struggling with her weight and feeling exasperated because it seems virtually impossible for her to do anything about it. With all good intentions, people (especially slender ones or those who have just lost weight on the latest diet), say things like: "It's easy; all you have to do is decrease intake or increase output—lower your calories or do more exercise," or "Just follow this or that diet or this or that exercise regime—it's so easy; all you have to do is eat only lemons and row a boat to Hawaii every day!" The contradiction here is obvious—Carrie is finding her weight-loss efforts frustratingly difficult, a far cry from the dismissive messages of her well-meaning advisers. The result is self-doubt that paralyzes one's natural inclinations toward health. Carrie responds to these invalidating comments by thinking, "If this is so easy, why can't I do it? Why is it so difficult for me and not for others?" Unfortunately, these questions are not rhetorical and usually get answered with blame of some kind, another form of invalidation.

This is the message that singles us out as *the* source of the conundrum: "It's your fault; *you* are the problem." This voice accepts no extenuating or mitigating circumstances and highlights our shortcomings as the *best* explanation for our troubles. Blaming ourselves keeps us mired in the muck of the problem and blinds us to the resources we possess that might help us to navigate a way out of the quagmire at hand. Consider Carrie, who now blames herself for being overweight. Carrie says to herself, "I have no self- control. I eat all this junk when I know it just makes me fat. I'm hopeless. I am a loser!"

Just as self-doubt leads to self-blame, a continual pelting of blame culminates in self-loathing. While taking responsibility allows us to take action to improve our situations, blaming keeps us stuck and often leads to depression.

Invalidation, then, is characterized by the following statements:

- I shouldn't feel or be this way. I am not like others. My feelings have no connection to reality.
- It's me; I am to blame; I am incomplete. There is something wrong with me or what I have done or am doing currently. If only I were smarter, braver or had that special something that others have.

Picture yourself in an interrogation room under a blinding bright light with a very unsympathetic character—rubber hose in hand—confronting you about the problem you are experiencing. He shouts, "You shouldn't feel this way—you are the problem!" This uncomfortable scene illustrates the effects of invalidation—whether self-inflicted or by others, it paralyzes us as though we are strapped in fast.

Validating ourselves frees us from the rubber hose of doubt and the bright light of blame. Validation does not mean that you should agree with everything you have done, or that you do not think you could have done something differently, or that you do not feel regret; it simply means you give yourself a break! Sure you could have acted or thought or felt differently, but you didn't, and you did the best you could under the circumstances at that time. Validation looks at those circumstances and acknowledges all the factors that contribute to your feelings or behaviors. Validation puts your actions in a context that legitimizes you as a human being—explaining your situation in a "big picture" way in which your actions are part of a larger scenario. The idea here is to rightfully justify your feelings and actions by looking at all the pieces of the puzzle—all the extenuating or mitigating circumstances. Validation clears a path for change because it diffuses self-doubt and dissipates self-loathing—it allows you to forgive yourself. It also enables you to identify and address the factors that may need to be dealt with for change to occur.

Stopping the blows of the rubber-hose contradictions and turning off the hot, blaming spotlight on Carrie requires only that she examine the factors involved in her weight dilemma—to *contextualize* her conundrum. Losing weight is one of the most difficult things to do on this planet, especially in the United States—many consider it even more difficult than quitting smoking or drinking! Not only are we subjected to a constant barrage of advertisements of high-fat, high-carbohydrate foods consumed by slender, fit people, we must endure their immediate accessibility at every turn. Moreover, nearly every occasion or holiday involves food, and of course it's usually not healthful and low in calories. Combine all of those larger social contingencies with the fact that Carrie prepares meals for three other people—two of whom are adolescents, and all of whom have no desire to watch what they eat—and it adds to a nearly insurmountable challenge that would test anyone's mettle. So *no wonder* she feels terribly frustrated and is having difficulty losing weight, given how tough it is to lose weight to begin with, the never-ending pressures to eat the wrong things and the complete (but unintentional) lack of support from her family. Losing weight requires the assembly of all one's resources, recruiting relational support and forming a plan that makes sense to the individual before going toe-to-toe with the weight problem. That process begins with validation, not blame. The factors identified in Carrie's situation let her know what she was really up against and what needed to be addressed for her to succeed in a weight-reduction plan.

Consider Janice, a thirty-two-year-old software executive who was recently promoted to a position that requires her to fly to regional meetings. Janice was very fearful of flying and up until her promotion had successfully avoided it. Janice experienced her fears as extreme panic and a most distressful feeling of going crazy.

Now think about invalidation. Here is what Janice and others said about her fears of flying:

- Flying is safer than driving; don't worry.
- Your fears are an overreaction. Get a grip; most people fly without fear.

The first invalidating statement misses the mark of Janice's feelings by at least thirty-thousand feet. Look at the contradiction between Janice's feelings of panic and the comment that flying is safer than driving and there is nothing to worry about. As with the proverbial "relax" and the sound of the latex glove, the idea of bouncing around in turbulence and the suggestion to not worry just don't add up in Janice's mind. Although meant to be reassuring, such comments discount the feelings of the distressed individual and add to his or her self-doubt: "If it is really safe and I have nothing to fear, I must really be crazy to be feeling this way."

The second message blames Janice for her fears and suggests that she is somehow deficient when compared to others who seem to have what it takes to pull off flying without a hitch. Feeling like you don't measure up to others and that you are missing something very important as a person are powerful forces working against you that interfere with your natural healing and coping abilities; they create self-loathing.

Here are some more-validating ways to look at Janice's fears of flying:

- Flying is anxiety provoking for nearly everyone, especially during takeoff and landing and bumpy air. The only difference between them and you is that they have experience flying with their fears.
- Okay, flying is statistically safer than driving, but there are no fender benders at thirty-thousand feet.
- No wonder you are afraid—who wouldn't be? Hurling through space at five hundred miles an hour in a two-hundred-ton metal can at thirty-thousand feet is pretty frightening if you give it any thought. In fact, it might be a little wacky to not be afraid to some degree.

As you will see in chapter 5, Janice accepted her fears as legitimate feelings in response to the frightening situation of flying and formulated a specific action plan to manage her panic and distress.

Validating your experience starts by setting aside your negative and judgmental ideas about yourself and embracing the attitude that you are, and have been, doing the best you can under trying circumstances—that your feelings and what has happened makes sense, given the context of your unique life experiences. This process begins by simply telling your story—a detailed account of the situation troubling you and the circumstances that surround it. Telling the story itself can provide validation, as the following fable implies.

When the great Rabbi Israel Baal Shem-Tov saw misfortune threatening the Jews, it was his custom to go into a certain part of the forest to meditate. There he would light a fire, say a special prayer, and the miracle would be accomplished and the misfortune averted. Later, when his disciple, the celebrated Magid of Mezritch, had occasion, for the same reason, to intercede with heaven, he would go to the same place in the forest and say: "Master of the Universe, listen! I do not know how to light the fire, but I am still able to say the prayer." And again the miracle would be accomplished.

Still later, Rabbi Moshe-Leib of Sasov, in order to save his people once more, went to the forest and said: "I do not know how to light the fire, I do not know the prayer, but I know the place and this must be sufficient." It was sufficient, and the miracle was accomplished.

Then it fell to Rabbi Israel of Rizhyn to overcome misfortune. Sitting in his armchair, his head in his hands, he spoke to God: "I am unable to light the fire, and I do not know the prayer; I cannot even find the place in the forest. All I can do is to tell the story, and this must be sufficient." And it was sufficient.

God made man because he loves stories.[12]

The validation that occurs in telling the story is itself curative and potentially powerful in resolving your concerns. You will hear your own voice telling of your experiences and find validation in doing so. Telling your story allows you to hear the invalidating messages from yourself and others, so that you may challenge them, set them aside, reach different conclusions and forge new directions.

Consider Anita, a twenty-nine-year-old nurse and mother who was so deeply depressed that her religious beliefs were her only defense against suicide. Her ORS score was a paltry ten. When asked about her depression and what was so bad in her life that she would contemplate suicide, Anita could only throw up her hands and say that she had no explanation for it—that it came on for no apparent reason "out of the blue." She reported that everything was fine otherwise: she liked her job, enjoyed her hobby of interior decorating, and loved her husband and children very much. She tried antidepressants but that didn't help.

Everyone told Anita that she needed to do more things for herself, enjoy herself and appreciate her blessings in life.

Anita's Story

I just feel terrible and don't care about anything. I should be happy—I am blessed in many ways. I have a nice home, my family loves me, but it doesn't matter. Nothing makes me feel better. I do what everybody says, but it doesn't help. It's just such a hopeless feeling. I am even more discouraged because my husband said he would go to the doctor or to therapy, but when it got down to it, he didn't. I didn't get depressed over it; I just got discouraged.

Anita starts out with the view that she has nothing to be depressed about—that everything should be peachy. Notice the invalidation embedded in her descriptions and in the comments of others. If she has nothing to be depressed about, there must be something deeply off-kilter about her, because her life is so perfect otherwise—the contradiction between others saying that she should count her blessings and her miserable feelings of depression is striking. She can only conclude that her feelings have no basis in reality. Furthermore, the impact of blame was devastating—Anita believed there was something wrong with her, not the circumstances of her life, and the result was hopelessness. Invalidation smothers more promising ways to approach problems. Anita challenges her invalidating comments, sets them aside and picks up on the last thing she said:

Maybe it bothers me, and I don't realize it. I know he has a problem that he can't help until he is ready to get help. Me being upset will not help things. Sam has erection difficulties, and when he does get an erection, he quickly ejaculates.

Challenging the invalidating messages resulted in a subtle shift. Before, her comments reflected that there was no reason for her depression. Now she begins to consider that her husband's erectile problems and premature ejaculation may be contributing to her depression. Anita moves on to consider the ins and outs of this new understanding of her dilemma:

> *I guess a lot of people would certainly be depressed in relation to not having sex with their partner. I mean, sex is more than the sexual part; it is also a time when a man and a woman are intimate together emotionally. It's there to reaffirm a relationship—it's an intimate pleasure that keeps a marriage strong in a lot of ways. There are a lot of times when I cannot even watch television. When somebody is kissing or whatever, I just can't even watch. It bothers me. Gosh, I wish we could be that way. But I have tried to talk to him and even fight with him about it, but he won't. If he could get a little mad and fight, we could make up! But no, he doesn't like to fight. I don't know if that is a good marriage or not. Fighting is part of being married. You know, we are like roommates! We don't fight and we don't have sex—no wonder I am depressed! The way I look at it, that's the way the Lord made man and woman, husband and wife. I think this depression is telling me I have to do something about my marriage and that I can't be happy with no sex for the rest of my life.*

Anita's story shifted from blaming herself about her depression to understanding her distress as related to longings for sexual intimacy with her husband, from an invalidating story of self-doubt and self-loathing offering little remedial action to a whole new set of options. Notice how Anita's comments evolved to the point where she replaced her own invalidation with the strong self-validation: "No wonder I am depressed." Validation helped Anita move from passive resignation to proactive involvement.

Anita confronted Sam and delivered an ultimatum that she was willing to do anything to help, but she would leave if he didn't seek help for his erection and quick ejaculation problem. He did, and the depression miraculously lifted through "bedroom" therapy. Anita's score on the ORS also elevated to a twenty-nine.

Validating the Struggle: Danger and Opportunity

We are continually faced by great opportunities brilliantly disguised as insoluble problems.

Mark Twain

Anita's story also illustrates another aspect of validation—the importance of human struggle and the apparent *meaning* of those struggles in peoples' lives. As crazy as it sounds, problems also provide possibilities for living our lives differently, for reaching new conclusions. Anita's depression was obviously painful, and it brought attention to the fact that she was not happy in her marriage and needed to address it. *The depression, therefore, was critical as a life-transformation vehicle.* In Anita's situation, the depression provided the impetus to either improve the marriage or perhaps end it. Sometimes it takes heartache and discomfort— where life doesn't just tap us on the shoulder, it throws us against the wall—to focus our efforts on changes that need to be made.

So, as paradoxical as it sounds, problems are not 100 percent bad. They may very well be an indication that your internal wisdom is trying to reach you. Problems or symptoms offer great possibilities for change—they are painfully human experiences that serve as messages that we need to do something to change the way we are living our lives or the way we are relating to our loved ones. Consequently, life struggles are important, perhaps representing a critical juncture that can open entirely new vantage points and understandings. Life problems put you at a crossroad and offer you choices not only about what is happening, but also about who you really are.

That is why the D Industry is such an obstacle to change. It obscures these important messages and discounts basic human struggles with ridiculous platitudes like: "Depression is a flaw of chemistry, not character." Depression is not a flaw but rather an important struggle, perhaps the most critical of a person's life. Depression represents a profound crisis; it calls into question our very identities and how we are conducting our lives. It is at once a crisis point, a real danger and an opportunity for incredible change.

The Chinese characters for the word crisis are *wei chi*: danger and opportunity. This combination of danger over opportunity captures the essence of any crisis or human struggle. Both elements exist in balance. When we choose to focus exclusively on managing the crisis, either through medication or other methods to relieve the problem, we lose sight of the inherent opportunities. These situations are the way human beings learn and grow. Don't let anyone ever take that away from you. This is not to say that it is wrong to want relief from the stress that problems bring us. Rather, I am only suggesting that *sole* focus on relief blinds us to the wisdom and possibilities to be found in experiencing these totally human foibles firsthand.

Okay, let's get down to the nuts and bolts. Validating your experience simply requires you, like Anita, to tell your story. The ORS offers some guidance on what to start with. Which line did you mark the lowest? What situation or circumstance led you to make that mark? Anita marked both the personal well-being and close relationships scales a very low two, a very good clue about what was influencing her depression.

There are two ways you can tell your story. You may simply write your story, focusing on the elements of your life you find most troubling, in as much detail as possible. Or you may tell your detailed, nuanced story to a tape recorder. In chapter 3, we will build on your self-validation and bring your story to someone who is a strong relational support.

Validation requires you to accept yourself at face value and search for justification of your experience—replacing the invalidation that may be a part of it. Read or listen to your story, reflecting on the following questions:[13]

- What are the obvious and hidden invalidations contained in my story? How am I or others discounting or contradicting my experiences? How am I or others blaming me for this situation?
- What other factors or circumstances have contributed to this situation or are extenuating or mitigating variables? How can I place my situation in a context that explains and justifies my behavior or feelings? How can I give myself credit for trying to do the right thing?
- How is this experience representative of an important cross-road in my life or a statement about my identity? What message is my internal wisdom attempting to tell me? What did I learn from this experience?

Put your experience in the following format:

- No wonder I feel or behave this way [fill in with your circumstance] given that [fill in the ways you have discovered to justify your responses].

Finally, ask:

- Now that I have validated myself, what different conclusions did I reach? Did any other courses of action emerge?

Consider Mark, a twenty-eight-year-old student who felt very depressed and was paralyzed by worrying about whether he would succeed at school. This paralysis virtually guaranteed his failure. Mark's score on the ORS was a fourteen, which reflected that he was in significant distress. Mark constantly told himself that his whole experience was stupid, that he shouldn't be worrying or having difficulties in school because he had been successful before. When Mark brought his feelings and distress to others, they reassured him with all good intentions that he would do fine and that he shouldn't worry about it. This, of course, just reinforced Mark's idea of how stupid the problem was.

Mark wrote his story so he could examine it carefully and ultimately validate himself. Mark's story revealed that he had returned to college to pursue a career that was very important to him. He finally knew what he wanted to do with his life after much early floundering—Mark wanted with all his heart to be a teacher. His previous college experience in business was meaningless to him and had led to a series of unsatisfactory, ho-hum jobs. This time, however, college meant everything: he was no longer a kid resting on potential, and if he didn't succeed at school this time it meant, in his mind, he was a failure and doomed to an unfulfilling life. Therefore, his paralyzing worry represented a far greater life tragedy than merely not doing well on a test or in a class. Not being able to concentrate and poor performance in school meant that Mark's whole life was on the line—his aspirations for a meaningful life and his very identity as a person. Imagine the self-invalidation of "this is stupid" coupled with others' well-meaning invalidation of "don't worry." It was like telling a person driving off a cliff that it was stupid to feel frightened and to not worry about the fall! It is like hearing "relax" from the doctor while you are ready to climb the walls.

After asking himself the suggested questions and reflecting about what he wrote, Mark fit his experience into the suggested formula: "No wonder I am worried and am depressed. This is not just a class; it's my career and my life. It is all of my self-worth rolled up into one do-or-die experience." Mark therefore found validation of his distress, which replaced the invalidation he received from others (don't worry) and himself (this is stupid). Mark no longer experienced the contradiction between what he felt as extremely distressing and what he and others described as trivial, a crucial step in the process of making changes in life. When Mark validated himself as a human being with legitimate concerns and feelings, he was able to redirect his energies to address his depression and schoolwork. Mark's story continues in chapters 5 and 6.

Let's go through the process with Sarah, a thirty-nine-year-old woman recovering from a heroin addiction who is also HIV positive. Sarah was seeing a counselor but felt hopeless and stuck because she could not motivate herself to attend a support group for HIV-positive folks. Sarah's score on the ORS was a fifteen.

Sarah told this story about her experience to a tape recorder:

I have experienced a rough way to go in my life. I was an IV drug user and not only became seriously addicted, but I also contracted HIV. It is controlled by drugs, but they make me feel like crap all the time. My husband also was a heroin addict and contracted HIV, which progressed into AIDS, and he died in my arms after a tortuous but valiant battle. I was straight while he was dying but started using again right after he died. It took me a long time to bounce back from that—I loved him very much. Now I am in recovery and working on staying straight, which I have done for almost a year. But I feel like I've got this barrier that keeps me from moving forward. I know I need to go to the HIV support group; it would be good for me to be around people again, but I can't motivate myself. My roommate just left and started using again, and I know I should get out more. I'm just lazy; that's what I think, and that is what my drug counselor says too. It's like I want everything to be handed to me; I don't want to work on my recovery. Like the HIV group—I know that it would be good for me, but I am just too lazy to do it.

Next, Sarah reflected about the questions (practice this thinking of Sarah's situation):

• What are the obvious and hidden invalidations contained in my story? How am I or others discounting or contradicting my experiences? How am I or others blaming me for this situation?

The obvious invalidations are both my own and my drug counselor's ideas that I am lazy—not exactly a validating explanation of my barrier and why I am stuck. I guess a hidden one is the idea that somehow I am not motivated to change in my life, which of course is ridiculous. Does anyone really think that I enjoy my life now and that I wouldn't give or do anything to change what has happened, especially what happened to my husband? Perhaps a real hidden one is how I blame myself for being a drug addict to begin with and how that caused everything to be miserable.

• What other factors or circumstances have contributed to this situation or are extenuating or mitigating variables? How can I place my situation in a context that explains and justifies my behavior or feelings? How can I give myself credit for trying to do the right thing?

Okay, let me start with the lazy thing. I think I have something with letting people in really close. I am a very friendly person. I have got a good heart. I wanna be friends with people, but the other part of this, I like keeping them away too. You know I have lost someone very close to me. There is a lot to be said about why I would never want to get close to anyone, especially given how I lost my husband and the context of that HIV group. So it's a risk to go to that AIDS meeting because I could meet somebody that would die. I guess another reason other than lazy is that I did not want to revisit the situation I experienced when my husband died. So even though there is something there that would give me some support and friendship, there is a risk that goes along with that, and I know that risk only too well! So I understand my bind in not wanting to go.

Now let me get at that miserable, unmotivated drug addict message. I do blame myself a lot for all that has happened. But the blame is such a burden. Taking responsibility for my addiction is a good thing and has allowed me to be in recovery. But you know what, I was responsible in a lot of other ways. Mike and I did not have children because we knew we had a problem—that was responsible. We both worked part time—we weren't crooks. I never stole anything in my life, to get drugs or for any other reason. And we had no idea about the whole HIV thing. It was not widely known in our circle of users that you could get HIV from sharing needles. So although I knew I was a heroin addict, I did not know that it would lead to Mike's death— neither did he. We were heroin addicts, but we weren't scumbag druggies! And the whole heroin thing really just snuck up on us too. We enjoyed the party lifestyle, but neither of us really intended to get as involved as we did, and soon it was too late to turn back.

- How is this experience representative of an important cross-road in my life or a statement about my identity? What message is my internal wisdom attempting to tell me? What did I learn from this experience?

Wow, heavy questions! This is a critical juncture in my life. It's like I have a choice: I can either stay a lonely, miserable recovering drug addict, or I can take some risks and decide to get a life. I had the using and party time of life, then finally dealing with Mike's illness and death brought me to the next plateau, and this depression thing is my next transition. This depression feeling I have now is like part of me saying "Hellooo!" and telling me to look the whole situation over and choose what path I am going to walk down. It is telling me that it is time to move on and make a new life for myself, to redefine my identity as a good person who happens to be HIV positive and in recovery.

Think of Sarah's situation, and put it in the suggested format:

• No wonder I feel or behave this way [fill in with your circumstance] given that [fill in the ways you have discovered to justify your responses].

First of all, no wonder I am discouraged and feel like crap. I am like Napoleon fighting these battles at all these different fronts. I am not just fighting addiction and trying to work and have a life, but I am also fighting HIV. No wonder I was struggling with attending that group—given that I lost my husband to AIDS and there is a good chance that someone in that group may also die. It is a risk to attend that group.

• Now that I have validated myself, what different conclusions did I reach? Did any other courses of action emerge?

Well, I guess I figured out that I am not that bad—I don't know how I ever forgot that. I need to give myself more credit and keep looking at the big picture. I also know now why I was reluctant to go to the group, and I think I need to talk about Mike some more, and that group will be a good place to do it since I am relatively sure that others will have lost people from this terrible virus also.

Replacing the invalidation that is often embedded in your story sometimes is so liberating that you may then do exactly what you need to do. This is what happened for Sarah. She moved beyond her barrier and began attending the support group.

CHECKPOINT: Validating your struggles, or understanding your troubling situation as the confluence of many factors, legitimizes your actions and feelings (without absolving you of responsibility for change) and is the first step toward meaningful growth.

Tell Your Heroic Story

It's not what you look at that matters, it's what you see.
                                        Henry David Thoreau

Now that you have honestly acknowledged where you are and validated yourself, it is time to cast yourself in the lead role of change by bringing forth your competencies and resiliencies—the heroic stories that reflect your part in surmounting obstacles, initiating action and maintaining positive change. The key here is the attitude you assume regarding your inherent abilities; you must foster a determined mindfulness of the strengths and resources that you *know* are there.

Although we often think of ourselves in black-and-white ways, human beings have the beautiful complexity of simultaneously possessing polar-opposite characteristics. The stories of who we are have multiple sides, depending on who is recounting them and what sides are emphasized. Unfortunately, the Killer Ds have persuaded us to believe in the story of what is wrong with us as the only or best version. It is neither. Many other stories of survival and courage simultaneously exist—stories that portray what is right with you.

Telling your heroic story, then, starts with the recognition of the existence of several competing descriptions of your experience.[14] Developing mindfulness about your competencies, resources and resiliencies does not mean you must ignore your pain or assume a Pollyanna stance. Rather, it only requires that you give voice to the whole story: the confusion and the *clarity,* the suffering and the *endurance,* the pain and the *coping,* the desperation and the *desire.*

Recall Erica and her real story of a horrific accident and its devastating consequences resulting in her "disability." But other stories, ones that not only competed with but also transcended the other, were simultaneously present and ready to be told.

Erica Revisited: Competing Stories of Heroism

Before the accident I was a police officer, a detective. I loved it. I have a degree in law enforcement. I worked on the street for fifteen years. I lived my dream until the accident— a drunk driver of all things! I was in a coma, and they told my family that I wasn't going to live, and then they told my family that if I did live, I'd be a vegetable all my life and that there was no hope for me.

I miss what I had. When I drive by the police station, there

*is a part of me that really hurts. I knew when I was a child I
was going into law enforcement. I even rode with state troopers when I was in high school! I worked hard all my life to
achieve my dreams. I went to school for two years and got an
associate's degree in law enforcement and finally a bachelor's
degree in criminal justice. Then I worked on the street for ten
years and finally became a detective. I was not only the first
female in the state to graduate from a major city police academy, but was also the youngest in my class. I was the first
woman to make detective in the state, too. I am very proud of
my accomplishments.*

At least three stories have emerged: the story of a catastrophic
accident and Erica's subsequent losses and disabilities; a heroic
story of a little girl who knew she wanted to be a police officer,
who did everything humanly possible to accomplish her goal and
achieve at the highest levels; and a remarkable tale of survival
about a person who came back from the dead to prove everyone
wrong—a woman who could not even talk when she awakened
from a coma, yet came to the session under her own power with
only the help of a cane.

Her account of heartbreaking loss and diminished abilities to
perform police work was real. While the terrible impact of the
accident was profound, *there was no reason to succumb to that
particular story as the only or truest one of Erica's life.* Instead, a
different story of amazing resilience and courage emerged as the
plotline of her life. Erica was recast as the heroine who over-
came all obstacles in her path and now must enlist those same
resources to conquer the new challenge before her. And, as
noted in chapter 1, she did. *Telling your heroic story paves the way
for change—bringing forth those qualities that are only lying dormant awaiting your recognition and activation.*

To help identify your inherent resources, consider positive

psychology researchers Drs. Christopher Peterson and Martin Seligman's refreshing look at the six human virtues and their component character strengths:[15]

- wisdom and knowledge—creativity, curiosity, open-mindedness, love of learning and perspective
- courage—bravery, persistence, integrity and vitality
- humanity—love, kindness and social intelligence
- justice—citizenship, fairness and leadership
- temperance—forgiveness, humility, prudence and self-regulation
- transcendence—appreciation of beauty and excellence, gratitude, hope, humor and spirituality

Using this list as a guide, let's revisit Sarah's story to enlist her natural strengths, to shine a spotlight on her competencies to address her difficult life. There is a story of drug addiction, serious illness and devastating loss. But what other stories exist? Reread her story:

I have experienced a rough way to go in my life. I was an IV drug user and not only became seriously addicted, but I also contracted HIV. It is controlled by drugs, but they make me feel like crap all the time. My husband also was a heroin addict and contracted HIV, which progressed into AIDS, and he died in my arms after a tortuous but valiant battle. I was straight while he was dying but started using again right after he died. It took me a long time to bounce back from that—I loved him very much. Now I am in recovery and working on staying straight, which I have done for almost a year. But I feel like I've got this barrier that keeps me from moving forward. I know I need to go to the HIV support group; it would be good for me to be around people again, but I can't motivate myself. My roommate just left and started using again, and I know I should get out more. I'm just lazy; that's what I think, and that is what my drug counselor says too. It's like I want everything to be handed to me; I don't want to work on my recovery. Like the HIV group—I know that it would be good for me, but I am just too lazy to do it.

Now consider the following questions and Sarah's answers. Think of other questions that ask about strength, clarity, endurance, coping and desire, as well as the virtues listed on page 51:

- You say "was an IV drug user." How did you stop? Halting an addiction is an amazingly difficult thing to do, and many never accomplish it.

I knew that if I didn't stop, I couldn't even begin to take care of Mike, so I just quit. It was hell, but I knew he needed me. Mike was a higher calling for me—taking care of him represented the best of what I could offer in this life. Although I started using again right after he passed, over time I knew there must be something else in this life for me—something better than what I was experiencing. That's when I stopped for good. I know there is a better purpose for my life.

- Sounds like you were very loyal to your husband and supported him throughout his illness. What does that say about you as a person? Many would have abandoned him.

I loved Mike more than anything. He was the only thing that saved me from pure oblivion. He was the kindest person I ever met, and he did not have a mean bone in his body—how many people can you say that about? I had absolutely no desire to do anything other than stay with him until the end. I guess it says that I am true to the end, and I know a good thing when I see it!

- You say you are HIV positive. How are you able to cope with that? Having a serious medical condition leaves many in the grip of depression and destitution.

It hasn't been easy, but I look around me and see what there is in this life to enjoy. Sometimes I babysit for my sister's kids and get so much joy out of watching and playing with them. I look forward to those experiences and think that I can have others if I just keep going and dealing with the fatigue and sickness caused by my illness and the medication.

Other questions:

- You have been straight for a year. How have you been able to pull that off given your illness, the loss of your husband and now even your roommate starting to use again? Those are all reasons for many to relapse.
- What does that say about you? What kind of person overcomes addiction, illness and loss and yet still perseveres?

The next question is always interesting. There are always others who see you for the treasure that you are even when you don't see it yourself.

- Who in your life wouldn't be surprised to see you stand up to these situations and prevail? What experiences of you would they draw upon to make these conclusions about you? What quintessential Sarah stories would they tell?

Well, my uncle Virgil wouldn't be surprised to see me overcome these things. He was the most wonderful man and was actually my great-uncle. He was my dad's favorite uncle; he thought the world of me, and I loved to visit him in the summertime out in the country where he lived. One story he loved to tell about me was when I was six and running around in the woods with my cousin, a very frightening thing happened. I stepped in quicksand and got stuck and pretty quickly sank to my waist then slowly sank more and more. We were way out in the woods, and my cousin ran all the way back to get my uncle, who rushed to get me. I was stuck, waiting in the quicksand, for about an hour. He was so relieved to see me that he cried for joy. He never stopped talking about when he found me. I was calm and collected and just as still as I could be—somehow I instinctively knew not to struggle or make a move. He always told me and everybody else what a trooper I was and how I had the heart of a lion. Uncle Virgil would not be surprised by my ability to deal with this stuff.

- So as you look over these stories of your life, what qualities and characteristics that these stories tell and others have noticed are there waiting to be enlisted in service of your change?

Well, I guess I have more going for myself than I thought. I was a very good partner to Mike, and it seems like there is no doubt that I have been a fighter, and I have always been a tough cookie, as Uncle Virgil used to say. I have already overcome a lot of adversity, and I am struggling but seeing that I probably can even go further toward a better life. Specific words that describe me are strong, tough, never say die, loyal, faithful and now, hopeful. Looking at the human virtues, I can honestly say that I can see all of them in me to some degree, maybe except the justice one.

Sarah is still straight, still coping with HIV and has entered another relationship. At last contact, she scored a twenty-five on the ORS.

Dim-Witted Plodders
or Resourceful Hunters?

Why don't the psychologists ever talk about courage?
—Charles Darwin

In the summer of 1964, John Ostrom and Grant Meyer, Yale paleontologists, were walking along the slope of an eroded mound in south-central Montana. They came across the fossil remains of a creature that Ostrom would later call *Deinonychus* (terrible claw). While uncovering dinosaurs has become relatively commonplace, the finding of *Deinonychus* shook the very foundation of paleontological thought and fueled the flames of a major revolution in the way dinosaurs were viewed.[16] Whereas before, dinosaurs were seen as ponderous, cold-blooded, dim-witted, shuffling monsters, *Deinonychus*, by its skeletal anatomy, pointed to the undeniable existence of an agile, aggressive, larger-brained and perhaps even warm-blooded hunter that was anything but slow, sprawling and stupid. As a result of the chance encounter with *Deinonychus*, the earlier orthodoxy, solidly in place in paleontology, was doomed, soon to be as extinct as the animals it presumed to explain.

On one level, the finding of the fossils of *Deinonychus* and the end of a wrong-headed perspective of dinosaurs is akin to the discovery of your heroic story and the excavation of what's right with you. The remains of your strengths and resiliencies are often buried deep within the stories that tell only of the dim-witted plodder; uncovering these remnants of your strong character compels an entirely different tale to emerge—like *Deinonychus*, one of an agile and intelligent hunter, searching for a better life. On another level, just as *Deinonychus* dramatically changed how dinosaurs were viewed, the research supporting the importance of your innate abilities to change can bring about a seismic shift in the mental health field—stopping the reign of dinosaur beliefs in the Killer Ds and instead understanding people as resourceful hunters who have prevailed, and who will continue to prevail, over adversity.

CHAPTER TWO BOTTOM LINE
Honor Your Heroic Self

Exercise Two: Discovering Your Inner Hero/Heroine

1. **Acknowledge where you are. Take the Outcome Rating Scale.**
   - Score your responses and total the four lines. Compare your score to the clinical cutoff, and reflect on the implications.
   - What areas of functioning show your current strengths?
   - What are the circumstances, situations, concerns or problems that led you to make the marks on the lines where you did?
2. **Validate yourself as a human being. Write your story or tell it to a tape recorder. Listen to or read your story, and reflect on these questions:**
   - What are the obvious and hidden invalidations contained in my story? How am I or others discounting or contradicting my experiences? How am I or others blaming me for this situation?
   - What other factors or circumstances have contributed to this situation or are extenuating or mitigating variables? How can I place my situation in a context that explains and justifies my behavior or feelings? How can I give myself credit for trying to do the right thing?
   - How is this experience representative of an important crossroad in my life or a statement about my identity? What message is my internal wisdom attempting to tell me? What did I learn from this experience?
3. **Express your experience in the following format:**
   - No wonder I feel or behave this way [fill in with your circumstance] given that [fill in the ways you have discovered to justify your responses].
   - Now that I have validated myself, what different conclusions did I reach? Did any other courses of action emerge?
4. **Tell your heroic story. Listen to or read your story and reflect on these questions that bring forth a different story:**

- What are the obvious and hidden strengths, resources, resiliencies and competencies contained in my story?
- What are the competing stories that can be told: the stories of clarity, coping, endurance and desire that exist simultaneously with the stories of confusion, pain, suffering and desperation?
- Who in your life wouldn't be surprised to see you stand up to these situations and prevail? What experiences of you would they draw upon to make these conclusions about you? What "quintessentially you" stories would they tell?
- So as you look over these stories of your life, what qualities and characteristics that these stories tell and others have noticed are there waiting to be enlisted in service of your change?

5. **After completing this exercise, retake the ORS.**
   - If your score increased by five or beyond the clinical cutoff, removing the obstacles of invalidation and not succumbing to only one side of your story have provided a hopeful context for change. Continue to give yourself validating messages and describe yourself in heroic ways. Feel free to take a break and allow the good things you are experiencing to wash over you and evolve naturally. You might next want to read chapter 6, step four ("Empower Yourself") on page 165. Or read on.
   - If your score did not improve by removing the obstacles, it only means that you need more relational support or something more specific to enlist your innate abilities to get you going. Read on.

3

Recruiting Relational Support

. . . appreciation is a holy thing, that when we look for what's best in the person we happen to be with at the moment, we're doing what God does. So, in loving and appreciating our neighbor, we're participating in something truly sacred.

—Fred Rogers

There's no doubt that people change on their own. It happens all the time. So if you want to go at it alone, stop reading now and proceed to chapter 4. But two heads are better than one. Having someone to exchange ideas and brainstorm possibilities with enables vantage points that might be difficult to attain otherwise. And it is just common sense that change is easier when it is supported by others, when we have people on our side cheering us on. Research shows that up to 30 percent of change can be attributed to the relational support provided by the understanding and encouragement of a caring person. In truth, a large portion of positive results from therapy are a direct result of the quality of the client-therapist relationship.[17]

Chapter 3 puts the research about the importance of an encouraging relationship into practice. This chapter helps you select a change or recovery partner who will support your efforts to bring about meaningful growth in your life. It also presents guidelines for discussing and improving your relationship with a potential change partner, so that he or she can encourage you on your path to transformation.

The Power of Relationship

The great tragedy of science—the slaying of a beautiful hypothesis by an ugly fact.

Thomas Henry Huxley

For years researchers have known that change tends to happen in therapy when a client feels connected to the therapist and believes that he or she is working on goals with approaches that seem credible—that are a good fit. Relationships that are positively rated by clients usually result in successful outcomes. Given this importance, effective therapists attend closely to the relationship and monitor its quality to ensure this powerful factor is in good order.

One way that behavioral scientists have studied the therapeutic relationship is by conducting exit interviews with clients after they have completed therapy, similar to how journalists and polling companies do exit interviews at voting places. For fifty years, almost like a conspiracy, clients have said the same thing when asked what was helpful about their therapy. They say things like: "It was helpful to have someone listen to me when I was at my lowest ebb. It was most useful to have someone believe in me, believe that I could be something different. The therapist provided just the encouragement I needed to get me going." These, of course, are all relational comments.

Noticeably absent are mentions of magic methods or pills or the divine wisdom of the doctor or therapist. The "stuff" of therapy is not nearly as critical to change as the caring and support of another individual during a rocky encounter with life.

Consider the Treatment of Depression Collaborative Research Program (TDCRP),[18] which was conducted to find out which treatment worked best for depression. This landmark study, funded by the National Institute of Mental Health, is considered by many to be the most sophisticated study ever done. It involved only experienced psychiatrists and psychologists in multiple cities across the United States and randomly assigned 250 participants to four treatment groups: cognitive therapy, an approach that seeks to reduce depressive symptoms by challenging irrational and distorted attitudes; interpersonal therapy, which focuses on developing more effective strategies for dealing with "here and now" interpersonal problems; treatment with antidepressant medication, which also included therapeutic support and encouragement (a sort of combined therapy and medication approach); and, finally, a placebo treatment group, which received a sugar pill along with therapeutic support and encouragement. After all the effort that went into designing a study that represented the state of the art in outcome research, the investigators were stunned by their own findings.

Overall, the four treatments—including the placebo—worked with about the same effectiveness! As in other studies of other "disorders," there were no differences in overall effectiveness among the different treatments.[19] This of course says nothing negative about any therapy model or any medication; each approach can be very effective for some people. Because of the similar findings for the placebo group in the TDCRP, some researchers have made the tongue-in-cheek suggestion that placebo should be the treatment of choice for depression!

Something else very interesting emerged from this study. Researchers found that the quality of the relationship between the client and therapist, as rated by the client, predicted whether or not the participant benefited from the treatment he or she received. Those "alliances," as researchers call them, that were viewed positively by clients as a partnership designed to achieve their goals resulted in significant improvements in the participants' experiences of depression.

To further emphasize the change potential of a good relationship, consider another large study of diverse therapies for alcohol problems, called Project Match.[20] In this huge study of seventeen hundred participants that compared various treatments for alcohol abuse, *no approach was found to be superior,* but the client's rating of the alliance was predictive of success (sobriety). Amazingly, the participant's evaluation of the quality of the relationship *even predicted* his or her drinking levels at a one-year follow-up. Or said another way, those individuals who had strong alliances with their therapists were more likely not to drink, even a year after treatment stopped! That is the power of a good relationship.

As the epigraph that began this section stated, an ugly fact (no difference among approaches, and the power of the alliance) killed the beautiful idea that one approach would be knighted as the one true champion of change. *In truth, the best medicine for depression or any other problem may be a good relationship with a caring person, perhaps especially with a peer who has traveled a similiar journey.*

CHECKPOINT: Good relationships mobilize people's inherent resources and resiliencies. Don't underestimate the power for change that resides in your relationships. Human relationships are there for a reason. People need people.

Finding a Change or Recovery Partner

In real friendship, the judgment, the genius, the prudence of each party becomes the common property of both.

Maria Edgeworth

Take some time now and think about whom you have relied on in the past and whom you might depend upon now. Who is helpful in your day-to-day life? Whom have you sought out in the past who was useful? Was it a parent, partner, teacher, neighbor, colleague, friend, rabbi? Who are the candidates to be your recovery partner? Who is the best candidate?

When picking your change partner (or partners), please feel free to do it any way you feel would be best. You may already know whom you will ask and need no format to help your deliberations. Follow your instincts. You know whom you can trust. You may need to do nothing more than tell your chosen partner what you are up to and begin the work of changing your life. So if you feel ready, go ahead and enlist a change partner and proceed to the exercise at the end of this chapter. Take what follows as food for thought.

On the other hand, you may want a little guidance or a more formal method to pick the best possible change partner. First, generate a list of candidates. Don't be shy here; you are bestowing a great honor on anyone you consider. It is an honor because you are saying that this person is not only trustworthy, but is also of such high caliber that you are contemplating him or her as a companion in your very personal journey to a more satisfying life. It is better to be overinclusive at this point, so list as many potential partners as possible—a candidate need not be your closest friend or most trusted family member. Once you have identified your candidates, recall the last conversation you had with each person in which you discussed a personal concern. If you have not had such a discussion with a candidate, imagine how you think that exchange might go. Reflect upon that conversation with the following relational dimensions in mind, which have been shown to be invaluable to change in therapy.

Understood, Respected and Validated

Feeling understood, respected and validated is critical to any change endeavor. It is simply a priceless experience that sets us free to consider the possibilities of a better future. Feeling understood means that your change partner makes a sincere attempt to look at the world through your eyes. In addition, like Aretha says, we all want a little R-E-S-P-E-C-T. Respect, according to one of the founding parents of psychotherapy, Carl Rogers, means to value another individual as a person with worth and dignity.

In total, your change partner must assume that you can and will make a more satisfying life for yourself and that you have the inherent capacity to do so. *He or she must believe that no one knows better than you—that you are the expert regarding your concerns.* Part and parcel of this attitude is the belief that you are doing the best you can under stressful circumstances and that your actions are understandable given your context. In short, your change partner must have a validating attitude toward you.

Recall that *validation* is a process in which your struggle is respected as important, perhaps representing a critical juncture in your life, and your thoughts, feelings and behaviors are accepted, believed and considered completely understandable given trying circumstances. Change partners at their best legitimize your point of view, even if, in hindsight, you have not made the best choices. Change partners help you replace any invalidation that may be a part of the load you carry.

Your **Goals**

The second aspect of a change-producing relationship is the complete agreement with your personal goals. Your change partner must embrace your goals because *those are the desires that will excite and motivate you to initiate action.* It begins the process of change, wherever you may ultimately travel.

Consider Mary, a twenty-four-year-old woman who lived in a supervised residence for the "mentally ill." She spent much of her time watching TV and eating snack foods, and her counselor was concerned about her. Consequently, he spent much of his time encouraging Mary to get out of the house, exercise and avail herself of the provided social activities. When asked what she wanted for her life, Mary repeatedly expressed her desire to be a BenGal, a Cincinnati Bengal cheerleader.

But her therapist just couldn't accept this goal. After all, it was just not possible. In fact, most people considered it laughable in a sad kind of way. But what was even sadder was that no one knew why Mary had such an interesting goal. Here she was in rural Minnesota in a group home for folks carrying serious diagnoses, and her heart's desire was to become a professional football cheerleader in a faraway city.

The work with Mary floundered. She rarely spoke and minimally answered questions. Her counselor brought his concerns to his colleagues, who recommended two things: first that he find out where the desire to be a cheerleader came from; and second, that he then find a way to accept her personal goal and recognize the motivation and energy it represented.

When the counselor asked Mary about her goal, she told the story of growing up watching the Bengals every Sunday with her dad, who delighted in Mary's performance of the cheers. Mary sparkled when she talked of her father, who had passed away several years previously, and the counselor noticed that it was the most he had ever heard her speak. The therapist took this experience to heart and often asked Mary about her father, to which she was invariably pleased to respond. In addition, the counselor decided to slow down his efforts to get Mary to social-ize or exercise and instead leaned more toward Mary's interest in cheerleading. Mary regularly watched cheerleading contests on ESPN, so her counselor decided to just sit with her and watch. He learned that Mary knew a lot about cheerleading and really enjoyed showing her considerable expertise.

After a while, Mary decided, on her own, to organize a cheer-leading squad for a community basketball team sponsored by the agency that managed the supervised residence. Mary maintains her involvement in cheerleading for the team, which, by the way, gets her out and away from the TV and actively involved in the community. Mary's story illustrates the importance of following our own goals, even if they do not make sense to others. Staying true to her desire to be a BenGal ultimately opened other oppor-tunities. Walking the path cut by our goals often reveals alternative routes that would have never been discovered otherwise.

Supportive and Encouraging

Finally, for a relationship to enhance your prospects for change, it must be supportive and encouraging in the ways that *you* think best. Keep in mind that you are the director as well as the star of this movie, the story of your life. It is your view about what is most helpful that is key. You might, for instance, prefer your partner to be a sounding board or confidant and not offer any ideas, suggestions or advice. Or you might want someone to brainstorm and problem-solve with you. You might desire that he or she only follow the tasks that this book suggests. Or, after he or she gains an appreciation of your situation from your point of view, you might want the person to read this book and offer input to your situation, if he or she is willing.

You may even want different things from different change partners. Perhaps you want your best friend to take a more passive role, while you want your grandmother to offer ideas and suggestions. The more specific and explicit you are about the role you want each person to take, the better. Don't worry, this can change over time, and you are never locked in to one idea of how your change partner can be helpful. It is an ongoing negotiation, a conversation with someone you trust about his or her role in supporting you on your road to a different future. Ensuring a good fit between your expectations and your change partner's role enhances the chances of your success.

The Relationship Rating Scale

The Relationship Rating Scale (RRS) on page 69 provides a shorthand way for thinking about your potential change partners. The RRS is divided into four areas that decades of research have shown to be the qualities of change-producing relationships.[21] The scale is a way for you to organize your thoughts about your candidates so you can make the best decision; it can also identify areas that may benefit from further conversation with your potential change partner.

Make copies of the RRS for future use. Think about the people you have identified as candidates, and using a separate sheet for each, rate them on the different relational domains represented by the four lines. As you did with the ORS, place a mark on each line according to your relational experiences with each person, with those that aren't so good to the left, and those that are good to the right.

The scoring system is the same as that for the in chapter 2: each line has a potential score of ten, with a grand total possibility of forty. A scoring template is provided along with instructions on the reverse side of the RRS. Take the template or a centimeter ruler and measure your mark on each line and then add them up.

There is no specific cutoff score between relationships that have "good" or "bad" change potential. Higher scores (above thirty) reflect those relationships that have better change potential, because they may naturally have the qualities deemed important in research about therapy. Some people are just better listeners and provide validation without giving it much thought. For example, Carlos knew that he wanted his best friend, Taylor, to be his change partner. Taylor had always been there for Carlos and seemed to instinctively know how to validate Carlos and get him unstuck. You may already have one of these "naturals" in your life and need only to request that person's support. The major difference between your usual interaction with the person and the one discussed here is that your conversations will be focused on your efforts to change the situation that troubles you. When you request your candidate to be your change partner, it may help if you offer to return the favor in his or her efforts to change. Consequently, you may also consider applying the dimensions of the RRS to yourself as a change partner.

Some candidates may require you to discuss the qualities you are looking for in a change partner. So even those with lower

RELATIONSHIP RATING SCALE (RRS)

Name _____

Score: _____ Date: _____

Relationship: _____

Please rate this relationship's change potential by placing a mark on the line nearest to the description that best fits your experience.

| I didn't feel understood, respected and validated. | **Validation** | I felt understood, respected and validated. |

└───┘

| We did *not* work on or talk about what I wanted to work on and talk about. | **Goals and Topics** | We worked on or talked about what I wanted to work on and talk about. |

└───┘

| I did *not* feel supported and encouraged in my change efforts; the role was not a good fit. | **Supportive/Encouraging Role** | I felt supported and encouraged in my change efforts; the role was a good fit. |

└───┘

| Overall, this relationship may *not* be the best one for my change efforts. | **Overall** | Overall, this relationship is right for my change efforts. |

└───┘

Directions and Scoring of the RRS

- Make copies of the RRS for future use.
- On a copy, "take the temperature" of the conversation with your change partner by rating the domains of the alliance. Place a mark on each line, where low estimates are represented to the left and high to the right.
- The three areas, plus an overall rating, are measured on four ten-centimeter lines. The four ten-centimeter lines add to a possible total score of forty.
- Your score is simply the total of the nearest centimeter marked on each of the four lines.
- With the above template or a centimeter ruler, measure your mark on each line and add them up.
- Higher scores (above thirty) indicate a good change potential; lower scores suggest the relationship may need some work to support your growth.

scores can be enlisted. A simple conversation may be all that is necessary to fine-tune the relationship to reach its maximum change potential. Perhaps you need only make your expectations clear about what role you would prefer the person to take. Jason, for example, knew he wanted his mentor and friend Connie to be his change partner on his quest to resolve his estrangement from his mother. Jason scored Connie a twenty-six on the RRS, but not because anything was wrong with her. On the contrary, Connie had been an invaluable resource when Jason had left an abusive relationship. Jason's lower rating was because Connie had been very opinionated about Jason getting out of that relationship, which led him to worry a bit about whether she could listen and be more laid back in this situation with his mother. The RRS helped Jason to articulate both what he loved about his relationship with Connie *and* what he was concerned about in his current effort to change. Jason simply asked Connie if she could back off a little bit to let him brainstorm his thoughts and feelings about what he could do. Connie was happy to abide by Jason's wishes, as most people who want to help will be.

You may want a person to be your change partner regardless of his or her score on the RRS and feel that no conversation is warranted. Trust your instincts. You know which people have helped you in the past and how to accommodate any relational quirks they may have. There are no absolutes here (or anywhere else). The RRS is simply a quick reference to help you in your decision process—to incorporate the research about change in therapy to build the best possible chance for growth.

After you rate all your candidates based on your last conversation or an imagined one, separate those with the highest scores (or those who you believe have the best potential) and set a time with each person to talk about becoming a change partner in your journey to create a better life. Tell them they are very important people in your life and that you want to tap in to the connection you have with them to help inspire the changes you want to make. Briefly discuss your situation, what you are doing with this book and what role you would like them to play. Pay particular attention to how the conversations unfold according to the areas outlined on the RRS.

Thank each person for his or her time, and then rate how the discussion went on the RRS. Reflect on how your rating of the actual conversation compared to your previous perceptions. The RRS provides a way to gather your thoughts about potential change partners; your gut reactions also provide invaluable information. Based on both sources, select the person or persons who you feel will make the best change partners. But hold on to all of the other folks as well because they can be a part of your solution team. Chapter 7 will discuss how these other important people in your life can become a solution chorus—a collective voice of further support in your quest for transformation.

Once you have made your choice, talk to your change partner and set a time to get started with the exercise at the end of this chapter (page 82). This exercise will allow your change partner to understand and validate your circumstance, appreciate your strengths and join you in your pursuit of a better future.

Improving Your Change Partner's RRS Score—The Quid Pro Quo Method

If I keep from commanding people, they behave themselves. If I keep from preaching at people, they improve themselves. If I keep from meddling with people, they take care of themselves. If I keep from imposing on people, they become themselves.

Lao Tzu

If someone you feel would be a great partner winds up with a low score on the RRS, you may need to do a little work to bring him or her on board. Many times, a simple conversation with the person may be all that is needed to highlight the areas that need improvement. The most frequent glitch is a role mismatch—the role you want the person to play is not the one he or she is used to. Feel free to have this conversation in any way you think will have the best results with your chosen partner.

You may prefer some guidance with this process. One method that can help you improve a relationship's change potential is called the "quid pro quo," which is Latin for "something for something." It is designed to allow a collaborative discussion about problems and to negotiate how these problems may be resolved.[22]

The quid pro quo method assumes that relationships need to be redefined periodically to accommodate all the changes that have occurred to each individual. In this instance, the alliance required to support your change project may be different from the usual way the relationship works.

It is best to do this face-to-face, but if the telephone is the only way, that is okay too. Begin by telling your change partner all the characteristics, attitudes and behaviors you would like to see more or less of that would make your change efforts easier. This is not easy. Use the results from the RRS as a guide. Do not editorialize, justify, rationalize or explain yourself; just say what you want more or less of to support your quest for growth. Take ten minutes to complete this segment. There will be pauses, and that's okay. Take your time and think about what you want to say. Fill the ten minutes however you like. You may start with general things and go to specifics or vice versa. It doesn't matter. What is important is that you share what will make the relationship better for your change efforts without diluting your message with excess verbiage. Your partner needs only to listen carefully and record your list of "more ofs" and "less ofs."

Next, prioritize your top three "more ofs" and "less ofs" using the RRS as a guide. Now the real negotiation begins. Start with the number-one priority on your list, the most important and meaningful issue in helping your quest for change. For example, let's say that the number-one issue is "I would like you to be more supportive."

After you've determined the number-one issue, you must define it in a way that clearly expresses what you want. Specifically and in concrete terms that your partner will understand, what exactly are you wanting more of or less of? What would you see that would tell you that things were beginning to turn toward the desired change? What would be the first step your partner would take to address the issue under concern? What would "more supportive" look like? Try to think of what the first indicator would be of your change partner beginning to be more supportive, and negotiate for it at that level. Think small because small, noticeable changes lead to big changes, much like a snowball rolling down a hill. A first, noticeable step toward being more supportive may be simply listening to you without jumping in with unwanted suggestions or advice. *This first aspect of negotiation entails defining specifically what the desired change is and clarifying what an initial step toward positive change would look like.*

Finally, ask your change partner the following questions:

"What can I do that will permit you or make it easier for you to listen to me and not give me advice? How can I set the stage, through my own behavior, for you to give me what I want? How can I stack the deck so that I may be dealt the cards I want?" Think for a minute about what a change of operations this exercise requires. Instead of telling your change partner about how your needs are not being met, you are asking your partner how you can help him or her meet your needs.

In our example (requesting more support), your change partner could respond in a number of ways: he or she could say that you need to do nothing or all that is needed is a reminder; or he or she could say something specific, like how about giving him or her a call from time to time. This is the beauty of conversation—you never know what will happen and how things will be negotiated.

Address the list of priorities one by one. Once an agreement has been made, put it in writing. Try out the agreement when you and your change partner perform the first task together, the exercise at the end of this chapter. Pay particular attention to how your partner responds to your new way of getting what you want.

CHECKPOINT: The quid pro quo has five stages: (1) Tell your change partner what you would like to see more of or less of that would make the relationship more suitable for your change project, (2) record your list and prioritize the top three, (3) start with your first priority and specify in concrete terms what the first step toward making the desired change would be, (4) ask your partner what you can do to make it easier for him or her to accomplish the desired change, (5) put it in writing and try it out. Return the favor by asking your change partner for his or her list of "more ofs" and "less ofs" about you.

Recall Janice with the fear of flying from chapter 2. Although she considered Cindy, a longtime running buddy, to be her best friend in the world, Cindy's rating on the RRS was only a twenty-seven. Janice decided to use the structure of the quid pro quo method and set up a meeting with Cindy. Janice reassured her that the RRS was not a reflection of the quality of their relationship; rather it only indicated that the relationship needed to be fine-tuned to create an "alliance" that would best support her change efforts. Janice also informed Cindy that she would be happy to return the favor and address any concerns that Cindy may have.

Step One: Using the RRS as a guide, tell your change partner what you would like to see more of or less of that would make your change effort easier.

Janice: *Okay, Cindy, first off I want to say that I love you dearly and cannot imagine my life without you. I want you to continue being my best friend—I want a lot more of that! Wow, this is tough! Regarding my fear of flying and my efforts to change, I would like for you to listen more, to interrupt me less, to minimize my problems less, to validate me more, to understand more what my thoughts and feelings are about, to put a smiley face on every situation less, to have an answer for everything less, to give less advice, to take over conversations less, to compare me to you less. [This process included many awkward pauses for reflection and took a full ten minutes to complete.]*

Step Two: Using the RRS as a guide, prioritize your list.

Cindy wrote down the list and Janice prioritized her concerns. The top three items were minimizing less, giving less advice and comparing less.

Step Three: Start the negotiation process with your first priority, and specify in concrete terms what an indication would be that your partner was taking the first step toward making the desired change.

Janice: *Okay the first thing on my list is "minimizing my problems less." How do I make this concrete? What would be a sign that you were doing this? Well, when I say something that is bothering me, it would be great if you would just listen and not say things like, "Stuff happens; everyone feels that way; what's new about that?" It would be an indication that you were not minimizing my problems if you just responded, "That sounds tough," or "That must be hard for you," or anything that didn't make me feel like my concerns were trivial.*

Step Four: Ask your partner what you can do to make it easier for him or her to accomplish the desired change.

Janice: *So what can I do to help you to be less minimizing and respond in ways that don't feel like you aren't trivializing my concerns?*

Cindy: *Wow! I felt a little defensive at first, but I can see how those things are not very helpful to you, but you know I really didn't mean them to be trivializing. I thought I was helping. I guess it would help me to be reminded when I do these things so I can break a bad habit. Something else that would help is, and don't take this wrong, but you tend to complain a lot, and you know I am kind of an upbeat person, and well, I guess I have a low tolerance for talking about problems. I think it would help if we limited talking about problems in some way. I know it would really help me minimize less if you would ask me if it was a good time to talk about your problems.*

Janice: *Sounds good. Yeah, I do talk a lot about this stuff, and I never thought that you might get tired of it; I guess minimizing it was a way to change the subject. Okay, we can set aside times for problem talk. You know just about all the rest of my "more ofs" and "less ofs" revolve around the same issue—validation. The giving-advice thing and the comparing-me-to-you issue are all related. When you tell me I just need to fly more or just get over it, or you tell me how it is no big deal for you, it is all basically the same thing. So I want you to just pause when I say something and think about it from my point of view and not jump in with some idea that works for you but does nothing for me. We are totally different people and what works for you doesn't for me. If I saw you pause and reflect, it would tell me you were taking great strides to give less advice and not compare me to you.*

Cindy: *Okay, and again I can see how my approach to your flying problem has been a big pain! I certainly didn't mean it that way. I thought seeing how I handle flying would help you do it. So let me see, what can you do to help me pause and reflect more and consider things from your point of view? How about this? You know, we tend to talk about your stuff most of the time, and I wind up changing the topic because I get tired of talking about it. Let's make a rule that we spend equal time talking about our own lives. You know, I have concerns too, but I don't discuss them much. Also I think writing this out will help me remember to slow down in the way I react to you.*

Janice: *That makes sense to me. I'll be sure to ask you about your concerns too. Okay, let's write this out and go for a run. This is hard!*

Step Five: Put it in writing and try it out.

Janice and Cindy wrote out their agreement and kept a copy for later reference. They completed the exercises of this chapter and Janice rated Cindy a thirty-seven on the RRS.

Relationships and Change

We can do no great things; only small things with great love.

Mother Teresa

A gas furnace explosion when Rosa was six had killed both her father and sister. Her mother had collapsed emotionally after the accident and spent most of her days in bed. Rosa had effectively grown up without a parent and, partly as a result, had been sexually abused by a neighbor.

By the time I saw Rosa, she was thirty-two and had been in therapy for most of her adult life. She held a highly responsible but unsatisfying job in a biotechnology company. She had tried to kill herself five times, leading to five stays in psychiatric hospitals. Rosa called her latest therapist eight or nine times a day, leaving agonized messages with the answering service, demanding to be called back. Rosa carried the queen of all "disorders," the infamous "borderline personality disorder." The literature on "borderlines" frequently admonishes therapists not to respond to their "manipulative" attempts to extort attention and not to reward their "infantile neediness." So Rosa's demands were rarely, if ever, met by her therapists, which provoked her into escalating levels of distress and self-harm. She carried this ominous diagnosis and was on a popular antidepressant when her discouraged and burned-out therapist referred her, with a sense of relief, to me.

I decided to encourage Rosa's calls and nurture rather than limit our relationship. I worked hard to court Rosa's favor during our first four sessions, and it wasn't easy. She embodied hostility intertwined with spoken and unspoken demands. She sat in my office tight-lipped, twisting a handkerchief in her hands. She told me from the first that she wanted her phone calls returned because she only called when she was in really bad shape.

I returned her calls when I had spare time during the workday and again in the evenings after my last client, talking each time for about fifteen minutes. Perhaps because I reliably called her back, she rarely called more than once or twice a day. Then, after our fourth session, I went on a backpacking trip with my son, intentionally leaving my cell phone behind and arranging for someone else to deal with any client emergencies. After setting up camp, I felt inexplicably worried about Rosa. So I hiked back to my truck in the darkness and drove to a pay phone in a nearby town to see how she was getting along. She was okay.

That call proved to be a turning point. Afterward, Rosa became proactive in both therapy and in her daily life. She started going to church regularly, got involved in a singles group and signed up for additional technical training that would allow her to change jobs. In short, she mobilized her own resilience and resources. Her thoughts of suicide stopped, and she discontinued the antidepressant. In sessions, at her direction, we talked less about how lousy she felt and more about how she could change her life. Over the next six months, she left her unrewarding job, where everyone knew her as a psychiatric casualty, and joined a medical missionary project in Asia. Six months later, she wrote to let me know that things were going pretty well for her in northern Thailand. "I picture myself in your office, just telling you stuff and you listening," her letter said. "Every time I called you, you called me back. It didn't always help, but you were there. And I realized that is just what a little girl would want from her daddy, what I had been missing all my life and wanting so badly.

"Finally, when I was thirty-two years old, someone gave it to me. I sure am glad I got to know what it feels like to have someone care about me in that way. It was a beautiful gift you gave me. You also made me realize how much God loves me. When you called me that weekend you went backpacking, I thought to myself, 'If a human can do that for me, then I believe what the Bible says.' So thanks for loving me—because that's what you did."

Rosa taught me to never underestimate the power inherent in a caring and supportive relationship. Relationships empower people to bring out their best. Allow yours to do the same.

❧ CHAPTER THREE BOTTOM LINE ❧
Add a Helper: Recruit a Change Partner

Exercise Three: Recruiting Relational Support

1. **Select a primary change partner.**
   - Choose someone based on your instincts of whom you can trust, or generate a list of candidates.
   - Rate each on the RRS, based on your last conversation or an imagined one.
   - Talk to each person about your change project and his or her possible role.
   - Rate each discussion on the ORS.
   - Select the one or two people who score the highest and pass your "gut" test; the others can also be enlisted when you need a solution team (chapter 7 will explain those circumstances).
   - If necessary, use the quid pro quo method or a simple conversation to improve the change potential of a relationship.
2. **Complete the exercise from chapter 2 (page 57) with your change partner.**
3. **After completing the exercise with your change partner, retake the ORS.**
   - If your score increased by five or beyond the clinical cutoff, removing the obstacles of invalidation and succumbing to only one side of your story have provided a hopeful context for change. Read the "Empower Yourself" section in chapter 6 (page 165) and feel free to take a break. Or read on.
   - If your score did not improve, it only means that you may require something more specific to enlist your innate abilities to get you going. Read on.
4. **After completing the exercise with your change partner, rate the experience on the RRS.**
   - Use the rating as a way to organize your thoughts and to consider whether or not to give your partner feedback

about what he or she could do to help your efforts to change.
• Do not use the RRS in any critical or punitive way—it could hurt your relationship with the person and undermine its change potential.

4

Valuing Your View of Change

People are generally better persuaded by the reasons
which they have themselves discovered than by those
which have come into the minds of others

—Blaise Pascal

I f there is one thing that is clear from all the research about
change, besides the fact that change mostly emanates from
you, it is that there is no one righteous road to the promised
land of meaningful growth. Many roads lead to Rome. In fact,
there are about as many paths as there are people.

Finding the paths that fit your personal sensibilities about
change is what this chapter is all about. Everyone has his or her
own philosophies about life—ideas and beliefs about what it
really takes to face challenges and make important changes. You

may not realize it, but you possess untapped wisdom about what it will take to transform your life. This internal knowledge about how change happens, when enlisted or when suggested methods fit these core beliefs, makes it far more likely for something positive to occur for two reasons: one, because it enhances hope and the expectation of good things—we tend to feel more hopeful when a change plan resonates with our own sensibilities; and two, because people, as the quote that began this chapter suggests, are far more persuaded by their own views than by those of others. Plans emerging from or fitting with your own ideas will more likely motivate you to implement them, and therefore will most likely work. Similarly, if you are trying to help someone close to you, following his or her theory of change will most likely yield the most benefit.

Unfortunately, just as we have been convinced to blame ourselves for our misfortunes, to invalidate ourselves, most of us have been persuaded to discount our own views, insights and wisdom and, instead, defer to the experts. The doctor knows best . . . or does she? Believing that another person knows what is best for you is at least partially tragic because *you* know your situation better than anyone else, in ways that others can never know—you alone live in your skin, and your special insights from that vantage point hold the keys to achieving your goals. This chapter shows you how to discover your personal theory of change (or a loved one's) and how that theory can provide a plan for action or help you select the best possible strategies.

Your Personal Theory of Change

It is the familiar that usually eludes us in life. What is before our nose is what we see last.

William Barrett

In chapter 3, I told you about the Treatment of Depression Collaborative Research Program (TDCRP). Recall that this study found no difference in results from the different therapeutic approaches—the participant's view of the relationship with the therapist was far more important in predicting success than the treatment method. However, something else emerged from the TDCRP that did influence whether or not people benefited from the treatment they received. The study found that when a match occurred between a person's beliefs about the causes of his or her depression and the treatment he or she received, more improvement resulted. So if people believed their depressions were caused by psychological factors, they were far more likely to be helped if they received talk therapy approaches. On the other hand, if they received medication, they were less likely to benefit—and vice versa. So aside from the touted benefits of any treatment, to achieve success it is critical that the approach fits the individual's ideas about his or her problem and its solution.[23]

Similarly, in a large study of alcohol abuse, no differences in results were found between the two most common treatments (twelve-step disease model versus a behavioral-learning model). An interesting finding did emerge, however. Participants benefited differently depending on whether the treatment fit with their beliefs about their drinking before the treatment began. Those who believed their alcohol abuse was a disease and thought they needed to abstain from drinking to recover did well in the twelve-step group but terribly in the behavioral group;

individuals who believed their drinking was a bad habit and thought they could learn to control their drinking, improved significantly in the behavioral group but did not do well in the twelve-step group.[24]

CHECKPOINT: It is your perspective on change, your map of the territory, that should guide you to both the desired destination and the routes of restoration. Your view is absolutely critical to the success of your self-change program. So rather than changing your own ideas to fit what is offered to you (if you go to psychiatrist, you'll get a pill; if you go to a cognitive psychologist, you'll get cognitive therapy), I suggest the exact opposite: elevate your perceptions above all others, and allow your own view of change to direct your choices. Approaches to your situation are helpful only if you see them as relevant and credible. They are potentially helpful "lenses" to try on for fit to your own "frame" and "prescription" for change. Any method must have your buy-in, and the best way to accomplish this is by matching your views.[25]

Disregarding an individual's theory of change explains why many attempts at change fail and why many therapies are unsuccessful. My colleagues and I studied clients called "multiple treatment failures" and wrote a book about it called *Psychotherapy with "Impossible" Cases.*[26] We found that success could occur in the most difficult circumstances when the person's own ideas were recruited and implemented. My favorite story from the project is the heroic tale of Hannah.

Hannah, a delightful and precocious ten-year-old, was originally referred for treatment by her mother, Kim. Hannah's parents were divorced. She was sleeping in Kim's bed and having trouble adjusting to a new apartment, school and friends. At a mental health clinic, Hannah was identified as coming from a "dysfunctional family." Diagnosed with "separation anxiety disorder," she was referred for weekly group therapy.

After a few weeks, Kim reported that Hannah was experiencing nightmares. The group therapist responded by also seeing Hannah individually. The therapist pursued Hannah's impressions of her parents' relationship and encouraged her to remove herself from their problems. Following six months of concurrent group and individual treatment, there was little improvement. In fact, things were worse; Hannah was having more frequent nightmares and beginning to struggle at school. Thinking it might help, Hannah's mother next requested a female therapist.

Kim's wishes were respected, and a female therapist assumed the girl's care. Individual therapy now revolved around playing games to see what "themes came out." The therapist suspected sexual abuse. Three more months passed.

Still concerned about her daughter's lack of progress, Kim requested a psychiatric evaluation. The evaluation noted that Hannah still slept in mother's room and that her night terrors remained. An antidepressant was prescribed to relieve Hannah's separation anxiety. Another three months passed with no change in her condition.

Hannah, in twice-weekly treatment for over a year and now on medication, had become, at the age of ten, an "impossible" case. Looking back, we can reconstruct how the customary practice of ignoring people's own ideas about their needs contributes to the evolution of impossibility.

First, the Killer Ds were in full force. Because the labels "*dysfunctional* family" and "separation anxiety *disorder*" were established, Hannah's therapists understood her behavior through those perceptual filters, discounting Hannah and her strengths in the process.

Second, the therapists followed their own ideas about change rather than asking for Hannah's. Her first therapist, following a family therapy tradition, investigated the relationship between Hannah's symptoms and her parents' conflict. The therapist followed this line of inquiry despite an unremitting problem and mother's view that it was not relevant. In addition, from the outset of her treatment, there was no evidence to suggest that Hannah was a victim of sexual abuse. Throughout all her therapies, sexual victimization was never brought up by Hannah or Kim, nor was it ever confirmed. Yet, because it was hypothesized by one of her therapists, a goal was set to explore for it.

In both the group and individual therapies, the clinicians neglected to ask Hannah for her ideas about her predicament. As many therapists have been trained to do, they assumed an expert role. They assessed Hannah, diagnosed her problems and prescribed therapy. What she thought—her theory of change—was either ignored or deemed immaterial.

Dedicated to her daughter's welfare and dissatisfied with the care provided, Kim discontinued the medication and sought help outside the clinic.

In my first meeting with Hannah, I asked her what she believed would be helpful for resolving the "nightmares and sleeping in her room" problem. To this, Hannah expressed astonishment that someone finally wanted her opinion. She then suggested she could barricade herself in her bed with pillows and stuffed animals. The barricade would "ward off" the nightmares and her fears. In session two, she reported that her plan was working.

Out of the Mouths of Babes

The excerpts that follow come from our third session. They reflect Hannah's observations about what was helpful, and not helpful, in her treatment experiences.

Barry: *Well, how is it going?*

Hannah: *Just fine. I'm sleeping in my own room.*

Barry: *That's great! That's wonderful! I'm impressed by that still.* . . .

Hannah: *Therapists just don't understand . . . you also have the solutions for yourself, but they say, "Let's try this and let's try that," and they're not helping. You know, you're like, "I don't really want to do that." So what I'm saying to all therapists is we have the answers; we just need someone to help us bring them to the front of our head.* . . . *It's like they're [the solutions] locked in an attic or something, like somebody locked them in a closet and nailed them down.*

Barry: *So the things the therapists told you to do didn't help?*

Hannah: *It didn't help. I didn't want to do them.* They weren't my ideas and they didn't seem right.

When Hannah tried to comply with her therapists' ideas, the therapy stalled. The ideas were not her own. Being told what to do certainly didn't motivate her to do something for herself. It interfered with her being able to explore her problems and discover her own solutions. Hannah now speaks to what it was like for her to find her own solution to the sleeping problem.

Hannah: *I feel a lot better now that I came up with the solution to sleep in my own room, and I did it, and I'm proud of myself. And I couldn't be proud of myself if you told me, "How about if you barricade yourself in with pillows? Maybe that'll work." I wouldn't feel like I'd done it, so basically what I'm saying is,* you don't get as much joy out of doing something when somebody told you to do it.

Hannah was obviously wise beyond her years—as we all are

when given the chance. When provided the opportunity, she revealed her inventiveness, derived her own solution and, through that process, enhanced her self-esteem. Hannah's "pillow brigade" of bed buddies worked, and she continued to sleep in her room without nightmares. She also returned to her previous level of academic success. Hannah's lessons can serve us all—not only therapists but parents, partners and friends as well.

Of course not all situations will resolve as easily as Hannah's. Enlisting your ideas and following them is not the new miracle cure. However, tapping in to your internal wisdom often leads to solutions that are more likely to be helpful. In over five hundred cases considered "impossible" because of their history of multiple treatment failures, my colleagues and I learned that success can occur when the individual's personal theory of change is recruited and honored.

If you are thinking: "This is interesting Barry, but I really just want to know what to do about my situation; how I think of it is not important to me right now. I just want to cut to the chase and look at my problem in a way that allows me to solve it." That's okay and perfectly understandable. In other words, you are saying that you feel stuck and want solutions—your theory of change is that you want a different way to look at and tackle your problem. *Then stop reading now and go on to chapters 5 and 6.* If that doesn't produce the results you want, come back here and discover your ideas about change.

Learning Your Theory

An intense anticipation itself transforms possibility into reality; our desires being often but precursors of the things which we are capable of performing.

Samuel Smiles

You have a uniquely personal theory waiting for discovery, a framework for change waiting to be unfolded and utilized for a successful outcome. Finding your theory is not magic, nor does it require an epic search for a hidden clue, because your most useful views about change are those that are strongly held. Discovering your theory evolves from your curiosity about your ideas, attitudes and speculations about change.

Theory of Change Exercise

All you have to do is start by answering the following questions. Sit down at your computer or with a pad of paper and start now. Don't hold back. Now is not the time to worry about spelling or sentence structure. Anything and everything can be useful. If you draw a blank while thinking about these questions, that's okay. Just let these ideas percolate as you evaluate the different ideas in the next two chapters.

- **What are your hunches and educated guesses about your situation? What ideas do you have about what needs to happen for change or relief to occur? Forget about change; what will help you feel just a little better?**

To learn your theory, sometimes it helps to think about your usual method of or experience with change.

- **How does change usually happen in your life? Think**

of a time that you made an important change in your life. What happened exactly?

Also think about what you have already tried to help or resolve your current difficulties or life circumstance. This thought process can provide an excellent way for articulating your theory of change and preferred modus operandi. Exploring what you have previously tried enables you to frankly evaluate those attempts at change and their fit with what you believe to be helpful.

- **What have you tried to help the problem/situation so far? Did it help? How did it help? Why didn't it help? Were the attempts in or out of sync with your ideas?**

Once you have completed the theory of change exercise, keep it close by and continue to work on it as you read and understand more. If you haven't started yet, that's okay. More information, including a full example later on, will help you pull it together.

Implementing Your View of Change

Once you have started to articulate your ideas about change, it is time to figure out how to implement your theory—how to put your ideas to work or find an approach that fits your beliefs about your situation and the change process. There are two ways to implement your view of change: *Just do it* and *find the fit.*[27]

Just Do It!

The first way to implement your theory of change is quite simple. After you find out what your ideas are, then, as the Nike ad says, "Just do it." Hannah provides a great example of *just do it.* Here are some other examples:

Scott was a terrific guy with a very dry sense of humor who was troubled by voices that told him people were trying to kill him and other scary things. Sometimes Scott was so fearful that he wouldn't leave his supervised apartment for weeks on end; other times he was actually hospitalized. After discussing Scott's views of his situation, I asked him what he thought it would take to get a little relief from the voices. Scott said that it would help if he would start riding his bike again. Scott had been a world-class cyclist in college before the bottom fell out of his life. I then asked him how he thought he could get it going, and Scott said if I would go with him to the bike shop to get the parts he needed to fix his bike, it would be a good start. I went with Scott, and we ultimately held sessions during biking trips. Scott still struggled with the voices at times, but he stayed out of the hospital, and they never kept him from biking. He eventually joined a bike club and moved into an unsupervised living arrangement.

I can personally guarantee that you will never find bike riding listed as a treatment for hearing voices in any book for mental health professionals. Another example:

Melanie was a very humble woman who had struggled with alcohol abuse for most of her life. She had traveled the route of treatment many times before and knew pretty much what she needed to do. There was one thing that hung her up though. Everyone had always told her that she needed to stay sober for herself—she couldn't do it for anybody else; it had to be for her and her alone. Unfortunately, this couldn't have been further from Melanie's perspective of the world. As Melanie was encouraged to discuss her views of staying sober, she unfolded a different map of the road to her recovery. She described a profound faith in God, a deep belief in Christian humility and a sincere religious conviction of selflessness. The reason for Melanie's impasse was now apparent. Being told that her sobriety must be done for herself, not others, was tantamount to sacrilege from Melanie's point of view. Doing anything solely for herself constituted a violation of her fundamental essence.

When completing the theory of change exercise, Melanie said that when she was successful with sobriety, it was because she was in service of others—her mom, her roommate and others who would not be in danger from her driving. Melanie's guiding philosophy of Christian humility served as a starting point for a brainstorming session on how she could serve others in her sobriety, including telling others her story and helping out at the local homeless shelter. Thereafter, Melanie stayed sober. Her faith in God and sincere conviction of humility and selflessness, rather than an obstacle, provided a viable path to continued sobriety.

People often have good ideas about their situations but have not been allowed the space to explore them or given the encouragement to implement them. Trust your ideas and follow them to their logical conclusions.

Find the Fit

The second way to implement your theory of change is a little more involved. It's akin to finding an outfit that is just right for a special occasion: it has to please your own sensibilities about what looks good, and it must fit your unique body shape and size. An outfit must also highlight your best qualities, its color and style bringing forth your finest attributes. In addition, the outfit needs to suit the situation in which you intend to wear it and must complement what you already have to create a coherent ensemble.

Many resources are available to help you find methods that strike a chord with your views. If you already know, however, that you feel stuck and are looking for different ways to understand and handle your concerns, then move on to chapters 5 and 6, and see if those ideas ring true for you. Otherwise, the easiest place to begin to *find the fit* is in the appendices of this book and at the Web site *www.whatsrightwithyou.com*. Using these two sources as a starting point, there are a couple of ways to find strategies that resonate with your views: First, begin your search by defining your specific type of problem, struggle or concern (depression, anxiety, smoking, family conflict, etc.). With your description of your theory of change in front of you, read the techniques in appendix A or on the "Smorgasbord of Ideas" page on the Web site that address your particular challenge. In both places, for example, you will find many ideas on addressing depression and other problems. As you go over the different strategies, pay attention to whether or not they make sense to you and your theory of change. If one stands out, then give it a shot.

You can also *find the fit* in a reverse fashion: read through the different approaches to therapy in appendix B and see if any of them match your ideas about change. Don't worry; for all their pomp and circumstance, schools of therapy are not really that complicated. My favorite therapists have reduced the major approaches to human dilemmas to their very essences, enabling you to quickly appraise whether they ring true to your own ideas. After all, when it comes down to it, so-called expert knowledge is not rocket science (but don't tell anyone). If one of the theories really rings a bell for you, search for more information on how it may address your situation on the Internet or at a bookstore.

You may also surf the Web in a similar fashion to *find the fit*. For example, if you plug in "depression" on a search engine, you will likely discover sites for cognitive-behavior therapy, interpersonal therapy, antidepressants and other alternatives. You then could explore what those approaches have to say and judge the degree of fit with your ideas. You can take some methods from each if you like; there are no rules here except to find something that makes sense to you and resonates with your personal philosophies.

Keep in mind that any approach you explore will describe itself as the greatest thing since sliced bread—as the "scientifically proven" inside track on human problems and the best and only remedy for the problem at hand. This is akin to walking into a store looking for something to wear for a special occasion and finding it has but one outfit to offer—one size, color and style fits all. Despite the enthusiasm and expertise of the salesperson, you would likely make a quick exit, unless of course this one outfit was a perfect fit for what you were looking for.

A couple of caveats: If you go to one of the popular search engines on the Web and type in a specific problem (e.g., depression or anxiety), your findings will likely suggest medication treatments. Pharmaceutical companies dominate the Internet, and drug therapies are privileged because of it. Sometimes it is difficult to decipher that drug companies are involved. For example, Depression Resource Center and WebMD Health are at least partially underwritten by Eli Lilly, the maker of Prozac. Many "patient organizations" are heavily funded by drug companies. For example, the Anxiety Disorders Association of America receives about 75 percent of it annual income from pharmaceutical companies; 91 percent of the budget of the National Depressive and Manic Depressive Association is provided by drug companies.[28] This only means that the information on their Web sites about treatments is heavily skewed toward medication and a biological view of problems. Because most of the information you find promotes medication doesn't mean that drug treatment is superior to other methods or should be chosen as a first line of action. Don't get me wrong, *there is nothing wrong with trying medication if it fits your theory of change.* The point is that you may have to look a little harder for alternatives, given the influence that drug companies have on the Web and everywhere else. Visit *www.whatsrightwithyou.com* for such alternatives.

Also be aware that many, if not most, of the sites that you find will be "disordered"! They will be heavily steeped in Killer D terminology and will talk about the challenges of life as if they were all medical problems. Don't allow the aura of expertise and science that shrouds these descriptions to fool you into believing that you have the latest fashion in disease or are damaged goods. Take what they have to offer but leave the Ds behind.

Lamont described himself as depressed and completed the theory of change exercise. He had a hunch that his depression was related to his marriage, which had seemed stale but was largely not spoken about. Since Lamont believed his depression was mostly a problem in his relationship with his wife, he pursued ideas from different family therapy approaches to find a good fit. One idea that resonated with Lamont was that the depression itself was a metaphor for what he wanted to say to his wife about their relationship (see appendix B). His lethargy and feelings of apathy reflected how his relationship with his wife had grown lifeless. That idea gained currency and motivated Lamont to start some much-needed dialogue with his wife that resulted in Lamont feeling much better about his life.

Although it was relatively easy for Lamont, finding a good fit can be tough; there are a lot of options out there. This is where your change partner can be invaluable. Again, think of it as finding the right outfit. There are many choices out there and many that you would look good in. Sometimes you need to get feedback from someone you trust about the outfit you have just pulled from the rack. Talking with your change partner about your theory can help your ideas evolve into a specific plan. He or she may help you harvest your good ideas and encourage you to implement them. Or by helping you flesh out your theory, your change partner can help your ideas coalesce enough to find possible strategies.

Margaret, at her wit's end with her teenage daughter Lisa, completed the theory of change exercise. Lisa was skipping school, coming home late, ignoring her mom's protestations and to Margaret's horror, cursing her out with the vilest language imaginable. Margaret had tried everything from rewards and punishments to quiet talks, from screaming tirades to impassioned pleadings—but to no avail. Lisa also refused therapy. Margaret's theory of change exercise revealed that she wasn't sure what would help, but that she knew that Lisa needed to be shaken up somehow. Margaret and her change partner massaged this idea until it began to take some form. The strategy that Margaret was looking for would really throw Lisa for a loop and enable her to see what she was doing to herself and her mother. Margaret and her change partner agreed that something a bit different from the direct approach seemed in order. They came across an unorthodox but potentially very fun idea called constructive payback—a tactic that turns the tables on tough adolescents by confusing the heck out of them (see appendix A). Margaret experimented with ways she could "pay back" Lisa when she acted up—like spilling juice on her as she was leaving for school, running the vacuum while Lisa was on the phone, leaving crumbs in her bed, etc. Margaret, in private, howled with laughter after these experimentations. Because this tactic is most effective when combined with an attitude of helplessness, Margaret apologized profusely when Lisa confronted her and explained her mishaps away because of her own stupidity, depression and senility. Lisa didn't know what hit her and began looking more at the impact of her behavior on her mother. She also stopped the four-letter-word barrage against her mother, although early on she did say, "Mom, I'm worried about you. You're going f——— nuts." Margaret just beamed when she told that story to her change partner. Although it was her least favorite word, she intimated, imagine that—Lisa was worried about her!

Margaret's chosen approach worked because it was a good fit for her; that tactic will not be a good fit for everyone. That's the beauty of having so many choices.

Sometimes finding the fit is a trial-and-error process. You thought the outfit looked great on you in the store, but when you try it on at home, you stare at the mirror in disbelief wondering, "What was I thinking?" That's okay, because sometimes you may have to implement a strategy before you can really determine whether it is right for you. There is never anything to lose by trying something; you only gain more information about your theory and what might work. Sometimes making the wrong choice helps you make the right one next time around.

Finally, even after a good deal of reflection or consultation with your change partner, how your theory of change translates into a plan or matches any approach may still not be clear. That's okay—no idea, no matter how helpful for some, is useful to everyone who tries to implement it. The theory of change concept is no different. If you are unable to mold your ideas into a plan or find a fit, or if this process seems too complicated, please don't be concerned. Sometimes it is just easier to explore different ideas about what do and then see if those ideas resonate with your own sensibilities about change. Chapters 5 and 6 offer many options for outfits that may provide the right style, color and fit for you.

Important! If you have realized a change by implementing your theory of change, there is one more step to stamping it in for good, and that is to "Empower Yourself." Go to chapter 6 and complete step four in the solution-building section (page 165), and then go on to chapter 7 to monitor and maintain your gains.

Theory of Change in Action: Amy

Hope is like the sun, which, as we journey toward it, casts the shadow of our burden behind us.

Samuel Smiles

Amy was a twenty-eight-year-old homemaker who had been in therapy on and off since her teenage years, which were fraught with drug dependence and rebellion. Amy carried many of the Killer Ds on her shoulders. Although her turbulent history was behind her, she remained troubled by her perceptions that she was incompetent at relationships because she was either a doormat for others or was "inappropriate" and out of control from time to time. Amy scored a nineteen on the PRS.

Amy Learns Her Theory of Change

- **What are your hunches and educated guesses about your situation? What ideas do you have about what needs to happen for change or relief to occur? Forget about change; what will help you feel just a little better?**

Okay, I have really changed over the years, especially since becoming a mother and an active member of my synagogue. Other people though, especially my in-laws, are still accustomed to my role as a "mental patient" and everyone's fall guy. I am doing well in my life now—I haven't had any drugs or alcohol in over five years! I am teaching a Hebrew class, and I just enrolled in the local university. They just don't see the real me because I have always been in therapy. They just typecast me and have a limited way of thinking about me because of my history. I give too much in relationships and often wind up being the butt of jokes. Then I stumble when I try to handle these situations. Sometimes I blow up and just make it worse or just start crying. I am tired of being the "resident scapegoat." I want to be taken seriously and respected.

This all comes to a head with my in-laws. To get some relief from this situation, I need to deal with them better. I have to stop crying or blowing up, and handle the jokes and ridicule in stride. I wind up reinforcing their view of me as a mental patient.

Amy and her change partner discussed the words that Amy used in her answers to the questions. "Resident scapegoat" provided an important clue about how she saw herself and what needed to happen for change to occur. Amy's response reflected resentment about being wronged by others and a strong desire to change others' perceptions of her. Moreover, she believed that if she was to experience some relief, she needed to manage her in-laws better when they ridiculed her. Finally, notice the words "role" and "typecast" in Amy's description; these are further clues that might help find strategies that are a good fit.

- **How does change usually happen in your life? Think of a time that you made an important change in your life. What happened exactly?**

Well, I have been through a lot of changes, including the birth of my daughter, becoming spiritual and a lot of other things. I have found confidence and self-respect in many areas of my life. I guess the change that is most relevant to my struggle with my in-laws is when I stood up to my best friend. She is my friend and all, but she seemed to take every opportunity to make fun of me, no matter how much I told her I didn't like it. Whenever my friend makes jokes at my expense and sees that I am bothered by it, she quickly tells me that she is only kidding and to lighten up. I try to explain that it is not funny to me—and then it is off to the races! I either cry or blow up or sit quietly the rest of the time.

I finally did something different from my usual ways of handling my "fall guy" role. I met my friend for lunch and received the customary put-downs, but somehow I laughed along with the jokes, although I was hurt by them. It was weird, but I felt more in control—I just decided that I was not going to fight city hall this time. I then refused, despite my friend's insistence and guilt induction, to go out of my way to drop her off at the mall (her car was in the shop) because it would make me late to the day-care center to pick up my daughter. I think I gained strength by my friend's dumbfounded response. The whole thing was almost like I was someone else, as if I were playing a different role. I played the part of someone confident and unaffected by her pressure. For whatever reason, my friend hasn't called me back. I may call her once I figure all this out.

Although I am very sad about the possible loss of this friendship, I feel very positive about the way I handled myself. I guess I see the way I handled that situation as an indication that I am actually changing; I didn't buckle under by apologizing or crying—it just didn't get to me the way it usually does.

I guess this change was spontaneous; it just seemed to happen in the moment, but usually I have to think things through and plan them out for something different to occur. I really like to get all my ducks in a row. Like when I decided to go back to school, I discussed it thoroughly with my mom and planned the courses I would take well in advance. So I think I need to plot things out for any change to really work for me.

I also know that I want others to be involved. I think I operate better when I have support. Through all my difficulties, my mom was always there, and she helped a lot. Someone else I know I can count on is my rabbi. I think I need to be able to bounce my ideas off someone else and further explore where they can go.

Note how Amy's theory continues to coalesce. She not only identifies a potential strategy (playing a role) but also presents a clear idea of what her plan would entail. With important changes, Amy likes to think things through and develop a specific attack with the support of her mom and her rabbi.

- **What have you tried to help the problem/situation so far? Did it help? How did it help? Why didn't it help? Were the attempts in or out of sync with your ideas?**

Boy, I have tried just about every technique imaginable for communicating my distress directly to others about their laughs at my expense. I've read self-help books and attended seminars on effective communication. You know, these approaches, as useful as they can be, not only didn't help, but were sometimes used as objects of ridicule! My in-laws would often ask me if that was something I learned from my shrink. I also participated in a codependency group for several months, but I didn't like it because it seemed to make me the bad guy in these situations.

I tried therapy. Although I identified these same issues, my therapist focused on my "boundary confusion" and poor sense of self. I worked hard in therapy, but I guess I disagreed with the implication that I was totally at fault for troubles in my relationships. Maybe I used to have poor self-esteem, but not anymore. The codependency stuff just was not a good fit for me. I just didn't understand how my caring about people liking me was a bad thing. And the therapy also seemed to turn everything around to me. I didn't understand how people making fun of me was because of my poor self-concept.

But the communication stuff I think is real important and it has helped me in other areas of my life, like with my husband. But it did not work in this situation because of my in-laws' views of me. They really disapprove of my troubled past, and it seems that they can only treat me like a "mental patient." I guess I really want to throw them a curve and change the way they look at me.

Exploring previous solutions also revealed many blind alleys to avoid, as well as more information regarding Amy's theory of change. Her previous attempts failed because they invalidated her and placed her at the center of blame for her troubles. This was not a good fit with Amy's view of herself, and as chapter 2 pointed out, blame rarely leads to action. The thing that did fit for her, direct communication, didn't work because of her in-laws' refusal to participate. Unfortunately, as sound as communicating directly is, it usually has to go both ways to be useful.

Amy Implements Her Theory of Change

One thing that emerged from Amy's writings and her explorations with her change partner was that she wanted to play a different role with her in-laws, and she wanted to throw them a curve. Amy thought long and hard about the role she played with her best friend, where it came from and how she could implement that success with her in-laws. Amy decided to *just do it,* but was unsure how. She talked with her rabbi to help her sort her thoughts, and a feeling of excitement, a sense of discovery, emerged from their conversation. They explored in detail the role that Amy wanted to play. Amy indicated it was someone who was bright, witty and, in a sophisticated way, didn't take any crap.

That conversation got Amy thinking about the role in a more specific way. Amy embraced the idea of playing a particular role and decided to see if she could *find the fit* with her idea. She searched for information and found a story about a person who decided to play the role of a famous person who could handle the situation with which the person was struggling (see appendix A). The woman in the story had chosen Joan of Arc, and it had been helpful.

Amy thought that it was a little weird, but gave considerable thought to who could shatter her resident scapegoat role. Slowly a name materialized in Amy's mind: Katharine Hepburn. Amy felt she had discovered a treasure. She beamed with pleasure and anticipation.

Because of her view that she did best when she planned things through, Amy turned her attention to writing the script for her role in an upcoming visit from the in-laws. Amy and her mother plotted how Amy could respond to specific situations. For example, when asked the typical question of whether or not she was still seeing a shrink, Amy might reply that yes, she was, and in fact, her therapist increased her sessions because she was on the brink of a total psychotic break. If asked what she learned most recently in therapy, Amy might reply that she was learning anger management techniques, explaining how she is supposed to break something in the room before damaging any people. She was to accompany this comment by picking up something breakable in the room and smiling that disarming, confident Hepburn smile. Amy and her mother nearly choked from laughter. Amy also decided to do all she could to look the part, including the trademark Hepburn scarf around her neck. The chosen approach, playing a role, fit Amy's particular viewpoint and the situation and consequently provided the motivation for her to try something different with her in-laws.

Amy gave an Academy Award–winning performance of Hepburn when her in-laws visited. By the end of the weekend, she found herself joking and enjoying herself with them without playing a role. The mold had been broken. She particularly relished her brother-in-law's dazed and confused look when she responded to his questions about her therapy. Amy's PRS score soared to a 32 after the visit.

Trust Your Instincts

What really nourishes our souls is the knowing that we can be trusted, that we never have to fear the truth, that the foundation of our very being is good stuff.

Fred Rogers

After several years of working in a factory, and a steady stream of promotions from laborer to second in command in a large department, I decided to quit my job and return to school full time. When I told my dad what I intended to do, he was both shocked and worried. He had seen me come back from a tumultuous adolescence, and he was very proud of me. I was well respected in the factory, I made a good income and my future was bright. To my dad, job security and a regular paycheck went a long way toward a happy life. After all, it had ended his poverty-stricken life and allowed him to carve out a piece of the American dream. Dad told me it just wasn't a rational thing for me to do;

you just don't give up a good job in hard economic times.

After a while, Dad stopped talking, and we sat in silence. Then he took a deep breath and asked me why. I told him that the part of my job I enjoyed most was talking to people and figuring out how we could work together to meet common goals, that people were my passion, not producing tires. I mentioned that people often sought me out to discuss their problems. I shared how a psychology course I took rekindled my long-held dream of being a psychologist, and that while it would be challenging and something no one else in our family had ever done, I knew I could do it because he had always believed that I could do anything I set my mind to.

Dad smiled and said he thought I was crazy nonetheless, and he would prefer that I just give up the whole idea. Then he talked about the times in his life when he had gone against the grain of what others thought was best—when he joined the Marines as soon as he was eligible, when he confronted soldiers who were abusing a Japanese prisoner, when he left his home in Kentucky to work in the factories and when he didn't take any guff from his department manager. For sure, he said, not all of these things worked out—he wasn't always right, but he had always trusted his instincts. And he said, "That's exactly what you should do."

Long after I graduated, my dad helped me restore a building I had purchased for my practice. When we were standing outside the building admiring our handiwork, Dad brought up the conversation we had some ten years prior. He kidded me about being nothing but "an overeducated hillbilly" and said, "It sure is a good thing you trusted your instincts instead of what I was comfortable with." And we both laughed.

❧ CHAPTER FOUR BOTTOM LINE ❧
Never Underestimate Your Own Ideas

Exercise Four: Valuing Your View of Change

1. **Learn your theory in three ways.**
   - What are your ideas about change?
   - What are your usual methods of change?
   - What have you tried so far to solve this problem?
2. **Implement your theory of change in one of two ways.**
   - Just do it! Take your ideas and implement them. Follow them to their logical conclusion. Monitor the effects and adjust accordingly.
   - Find the fit. Find a good fit with your ideas by searching either your specific problem or situation, or by looking at different approaches to change. If no action seems apparent from these searches, discuss your ideas with your change partner and see what evolves. If no plan emerges, don't worry. Go to chapters 5 and 6.
3. **Take the ORS again and compare your results. Sometimes just understanding your own views and where they can take you is enough to propel you into a more comfortable place. Or you may have implemented your theory and realized results. If your ORS score has risen by five or above twenty-five, please go to step four in chapter 6 (page 165) and "Empower Yourself."**

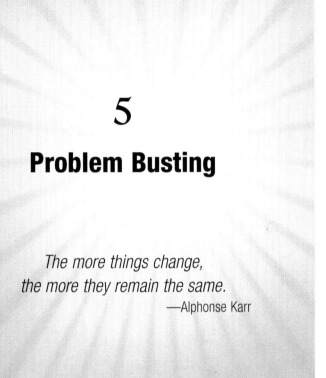

5

Problem Busting

The more things change,
the more they remain the same.
—Alphonse Karr

M<!-- -->any people like having something they can hold on to when they are on unfamiliar ground—such as when they are trying to change their lives. This chapter provides the first of two formats to help you find your way when you feel cast adrift in the sea of information about your problems and advice on what you can do about them. Chapters 5 and 6 give you an insider's view of therapy and teach you the tricks of the trade of how to focus your efforts to make significant personal changes.

This chapter provides specific instructions about how to examine your life experiences, recognize the patterns involved in problems and try different strategies to forge new directions in your life. This approach is deceptively simple but offers fresh ideas for solving old problems. It holds the ideal that people, no matter how troubled they are, no matter how distressing their situation, no matter how hopeless they feel, can move to a different place in relatively short order. An inspection of the very solutions we choose to address our troubles allows the possibility of a different future to enter a stale present, like fresh air from an open window after a long winter.

The Solution Is the Problem

Daring as it is to investigate the unknown, even more daring it is to question the known.

Kaspar

Over thirty years ago, a group of maverick clinicians collectively known as the Mental Research Institute (MRI) made a remarkable discovery.[29] They discerned that the simple examination of the relationship between a problem and the solutions applied to address it enables a unique problem-solving vantage point. Moreover, they concluded that because of the intimate connection between the solution and the problem, one needs only to change the solution to affect the problem—no matter how long the problem has been around!

Here is how this unique perspective unfolds: Problems begin from some ordinary difficulty, of which there are always many—the next one is in the mail. This difficulty may be an everyday situation like a relationship concern or nervousness, or it may come from an unexpected event, like the loss of a job, a car wreck or an F on a report card. Most often, the difficulty is associated with everyday stuff and the trials and tribulations regularly experienced in living, working and raising a family.

When difficulties arise, we ordinarily fall back on coping styles that have previously worked for us. Usually they continue to work, but sometimes they don't. For a problem to appear, only two conditions need be fulfilled. First, a difficulty is mishandled (an attempted solution doesn't work). Second, when the difficulty persists, more of the *same* ineffective solutions are applied.

Consider Jim, a thirty-six-year-old attorney. When he was a law student, Jim began experiencing insomnia during times of high stress. But this time was different. The insomnia just would not go away. Jim knew why he was having trouble sleeping: a far more demanding person had assumed authority over his work just when Jim was closing in on becoming a partner in the firm. In the past, Jim would struggle for a couple of nights, and then after implementing one of his strategies, his normal sleep patterns would return. Jim tried these methods, like watching TV or reading or soaking in a hot bath until he was tired, but he'd be wide awake as soon as he turned off the lights and hit the sheets. All of the methods he had successfully used before to rid himself of the insomnia didn't do the trick this time.

After a week of no sleeping, he found that his fatigue began affecting his work performance. Jim searched the Internet and asked people for their remedies. He tried relaxation tapes, soothing music, hot baths with special oils and the perennial favorite, a glass of wine before bed. Another week of sleeplessness passed, and it was obvious that the "new" methods hadn't budged the problem. Jim became more distressed, and he noticed that he was becoming perpetually crabby. His colleagues joked about his need for a vacation—not exactly the kind of image he wanted to portray while being considered for partnership.

Jim redoubled his efforts; he went to yoga class and bought new relaxation tapes; he tried natural sleep remedies and started drinking more wine. The wine helped a little but often left him feeling not rested and a little queasy in the morning. He found himself wanting a glass of wine earlier and earlier in the evening. Finally, after four weeks of insomnia, in desperation, Jim saw a doctor who prescribed a popular sleeping pill. Sometimes medication breaks the cycle of insomnia and can be quickly discontinued, but it didn't work that way for Jim. The pill helped at first and provided much needed relief, but the insomnia soon raised its ugly head again, and Jim found himself lying awake even after taking the pill. Jim, now looking a wreck and worrying about becoming addicted to sleeping pills, believed his chances at becoming a partner were all but gone.

Problems, then, develop from everyday life, chance events or transitional circumstances. Jim experienced difficulties falling asleep in response to the stress of a new supervisor and a pending partnership. He tried the things that had worked before, as well as a host of similar strategies. None of the methods produced positive results, and some even made things worse or introduced new problems. All of his solutions revolved around the theme of making himself drowsy or relaxed enough to fall asleep; all were designed to "make" him sleep.

Over time, the original difficulty grows in size and importance, perhaps to a point where it bears little or no resemblance to the original difficulty. The more the ineffective solution is applied, the bigger the problem gets. In essence, *the solution becomes the problem.* Our attempted solutions, the very acts we hope will improve problems, actually contribute most to the problems persisting and even worsening. For Jim, the original difficulty grew and grew until it affected not only his job performance and relationships at work, but also his ability to earn a partnership.

The problem evolves into a vicious cycle: the more the problem occurs, the more attempted solutions are applied. Attempted solutions that fail to produce a desired change become the impetus for more of the problem. Simultaneously, the worsening problem beckons more solution attempts. And so on. This vicious cycle occurs despite the best intentions and diligent efforts of those involved. Jim sincerely worked hard at solving his sleep problem and gave it his all. He continued pouring on the solutions despite evidence that none of the strategies were useful. Why?

Consider the puzzle depicted in figure 5.1.

FIGURE 5.1 The Nine-Dot Puzzle

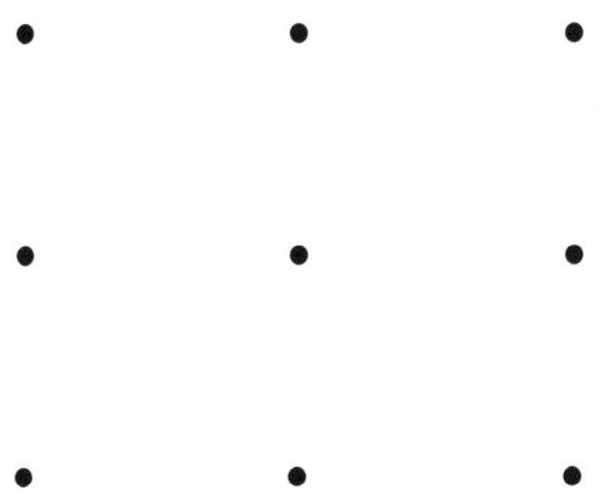

Connect the nine dots in figure 5.1, using only four straight lines, without taking your pencil off the paper. If you have not seen this puzzle before, please take a few minutes to try to solve it. Now, turn the page and look at figure 5.2, which shows the solution. Few people think of extending the straight lines beyond the dots, even though nothing in the instructions prohibits it. Most people, in effect, superimpose an imaginary square on the dots, which precludes resolution. By acting on the erroneous assumption that the lines cannot extend beyond the dots, you guarantee two things: frustration and failure. Those are the identical outcomes you face when you are stuck in a problem and continue to use the same solution strategies. These were just the things that Jim experienced.

FIGURE 5.2 The Nine-Dot Puzzle: The Solution

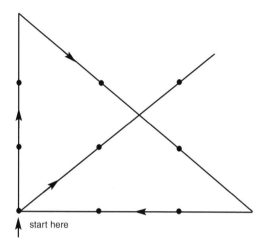

start here

Like Jim and his insomnia, you probably recognized early on that the solution to the puzzle in figure 5.1 using your current strategy seemed impossible. Even so, you likely continued to apply the same solution over and over again, just as you do when approaching problems in your life. You may have tried harder, or worked faster, but your solutions based on the restrictions of the imaginary square were doomed to failure. Jim pulled out all the stops, but as long as he tried to force himself to fall asleep by whatever method, he was only doing "more of the same" and remained destined to struggle with insomnia. Doing more of the same makes things worse.

Being freed from the constraints of the imaginary square shifts our view of the nine-dot puzzle and makes its solution immediately obvious. Looking at the relationship between the problem and our attempted solutions opens new options for consideration. *New directions appear as we discard the blinders of our current solution attempts.*

This simple view of how problems develop is understandable *and* hard to accept. At one time or another, we all handle things inappropriately. Yet what makes some of us persist with an ineffective solution even when experience says it's failing?

The Killer Ds provide a rapid answer. We are told that mental deficits, chemical imbalances or personality disorders explain such self-sabotage. But there is a far more simple explanation. The connection between the problem and continued ineffective attempted solutions, the so-called problem cycle, is a normal human response to difficult times. We are only loyally obeying a commonsense law: "If at first you don't succeed, try, try again." The task here is to learn to disobey the law and think outside the box.

The Three Solution Boxes

Many, but not all, problems and their solution attempts fall into three general themes. Consider Jim's dilemma. His solution attempts characterized a common pitfall: *trying to force something that can only happen naturally.* In this category of unhelpful solutions, the person is troubled about a normal bodily function like sexual performance, bowel or urinary function, appetite, sleep, etc. Normally these things fluctuate, and usually they correct themselves. But when people make willful, concerted efforts to fix these difficulties when they occur, they put themselves in a position of trying to coerce something that can only occur spontaneously or thoughtlessly. You cannot will yourself to sleep or force yourself to have an orgasm or erection any more than you can make yourself hungry. The trick here is to do something that interrupts the willful attempts that perpetuate the problem. We will return to Jim later in the chapter for ideas to address these situations.

Another common solution theme is: *trying to master a fear or control an emotion or thought by avoiding it.* Janice's trouble with flying exemplifies this category of solutions. People struggling with a fear or anxiety (flying, being around others, speaking in public, etc.) often orchestrate their lives to prevent the situation from happening. They live in dread of experiencing the situation, choreograph their daily lives to avoid it, and thereby increase the problem's importance and impact exponentially. In the case of fears and anxieties, people often believe that others handle these things in stride and possess some magic sword that enables them to slay the dragons lurking in elevators, planes, talking to the opposite sex, etc.

Those who experience negative feelings (anger, sadness, etc.) or intrusive thoughts (I am worthless; I hate my job) often believe they will be swept away by the feelings or thoughts if they allow them to occur—that they will lose total control and drown once the floodgates are opened. Consequently, they spend a considerable amount of energy holding down the fort, attempting to ward off the feelings or thoughts or to stop them when they appear. Unfortunately, despite their constant vigilance, they find that the unwanted feelings or thoughts are always lurking, ready to strike at the most inopportune moments. There is always a breach in the wall. In many ways, the intrusive thoughts and feelings are made all the more powerful by all the effort to prevent or avoid their occurrences. It can be useful to expose the struggling person to the avoided situation or emotions in a way that perfect mastery or success is not an expectation— to allow the person to confront the troubling circumstance, learn from it and move on. We will revisit Janice and her fear of flying to offer suggestions about these situations.

The final solution-attempt category describes how people

often address problems with others: *trying to solve a relational problem by persuasion, argument or contention.* This group of strategies covers disputes or disagreements in which one person is trying to get another person to do something he or she is not motivated to do, or when one person sees a problem and the other doesn't. These attempts usually start out innocently with one person bringing the problem to the other's attention, but then typically go south from there. Frequently used in marital and parent-child conflicts, solution attempts from this category often degenerate into criticism, defensiveness and hard feelings. People caught in this rut believe they need only make their point more adamantly and it will be heard—if they confront, persuade and cajole enough, the other person will finally see the light.

Consider Shanda and Louis. They have been married for nine years. Since the recent birth of their first child, Shanda has become increasingly aware that Louis regularly points out imperfections in her methods of doing things. The first thing Shanda does to address the problem is mention it to Louis. She explains that when they were first married, she appreciated the benefit of Louis's knowledge and experience, but now she feels he is treating her like a child. Shanda asks Louis to please hold his critical comments in abeyance. Louis agrees to stop criticizing her.

At first Louis is as good as his word, but he soon begins sharing his observations and making suggestions about better ways for Shanda to do things. When Shanda points this out to him, he accuses her of overreacting and not being able to accept constructive criticism. Shanda starts defending herself every time Louis makes any comments and continues to make Louis aware of his now "critical and paternalistic nature." Louis responds by sharpening the edge of his critical comments, and the interaction between the couple becomes sparse. When they do converse, Louis is more apt to criticize Shanda, now about her crazy feminist ideas, as well as the way she does almost everything. The couple's discussions become plagued by an unspoken tension. Shanda decides to try a different approach. She goes on "strike" and discontinues doing anything that Louis criticizes her about. When Louis comments that the spaghetti sauce needs more garlic, Shanda announces that she is no longer cooking. Louis blows up in anger, and they both say many things they later regret. Now an unspoken hostility underlies the relationship.

Shanda believed she was trying many *different* strategies to improve her situation. In reality, she was only trying slight variations on a single theme: "I will make my dissatisfaction apparent to him, and he will respond with less criticism." Or more generally, Shanda is trying to solve the criticism problem by persuasion, argument and contention. She wound up with increased criticism and a hostile backdrop to all her interactions with her husband. A relatively benign situation can grow into serious conflict despite the good intentions of the people involved.

To address this couple's situation, as well as Jim's and Janice's, a fresh perspective is needed to break out of "nine-dot" rut—the theme to which your solutions are enslaved. The four-step problem-busting model will help you challenge your loyalty to ineffective solutions—to break the law of "try, try again"—and unleash your creativity to solve the problems that concern you the most.

The Four-Step Problem-Busting Model

The dogmas of the quiet past are inadequate to the stormy present.

Abraham Lincoln

Step One: Who is doing what, to whom, and how does that behavior constitute a problem?

The first step is a *concrete, action-oriented* answer to the question, "Who is doing what that presents a problem, to whom and how does such behavior constitute a problem?" Asking this question enables you to identify the first crucial part of the problem cycle. What you want to know is what each individual involved in the problem is specifically saying and doing in *performing* the problem, rather than general statements or abstract explanations. For example, saying that you are depressed doesn't really say much about your unique experience; depression can have as many different expressions as there are people. What you want to consider is how you "do" the depression, how it actually looks, sounds and acts. Thinking of examples is often the best way to get specifics; particular instances of the problem will help you describe what it looks like in detail and how it affects you and others.

One way to get at your personal experience of your concern is to consider *how* the problem constitutes a problem, especially with general or vague situations. How a situation is a problem may often seem plain, but is it really? Again, consider depression. What does it really mean? How is the depression a problem? How does it manifest itself? Is it a sleep problem, a performance problem, a feeling problem, etc? How the situation constitutes a problem helps define it more clearly and identifies the aspect your new solution should address.

Recall Mark from chapter 2, the twenty-eight-year-old college student who was depressed. When Mark considered how his depression was a problem, he noted that it affected his ability to concentrate on his homework and tests. Pursuing the "how" allows you to step further into the problem cycle and pinpoint the area where action may have the most effect. For example, if Mark is able to do something different about the concentration problem, it will very likely help his depression. The pursuit of specificity, then, helps define general problems in such a way that allows more solution options.

Sometimes when we consider things in such a microscopic way, new understandings occur to us. We tend not to think of our situations in such detail and become so familiar with the misery of the problem that we barely notice its mechanics. Dismantling the problem and examining its parts can lead to new insights. For example, consider Ken, who told me he had been struggling with depression for several years related to his son's chronic trouble with the law, as well as to a long-term relationship with a married woman who always talked about leaving her husband without ever doing it. After I asked him a series of questions designed to have him reflect on the specific details of how he "does" the depression, he ended the session with a surprising conclusion. He said that he knew what I was driving at: that if he was going to conquer his depression, he would have to stop bailing his son out of trouble and deliver an ultimatum in his relationship. And he did. Of course, I wasn't driving at anything; sometimes taking the pieces of the puzzle apart provides just enough of a different perspective to get us going in a new direction.

Exploring the "how" of the problem further fleshes out the details and helps you understand the impact the problem has in your life, thereby either providing more motivation to take action or suggesting other steps to mediate the problem's effects. For Jim, the problem, specifically, was his inability to fall asleep in a timely fashion. His insomnia was troublesome because it affected his demeanor at work, as well as his job performance. He considered the effects of his insomnia and shared his difficulties with a couple of trusted colleagues. They were relieved to know why Jim seemed on edge and offered their support. Knowing how the insomnia affected him allowed Jim to do something to help buffer its effects.

To get into the spirit of this perspective, answer the following questions as if you were explaining your situation to a person who is completely naive, and perhaps even a little thick:

- Can you describe a recent example of the problem?
- If you recorded the problem on a video camera, what would you see and hear?
- What happens first? Then what happens? Then what?
- How often does it occur? How long does it last?
- Who is usually around when it happens?
- What are they doing or saying?
- What stops it?
- How or in what ways is it a problem? How does it affect your life?

You may not know all the answers to these questions. That's okay. You may need to do a little homework: Take a period of time, say a week, and observe the problem with the above questions in mind and gather as much information as possible. Become a fly on the wall and pay attention to the natural progression of the problem so you may better understand it. As we will see shortly, "observation tasks" like this one can be problem busters in and of themselves; sometimes the methodical monitoring of a problem can have the strange effect of diminishing it or solving it outright.

Step Two: Explore all the ways you and others have tried to solve the problem.

The next step in breaking the problem cycle is to contemplate what you and all the people closely involved with the problem have been doing to resolve it. This may include family members, friends, fellow workers, professionals and so on, depending on the circumstances. Again, this exploration focuses on actual behaviors, what people are doing and saying in their attempts to prevent a recurrence of the problem, or how they deal with it when it does happen. Identifying the theme of solution-attempts helps you avoid similar strategies and provides guidance in selecting problem busters. Understanding your solution attempts is the core of this approach.

Investigating Mark's solution strategies revealed that he had first tried reminding himself of his past successes in school; he had completed another degree many years earlier. Mark also told himself how stupid he was for worrying and then really poured on the pressure by thinking about how bad he would feel if he failed. Mark seemed to try reassurance, followed by self-criticism and pressure, and then attempts to force or will himself to concentrate. Others had followed a similar theme of solution attempts. Mark's troubles with concentration occurred within a vicious cycle consisting of efforts to both reassure and browbeat himself, which decreased his ability to concentrate, which led to more worrying and more reassurance from others and so on. Mark's problem with concentration could be understood to fit the category of "trying to force something that can only happen naturally."

Pursuing solution attempts also offers an opportunity to explore solutions that have worked, even fleetingly. If you discover a past or current solution that was helpful, stop reading now and go to chapter 6. It will show you how to capitalize on the successes you have experienced and build a solution based on this "exception" to the problem. This is precisely what happened in Mark's situation. While looking at his solutions, Mark identified an exception to his problem with concentration. He noted that when he studied with others, his concentration seemed better.

Exploring solution attempts may also encourage you to consider avenues you haven't tried but were thinking about. Consider Erik, a thirty-six-year-old single parent tormented by his seventeen-year-old's pot smoking. Erik tried a variety of things with Brent, including lectures, groundings and education at a drug treatment center, but none had influenced Brent's pot use. Erik had been considering another strategy but had been reluctant to try it. When answering the questions below with his change partner, he shared his idea about subjecting Brent to a urine test and requiring clean urine in exchange for driving privileges. In the ensuing discussion, Erik decided that Brent had pushed him around for too long and made Erik feel guilty about the breakup of his marriage. Erik's change partner encouraged him to implement the idea—and problem resolved! Often, new insights about problems occur as a result of considering the problem and its solutions in detail. Therapists bank on this idea.

Questions for exploring solution attempts:

- What have you done about the problem?
- How did each of these things work?
- What have other people suggested doing about the problem?
- What is the theme of your solutions attempts?
- Have you considered trying something else but haven't followed through with it?

Step Three: Find your minimal goal. Knowing what you want in advance will let you know when your efforts are successful.

This step is important regardless of the methods you choose to address your concerns. Finding a minimal goal, however, may be the most difficult aspect for you. Some people just do not think in terms of specific goals; they find it much easier to obtain a general or abstract formulation of what they are looking for rather than a definitive signal that the problem is resolving and their change efforts are working. For example, a depressed person might say, "I just want to feel better!" Okay, nothing wrong with that, but how will you know when that happens? What will be different? What will others notice? A more specific goal for this hypothetical depressed person might be: "I'll know that I feel better when I start going out with my friends at least once a week." Despite the inherent difficulties, setting such a benchmark allows you to judge when things are moving in the right direction—whether to drive full-speed ahead or to make a U-turn at the first opportunity.

Often, considering "how" the problem constitutes a problem tells you where your minimal goal might best be focused. Recall that Mark's depression was a problem because it interfered with his concentration and study. Thinking about what would indicate the first sign of improvement gave Mark the goal of being able to study for one hour without losing concentration for more than a few minutes.

It is most helpful to think small. Since a small change leads to additional changes, the logical place to start is with a first sign. The wonderful thing about thinking small is that the most easily attainable signal of change often comes to represent the larger problem. Accomplishing this first step becomes symbolic of resolving the entire problem; it creates a momentum and energy for change, like the first domino falling in the seemingly never-ending line of the problem. Recall that research shows early change to be very predictive of continued change; *small chinks in the armor of the problem inspire hope that more change is on the way.* For example, Eduardo, a twenty-seven-year-old salesman, said that his depression was a problem because he was unable to follow through with his work responsibilities. When considering what would indicate that things were on the right track, Eduardo first noted that he would make his schedule on Mondays and then follow through with his appointments the rest of the week. Then Eduardo rightfully concluded that this goal was too big and reflected about what would be the *first* sign that things were beginning to turn in the right direction. Eduardo concluded that

Beliefs based on our experiences sometimes become rigid, inadvertently restricting our options and leading us to continue using solutions that are not working. Questioning rules and defying conventional wisdom, when those approaches are not working, are often what it takes to make meaningful change.

Start thinking about what you can do differently by asking two questions:

1. What can I do that will stop the current solution attempts?
2. What other solutions can I try that will run counter to the theme of solutions currently employed?

The key here is to do things that are truly different, not just variations on a theme. To change 180 degrees in how you approach a problem, you must *unleash your creativity.* First acknowledge that something different is required, and then pull out all the stops and experiment with your responses to the problem. You will amaze yourself with your ingenuity and resourcefulness. I once saw a couple who were extremely upset about their thirteen-year-old son's intimidating temper tantrums and power plays; he became so loud, angry and disruptive they thought of him as the Incredible Hulk. The family had been through therapy and had tried many conventional methods to no avail.

In an attempt to stop their current solution attempts, I asked them to unleash their creativity and try something else that flew in the face of all the traditional methods that had failed. When I saw them next, they laughingly told me about what they had done during the last Incredible Hulk episode. Right when their son started to rant, the couple quietly stood up, went into their bedroom and locked the door. They began making squealing, grunting and groaning noises. The tantrums stopped.

Why? Because of the relationship between the problem and the applied solutions. The parents changed the way they approached the problem (endless talk, pleading, punishments) and enabled a different response from their son. Many times a small adjustment, strategically employed, is all that is needed for some much-needed relief and a more emotionally endurable situation.

Your task is to change how you "do" the problem—to change something when the problem occurs. Changing the doing can be as outrageous as the grunting and groaning parents, or it can be very subtle. For example, in searching for something different about his insomnia, Jim might simply try sleeping in another room, wearing different clothes or no clothes to bed. He might go to bed as soon as he gets home from work or decide to stay up all night watching movies. Shanda might put one of her running shoes in the refrigerator when Louis criticizes her or simply thank him for sharing his opinion. The idea is to unleash your creativity and experiment, knowing that when you change the solution, you will change the problem as well.

Instead of his usual angry tirade when his wife came home late from work, Wade greeted his apprehensive partner with a long, passionate kiss and whispered in her ear how it turned him on to have such a successful wife. She started coming home on time more often. Bill was long past feeling frustrated about standing and standing in public restrooms, trying to go; he felt hopeless and demoralized. Experimenting with the idea of changing the doing of the problem, Bill worked himself up to a good anger—about how this problem interfered with his comfort and added a big hassle in any situation away from his own bathroom. Bill allowed himself, when standing in front of the urinal, to become incensed—downright pissed off. And he started to go. Changing the feeling, from passive resignation to anger, paid off. Doing something different allows different possibilities.

Problem Busters: The Three Solution Categories

Start by doing what's necessary, then what's possible, and suddenly you are doing the impossible.

Saint Francis of Assisi

Don't worry if your solution attempts don't fit the following three categories or if none of these methods seems like a good fit. Remember that there are many stores with many racks of outfits in many different styles and colors. There are a million ways you can do something different and interrupt solutions that are not working. For more ideas, consult the appendices, which offer my favorite solutions as well as those of the two best therapists I know. If these ideas don't fit, don't worry about that either. Remember that *what* you do is not as important as actually doing something different—which outfit you choose is not as critical as actually trying one on for size. Feel free to experiment! With your change partner, discuss the options that strike a chord and brainstorm possibilities. Visit *www.whatsrightwithyou.com* and other sites for more ideas; you'll find something that makes sense, something that resonates with your own sensibilities about change.

Trying to Force Something That Can Only Happen Naturally

Recall that this class of unhelpful solution attempts is often applied to problems of bodily function that generally have to be allowed to happen rather than made to happen. Jim and his insomnia problem exemplify this category.

Observe the problem: Consider doing absolutely nothing about the problem except observing it and recording data about it. Don't try to change it at all. Observation tasks represent "something different" and often interrupt ineffective solution attempts, especially when people are pressing too hard. For Jim, this might include observing his sleeping problem for a week, recording the time he goes to bed, noting how long it takes him to fall asleep or what he thinks about while lying in bed. The idea is to stop the self-harassment of trying to force the natural activity by performing a task that prevents the *expectation* of success. Sometimes taking the edge off, backing off the screws just a bit, is enough to allow normal body functions to take over. A variation of this strategy is to *intentionally* fail at the problem at hand. For Jim, this would require him to try *not* to fall asleep—to intentionally fail to sleep! I know it sounds a little wacky, but these methods, when sincerely attempted, can bust the problem cycle and allow natural processes to take over.

First of all, intentionally failing immediately reduces pressure. If you are already awake, you know you can do it. It is impossible to "fail" at intentionally failing. You create a "win-win" situation. See if you can follow this logic. If you try to stay awake and do, you have succeeded in meeting your goal. If you fail and fall asleep, that is really fine also. Basically, what you do by using this counterintuitive strategy is to get out of your own way. Trying to solve your problem has become the problem. So you try to do something confusing and ambiguous. This frees you up to let nature take its course without your well-meaning interference.

I have seen people use these strategies successfully for problems ranging from trouble having an erection or an orgasm (observe yourself and intentionally remain flaccid or intentionally remain unaroused) to writing blocks (intentionally write a C paper) to difficulties in public speaking (intentionally become nervous, perspire and perform poorly). Sometimes, intentionally failing creates the opposite effect.

Even if these strategies do not result in problem resolution, at the very least they allow you to gain more distance from the problem and learn more about it. When we are in the throes of a troubling experience and pressing for resolution, we miss the opportunity to learn from the encounter. When the longing (and pressure) for resolution is taken out of the picture, it allows us to pay attention in a different way, permitting new revelations and understandings to emerge. For example, intentional failures have resulted in a variety of insights: maybe it's the wrong sexual partner or some unexpressed anger is interfering (in erectile or orgasmic difficulties), perhaps the chosen career is not what it's cracked up to be (in writing or concentration or performance blocks) or maybe one's body image is not so great (in problems of "showing oneself" in public restrooms). All insights that result from this task or any other can be useful to your change efforts. Doing something different allows such insights to come forth.

Let's look at Jim's solution attempts.

- Who: Jim
- What: Insomnia
- To whom: Jim
- How: Impacting job performance and possible partnership
- Solution attempts: Winding down (reading, TV); relaxation strategies; wine; pills
- Theme of attempts: Trying to force or make himself sleep
- Minimal goal: Falling asleep within one hour, one time
- What can Jim do to stop trying to force himself to sleep?
- What can he do that would run counter to these attempts?

To interrupt his solution attempts, Jim decided to try The Ordeal Technique (see appendix A). Instead of allowing himself to languish in insomnia, at the first hint of not being able to sleep, this problem buster required Jim to perform the most unpleasant and dreaded task in his household. The task should not take more than thirty minutes. But the kicker is that you must complete the thirty minutes no matter how tired or sleepy you become. Once the task is completed, then you may go to bed.

The first night Jim got up immediately and started his most procrastinated and hated task: cleaning the oven. After thirty minutes, he stopped and went to bed. But he still couldn't sleep, so he got back up and finished the job in the next thirty minutes. He went back to bed and fell blissfully asleep. The next night, Jim once again experienced difficulty falling asleep. This time Jim was ready to tackle the dreaded scum in the shower stall. Although yawning throughout the task, Jim made it the whole thirty minutes and fell to sleep instantly when he collapsed in the sheets. The following nights Jim slept, without difficulty, but he kept a list of the most horrendous cleaning tasks next to the bed, waiting for his next encounter with insomnia.

Trying to Master a Fear or Control an Emotion or Thought by Avoiding It

Remember that this group of ineffective strategies is usually applied to any fear or anxiety (fear of elevators, rejection, etc.), any negative emotion (depression, anger) or any negative thought (I am a failure, etc.) that a person is trying to control.

Invite what you dread: Let's start with fears and anxieties. There are two aspects to *inviting what you dread*. The first encourages the individual to expose him- or herself to the dreaded event while simultaneously requiring nonmastery. A person fearful of driving might sit in the car in the driveway for a maximum of thirty minutes contemplating the hazards of driving. An individual afraid of elevators might step into and out of an elevator for thirty minutes while considering the dangers of being stuck. A person paralyzed by fears of rejection might visit a bar or attend a singles event and think about the pitfalls of approaching potential dating partners. Sometimes it is useful to have your change partner accompany you in this first step if you believe his or her support might be helpful.

This strategy seeks to gradually increase the exposure to the feared situation, but mastery is still not required; completion of the task or confidence in one's ability to do it remains unnecessary. The next step may require our first person to drive to the end of block and back for thirty minutes while exploring the dangers of driving, the second may ride the elevator for one floor and back for thirty minutes and the third might approach the most attractive people in the bar and just say "hi" and quickly exit to approach the next person.

Behavior therapists (see appendix B) call these things exposure therapy, and they simply interrupt the uniformly unsuccessful approach of avoidance. This strategy allows people to experience that total mastery is not necessary to face the fear. Many times the feared events lose their sting, and people accomplish their goals—they wind up driving, riding the elevator or getting a date.

The second aspect of *inviting what you dread* with fears and anxieties is to carefully observe others and rate their level of fear or anxiety on a scale of one to ten, where one is calm, cool and collected and ten is freaked out to the max. In each of our examples, the person with the fear would observe others and determine how comfortable, or uncomfortable, they are when driving, in elevators or in singles situations. This continues the exposure solution, further permitting the individual to face the situation without mastery and now allowing firsthand observation that others are not the cool, calm and collected stalwarts once believed—that perfect mastery is never required. Others really don't have a magic sword to ward off the flying or elevator dragons. For example, when Susan rated others on the elevator, she was shocked to see how generally uncomfortable people are: their eyes dart around; they cough and clear their throats; they sigh and fidget and squirm. People are just plain freaked out by being closed in a small space with no control over what may happen. But they do it anyway. Often, people come to realize that the only difference between themselves and others is that the others have figured out ways of doing the activity in question while experiencing the fear. Sometimes other insights occur to people while performing these problem-busting ideas.

Now let's *invite what you dread* with negative emotions or thoughts. This method is sometimes called "symptom prescription," and it is a great way to interrupt the avoiding solutions. Trying to make yourself *not* experience something is nearly impossible. Try not thinking of a pink elephant. The more you try to stop the negative feelings or thoughts, the more they work their way into your life. It is certainly understandable that you just want the feelings or thoughts to stop—no one wants to feel depressed, and no one desires unpleasant thoughts to dominate their waking hours—but the very energy expended to dispel the feelings and thoughts contributes most to their continued oppression of your life.

A useful way to control negative feelings and intrusive thoughts is to make them happen, to bring them on with a vengeance. This occurs when you set time aside each day, for at least fifteen minutes but not more than thirty minutes, and consciously make the negative feelings or thoughts come on and stay on. At the end of thirty minutes, go on to another activity, or have your change partner call you to redirect your attention. If the thoughts or feelings occur outside of this time, then pour fuel on the fire and intensify them for at least fifteen, but not more than thirty, minutes. Think about this for a minute. When we are troubled by unwanted thoughts or feelings, they seem to be completely outside of our control—they hit us out of the blue, which only makes us continually look up, like Chicken Little, waiting for the sky to fall. *Inviting what you dread* is a dramatic shift that makes an involuntary action voluntary; something that has been out of your control is now under your control. This process makes you the master instead of the servant of your feelings or thoughts. Rather than opening Pandora's box, many find that giving the thoughts or feelings dedicated airtime reduces them over time, allowing them to fade into the background.

Sandra felt so depressed that she went to bed as soon as she got home from work. Her depression was such a paradox to her because her life was going so well! Her new job in a new exciting city should have made her happy. In fact, Sandra wound up incessantly trying to convince herself to be happy while simultaneously avoiding all that was negative about her circumstance. This only resulted in more and more feelings of hopelessness and more and more sleep. She knew things were not getting better, so she examined her problem cycle, the problem of her depression (specifically sleeping too much) and her solutions (primarily avoiding any feeling of depression because she shouldn't feel that way). Sandra decided to try *invite what she dreaded* and set time aside each day when she arrived home from work. Sandra thought about her move, the new city and how much she missed her parents and her friends. She started to cry, and instead of quickly drying her tears, she let herself go. Sandra did this every day and found that the intensity of the feelings diminished, and her tears slowed down. As this occurred, she felt more energetic and slept less.

There is often much insight to be gained from *inviting what you dread*. When we are feeling tormented or oppressed by our feelings or thoughts, we may miss the opportunity to explore what they may mean. What is my internal wisdom telling me? What lessons am I supposed to learn from this experience? When we intentionally bring on the thoughts or feelings, it frees us up to consider and reflect upon these questions. Sandra learned a couple of things. One was that she needed to proactively address the things she missed about leaving home: she decided to plan trips home and stay in better contact by e-mail.

Sandra also realized that her breakup with her hometown boyfriend was more important than she had thought. She concluded that she needed to start dating if she were going to adjust to the new city. This doesn't always happen, but allowing ourselves to experience our inner worlds permits insights into our dilemmas and often lights the way for continued success.

Trying to Solve a Relational Problem by Persuasion, Argument and Contention

This group of ineffective solutions is applied when one person—a parent, partner or friend—attempts to change an unwanted behavior of another person. It starts with simply bringing the problem to the other's attention, then escalates to *really* bringing the problem to the person's attention by confronting, persuading, reasoning, arguing and defending one's position. Shanda and Louis illustrate this group of ineffective solutions.

Giving up power to gain control: In an argument, the person who is "right" doesn't necessarily win. Either the best arguer wins or both people lose because they wind up more angry at each other and less able to see the other's point of view. Recognizing this, *giving up power* suggests the perspective, "I know I can't make you, but I would sure appreciate if . . ." From this vantage point, everything is a request—not a demand; you verbally admit that you cannot truly control the other person. He or she has to choose to change. Successful implementation requires you to overcome the temptation to confront, reason or argue with the other person, because agreement and harmony will likely never evolve from contention or hostility.

Giving up power breaks old rules and allows you to "gather" yourself before employing more active changes in your solution strategies. By ending needless, unproductive conflict, this strategy helps you to stop, observe and think before pressing ahead in more productive ways. This can be change-inducing all by itself. Without offering counterpoint to the other's actions, comments or accusations, the "buzz" he or she may get from the argument is eliminated. This may be particularly relevant with teenagers, but sometimes adults also derive some satisfaction during heated discussions.

Going with the flow: This problem buster extends *giving up power* a little further. It entails accepting the other person's actions and avoiding taking a contrary position. It requires you to do a reversal and say in words and in action, "You don't have to change; it's okay with me the way things are. I'll even help you stay the same." *Going with the flow* fits many relational conflicts because people often respond to any request for change with natural defensiveness, especially teenagers and partners who are experiencing problems that have been rehashed a million times. If you bring anything up to them, they feel forced, pressured and threatened. They respond to the perceived pressure by clinging to their points of view so intensely that they often do the opposite of what is requested. This pressure to change may prevent the other person from considering the alternatives and possibly changing the problem on his or her own. This method, however, makes it clear that the direct pressure is off.

Going with the flow can take as many forms as there are situations. By virtue of encouraging things to stay the same, the context in which the problem occurs is dramatically changed. Each strategy reflects an attempt to accept and even encourage the very behavior you don't like. Instead of refusing to buy a pack of cigarettes for the partner you are trying to convince not to smoke, you bring home two packs. Instead of balking at your lover's desire to back off the frequency of contact, you suggest that reassessment is a good idea and decrease the frequency of contact even more. Instead of criticizing your spouse's tendency to not talk about the relationship, you suggest the silence about the relationship lets you know that things are good and then make yourself less available for conversation.

Consider how *going with the flow* could be useful to address unwanted criticism. You could simply find something about the criticism to agree with or could ask the person for feedback before he or she had an opportunity to criticize. Another variation to deal with criticism is called *agree and exaggerate*. This technique suggests that you agree with the criticisms and even expand or exaggerate them. "Yes, I'm a terrible driver, and I can't believe you're brave enough to ride with me." "Not only am I a lousy cook, but I'm generally a rotten husband. I'm amazed you continue to put up with me." You are only agreeing with words; you are not in any way changing your behavior. It is very important that you not sound sarcastic. That just creates hostility.

If you agree, and the criticizer accepts it, you still do whatever you want, the argument's over—and you didn't get angry and defensive. So you win. If the other person disagrees with you (remember, you are now accepting criticism), that means he or she is absolving you of blame. So you still win.

This idea, like all other problem busters, is not for everyone. Any strategy must fit your own sensibilities of what is right. Feel free not to use them and think of your own ways to stop your current solution attempts. Or consult the many options in the appendices or at *www.whatsrightwithyou.com*.

- Who: Louis
- What: Criticism
- To whom: Shanda
- How: Feels childlike in response
- Solution attempts: Confrontation, arguing, defending herself, going on strike
- Theme of attempts: Bringing the problem to Louis's

attention; trying to solve a relational problem through persuasion, argument and contention

- Minimal goal: One pleasant conversation; reduce criticisms and restore harmony
- What can Shanda do to stop trying to bring the criticism problem to Louis's attention?
- What can she do that would run counter to confrontation, arguing, defending herself and going on strike?

Shanda first implemented *giving up power,* which resulted in a much-needed break from tension with Louis; pleasant conversations occurred again. This really got her creative juices flowing. Shanda also implemented *going with the flow* and started asking Louis for advice in areas he knew a lot about. Finally, Shanda liked what she read about *agree and exaggerate,* especially for Louis's more cutting remarks. One time, when Louis came home from work, their son was screaming, the house was a mess and dinner wasn't even started. Louis said, "I can't believe that you don't have dinner started. You're so disorganized." Shanda replied, "Not only am I disorganized, I can't even manage our son. I'm a terrible mother and wife." Louis looked surprised—and then simply changed the subject. He didn't say another word about it; he just started helping with dinner. Another time, a similar scenario occurred, but this time Louis commented that he thought Shanda was a great mother and that he couldn't imagine having a better wife. Shanda felt in control of these situations now and noticed that Louis's criticisms occurred less and less.

Important! After you have implemented your chosen problem buster, retake the ORS and compare it to your previous rating. If your score has increased by five points or above the cutoff line, or if you feel that things are on the right track, there is one more step to ensuring progress in the new direction. Go to chapter 6 and complete step four ("Empowering Yourself") in the solution-building section (page 165) and then proceed to chapter 7 for a discussion of the long-term maintenance of your gains.

Janice: The Whole Enchilada

How much pain have cost us the evils which have never happened.

Thomas Jefferson

To further illustrate this problem-solving approach, let's return to Janice, first introduced in chapter 2. Janice was a thirty-two-year-old executive recently promoted to a position that required her to fly to regional meetings. Janice was deathly afraid of flying.

Step One: Who is doing what, to whom, and how does that behavior constitute a problem?

I am just petrified of flying, and I have successfully avoided it all my life. My family just accepts it, and it has never been a problem until now. I guess it starts out with something about flying coming up, either on TV or in conversation. Then I leave the situation if possible. But if I can't, or even if I can sometimes, I start to get an uncomfortable queasiness in my stomach, which turns quickly into heart palpitations and panic, which continues until I get this feeling like I am going crazy. It lasts about an hour and usually ends when I throw up. No one says anything because I am good at covering it up. Since the promotion, it is getting worse and happens three or four times a week. How is it a problem? Are you kidding—if I don't do something about this and start to fly, I'll lose my promotion.

- Who: Janice

- What: Feels like she's going crazy when she even thinks about flying
- To whom: Janice
- How: Prevents her from flying and jeopardizes her promotion

Step Two: Explore all the ways you and others have tried to solve the problem.

Okay, the main thing I have done is avoid anything and everything about flying. I travel by car and train. Faraway relatives have to visit me if they want to see me. If a TV program or news show says anything about flying, I immediately change the channel. I guess you could sum up my attempts at flying by saying I haven't really attempted anything except avoidance. Essentially I have tried to master a feared event by avoiding it. Now, in retrospect, no wonder I don't have any control over it. It has grown into this ominous monster. But really, the whole strategy worked just fine until now.

Other people have told me that it is nothing to worry about, that all I need is to fly, and the anxiety will go away once I see that it is safe and that flying is safer than driving a car. Yeah right!

One thing that I thought might help is some kind of relaxation technique, but I haven't investigated anything about that.

Step Three: Find your minimal goal. Knowing what you want in advance will let you know when your efforts are successful.

I just want to be able to feel in control of my fears and diminish them to the degree that I can fly to regional meetings every three months. Okay, that's the big goal, but the first step . . . hmm. Let's see, I am at a twenty-two overall on the ORS and my Individual scale is about a four because of this problem. If it were to move to a five, what would I be doing differently that would encourage me to see some improvement? Okay, I would be able to tolerate the mention of flying and discuss it with others. I would no longer avoid the topic altogether—that would be a great start.

Step Four: If first you don't succeed, try something else!

Okay, let me consider those questions.
1. *What can I do that will stop the current solution attempts?*
2. *What other solutions can I try that will run counter to the solutions currently employed?*

I know that I need to somehow stop avoiding it and try something else. I had a little trouble coming up with ways to counter my avoidance, other than talking about it, so I involved my change partner. We discussed my solution attempts, and we brainstormed the options. We agreed that I would try "Invite what you dread." I started by spending at least fifteen minutes, but not more than thirty minutes, considering the dangers of flying and feeling my fears intensely. It was scary at first, but this not only interrupted my current solution attempts, it also created a situation that put me in control of my feelings. At the end of the allotted time, I simply stopped and went on to something else. I had scheduled a call to my change partner to ensure that I could change gears. I discussed all the dangers of flying with my partner and began to discuss my fears of flying (for the first time) with others. After discussing my fears, I found that many people also fear flying but do it anyway! I also started a relaxation exercise that I found in a bookstore and began visualizing myself getting on an airplane.

The next step was the airport. To continue to run counter to my avoidance, my change partner and I came up with ideas that put me closer and closer to the actual flying experience. I made weekly trips to the airport and observed people and rated them on how nervous I thought they were. Cindy, my change partner, went with me the first time. I couldn't believe how freaked out so many people looked. I guess flying is not as easy for others as I used to think. I also thought about the dangers of flying while I was there and practiced my relaxation and imagery. Finally, I bought a ticket and got all the way to the boarding process but purposely didn't board. I invited what I dreaded once again and implemented the relaxation strategy. I rated others' anxiety and was reassured by all the constant movement, eating and clock watching. The ticket rebooking fee was well worth the money.

Then I was ready for the first regional meeting. Before I got on the plane, I thought about the dangers for about fifteen minutes and stopped. When I got on the plane, I rated the people around me and saw that on takeoff and during turbulence, there was almost mass hysteria! I was nervous, more than nervous really, but I did it!

That's Just the Way I Have Always Done It

Whoever acquires knowledge and does not practice it resembles him who ploughs his land and leaves it unsown.
Sa'di Shirazi

Consider this experiment: There is a large cage containing five monkeys. Inside the cage, there is a banana hanging on a string and a set of stairs underneath it. Before long, a monkey will go to the stairs and start to climb toward the banana. As soon as he touches the stairs, all of the other monkeys are sprayed with cold water. After a while, another monkey makes an attempt with the same result—the other monkeys are sprayed with cold water. Pretty soon, when another monkey tries, the other monkeys will try to prevent it. Now, put away the cold water. Remove one monkey from the cage and insert a new one. The new monkey sees the banana and goes to climb the stairs. To his horror, the other monkeys attack him. After another attempt, he knows if he touches the stairs, he will be assaulted. Next, remove another of the original five monkeys and add a new one. The newcomer goes to the stairs and is attacked. The previous newcomer joins in with enthusiasm! Then replace a third monkey with a new one, then a fourth, then the fifth. Every time a newcomer takes to the stairs, he is attacked. Most of the monkeys beating him have no idea why they were not permitted to climb the stairs or why they are participating in the beating of the newest monkey. After replacing all the original monkeys, none of the remaining monkeys has ever been sprayed with cold water. Still, no monkey ever again approaches the stairs. Why not? *Because as far as they know, that's the way it's always been done around here.*

The idea that the solution is the problem frees your change endeavor from the encumbrances of the Killer Ds. Problems are merely an unfortunate result of what cofounder of the MRI, John Weakland, colorfully described as "the same damn thing over and over again." It is painfully apparent that life is full of opportunities for problems to develop. You don't have to be mentally flawed or emotionally disordered or chemically imbalanced to experience the distress and discomfort of life. Neither do you need to be diagnosable to get stuck in a problem and need to explore different options for becoming unstuck. In many ways, life is about experiencing these life struggles. Period! We grapple with their meaning, adapt ourselves the best we can and continue to enrich and be enriched by the relationships that matter most to us. Don't get stuck doing things because that's the way it's always been done.

CHAPTER FIVE BOTTOM LINE
Do Something Different

Exercise Five: Problem Busting

1. **Who is doing what, to whom, and how does that behavior constitute a problem?**
   - Can you describe a recent example of the problem?
   - If you recorded the problem on a video camera, what would you see and hear?
   - What happens first? Then what happens? Then what?
   - How often does it occur? How long does it last?
   - Who is usually around when it happens?
   - What are they doing or saying?
   - What stops it?
   - How or in what ways is it a problem?

2. **Explore all the ways you and others have tried to solve the problem.**
   - What have you done about the problem?
   - How did each of these things work?
   - What have other people suggested doing about the problem?
   - Have you considered trying something else but haven't actually followed through with it?

3. **Find your minimal goal.**
   - What will you see as a first sign that a significant, although small, change has occurred?
   - What will be an indication that things are beginning to turn toward problem improvement?
   - Look at your lowest rating on the ORS. If this problem is represented by your mark, what would a mark just to the right signify; what would be happening that would lead you to make such a mark?
   - How will you know that you can put this book down? What will be different?

- What will you be doing differently when this situation is less of a problem in your life?
- What do you think that your significant other, family member or friend would say is the first sign that things are getting better? What do you think he or she will notice first?

4. **If first you don't succeed, try something else!**
   - Ask two questions: (1) What can I do that will stop the current solution attempts? (2) What other solutions can I try that will run counter to the solutions currently employed? Unleash your creativity and *try something else.*

5. **Retake the ORS after implementing your problem buster.**
   - If there is an improvement of five points or greater or beyond the cutoff (twenty-five) go to step 4 of chapter 6 to "Empower Yourself" (page 165) and then on to chapter 7 to encourage your change over the long haul.
   - If no improvement is reflected on the ORS, then you may need to give your strategy a little more time or try different methods of change. Chapter 7 discusses what to do when no change is happening.

6

Solution Building

*What can be done with fewer means
is done in vain with many.*

—William of Ockham

The problem-solving method presented in the previous chapter takes a detailed look at troubling situations and the intimate connection between solution attempts and the very problem they intend to help. To identify the problem cycle, the Mental Research Institute (MRI) approach puts a magnifying glass on *when* the problem is happening. Oddly enough, the perspective of this chapter, so-called solution-focused therapy (SFT), hones in on just the opposite: when the problem *isn't* happening. SFT is the revolutionary notion that the solution to the problem does not necessarily have any relationship to the problem at all. In fact, from this vantage point, the problem is almost irrelevant.[30]

Consider this old Japanese folktale: A farmer working in the rice fields high above a coastal village saw a tidal wave rapidly approaching. The villagers could not have heard her had she yelled to them, nor did she have time to run to the village to warn them. What could she do? What would you do? She set the rice on fire. When the villagers rushed to save the vital crop, they were spared certain death from the tidal wave.

There is, of course, no relationship between the impending doom of the tidal wave (the problem) and setting the fields on fire (the solution). SFT teaches us that solutions can occur for the most troubling situations without any examination of the problem whatsoever. This surprising idea releases you from the hunt for the problem and its causes, and instead encourages you to cast a wider net to capture solutions that are already happening, so-called *exceptions* to the problem. SFT uses these exceptions—capitalizing on your existing experiences and strengths—to create solutions to life difficulties.

So these two approaches, the MRI and SFT, are really two sides of the same coin. The MRI, through a detailed look at the problem, encourages you to *change* your solutions that *don't* work. The SFT, by a thorough evaluation of your life *away* from the problem, encourages you to *amplify* those solutions that *do* work. The MRI is a problem-busting method; the SFT is a solution-building technique. As I did with the MRI approach in chapter 5, in this chapter I will give you an insider's view of how to apply this novel idea in the same way therapists are taught. Chapter 6 shows you how to look for solutions that are already happening—to mine nuggets of gold from your every-day life to forge a ring of hope, a necklace of a plan and bracelets of change.

The Four-E Method of Building Solutions[31]

All things have small beginnings.
                    Marcus Tullius Cicero

Step One: Elicit the Exception

The Greek philosopher Heracleitus is often credited with saying that nothing is permanent but change. Problem names (depression) or diagnoses (generalized anxiety disorder) imply the permanence of troubling situations. In reality, the severity, duration and frequency of problems are in constant flux. These changes or instances of freedom from the problem, even momentarily, are called *exceptions*. An exception is a specific circumstance in which the problem does not occur, or occurs less often or intensely. An exception can be considered a small success in daily life. From a practical standpoint, it is often easier and more productive to increase existing successes, no matter how small, than it is to focus on a problem and try to eliminate it; sometimes a dogged pursuit of the problem blinds us to other solution possibilities. Therapists have long used these small blips on the screen of the problem to build effective solution strategies.

It is common for people struggling with problems, however, to view the situation as rigid and unyielding; changes in the problem are dismissed or even completely unseen. With some reflection, you can describe and take advantage of these changes, the ebb and flow of the problem's presence and ascendancy in your daily affairs; you can *elicit exceptions*.

Stop and think about your situation. When is the problem not quite so bad or absent altogether? Even in seemingly dismal situations, exceptions can usually be discovered. For example, the teenager who reportedly "disrupts class constantly" and "never does any schoolwork" has probably behaved appropriately in class at *one time* or another and has completed *some* assignment along the way. Couples who say they argue all the time have probably been successful in *some* recent situation. An individual struggling with depression or anxiety can often identify *some* times when it is a bit less distressing or intense, if just for a moment.

These instances of liberation from the problem form the foundation for building solutions and changing your life for the better because *somehow you are already solving the problem.* There is part of you that is dealing with the problem differently, even if you are initially unaware of it. Sometimes just recognizing the problem's inability to control your life 24/7 can inspire insights about the problem and ideas for further changes.

I once saw Ellen, who because of many horrifying and downright disgusting experiences, often cut herself on her wrists and arms to relieve the emotional pain she felt. During our exploration of the exceptions to her cutting, I suggested that she was the master in charge, the one at the control panel. Apparently there was a part of her that managed to stand up to the urges to cut when she was feeling miserable—because she felt bad most of the time but only cut herself a couple of times a week. Our job, I said, was to learn more about *how* the master in charge helped her *not* cut when she was in extreme emotional pain. To my surprise and delight, Ellen returned and ended her therapy. She told me that the more she considered herself as the master at the control panel—that she was the one who managed not to cut herself most of the time—the more she realized that she could overcome the cutting. And she did. Although not all situations will resolve as quickly as Ellen's, awareness of your ability to overthrow the problem, even for a short time, can lead to further insurrections and a revolution of change.

In addition to the changes in the problem itself, seemingly

unrelated, serendipitous events can provide powerful opportunities for growth. A client named Rick taught me this lesson a long time ago and led me to pay considerably more attention to *any* fortuitous event as an exception and a possibility for important change.

Rick had been in treatment for depression for seven years and had tried a variety of medications and therapies to no avail. When I first met him in the waiting room, he shook my hand limply and said hello almost inaudibly. Rick was the walking personification of "depressed." In our conversation, he described his long-standing depression and his fears that he would ultimately be institutionalized. Adding to his woes were his marital problems. For nearly two years, Rick and his wife, Maggie, had slept in separate bedrooms and spoke to each other only when absolutely necessary. Thinking it might provide a different opportunity for improvement, I asked Rick to invite Maggie to our next session. He agreed to give it a try.

When I next saw Rick a week later in the waiting room, I did an immediate double take. I didn't recognize him! He spoke to me with enthusiasm, was quite animated and had a sparkle in his eye and a spring in his step that made me think for a moment that I was in a Broadway musical. I couldn't wait to shut my door and ask what in the heck was going on to explain the radical change.

He laughed at the astonished look on my face and told me he didn't have a chance to talk to his wife about attending the session because a funny thing had happened the previous Friday night. They received a phone call from a couple who had been their best friends when they lived in a different city. Over the years, they had lost contact. The couple was in town for a wedding and on a lark decided to look up Rick's number and see if they could come over. Rick and Maggie were excited to hear from their old friends and delighted to invite them over.

I don't know about you, but when my wife and I have company after we've had a fight, we behave like we have the best marriage on the planet: "Can I get you anything else, sweetie, honey, baby, blah, blah, blah?" Well that is exactly what Rick and Maggie did. Not having seen each other for many years, the two couples swapped old stories, laughed till they cried and allowed the evening to slip by unnoticed. As the night wore on, and after a few glasses of wine, the talk of old times seemed to rekindle some buried feelings, and Rick and Maggie were genuinely enjoying their friends and each other. When they finally realized the time and noted how much wine had been consumed, all agreed that it was not safe for the couple to drive back to their hotel. The visitors stayed the night.

This created an interesting dilemma. There were only two bedrooms in the house, which had been occupied separately by Rick and Maggie for the past two years. Continuing the charade, which didn't seem like a charade now, of their happy marriage, Rick and Maggie were forced to sleep together in the same room. For the first time in two years, the two spoke to each other about matters other than business, and for the first time in who knows how long, they felt warm feelings for each other. Before the night was over, they made love. The talk and warm feelings continued into the next day, and they slept together again that night. And so on.

So Rick told me this story and how his relationship had been improving since that evening. We talked about how this change occurred and what his ideas were for maintaining momentum. By the end of the session, Rick announced that his depression was no more! Change did not occur because of some marvelous therapy-related insight or technique about his marriage or the depression; rather, it arose from a serendipitous event that created an opportunity for Rick and Maggie to rekindle their marriage. And they made the best of it. Just as setting the rice fields ablaze seems unrelated to certain death from a tidal wave, unexpected visitors may appear unconnected to improving a marriage and overcoming depression. Change happens in mysterious ways.

So any change can provide possibilities for problem resolution; any exception to the problem has the potential to grow into a solution. This first step, *elicit the exception,* requires you to take a long look at your everyday life and make a concerted effort to discover change that is already happening—for whatever reason it initially occurs. To accomplish this task, you must believe, like Heracleitus, in the certainty of change and welcome *any* experience of it as an exception and a possible source of solution.

Yet as much sense as this approach makes, it can be hard to implement because it stands in stark contrast to everything else we have ever been told about solving a problem. We are taught to concentrate solely on the problem—what's wrong—rather than to see the significance of times without the problem—what's right. Under the spell of the Killer Ds, most approaches focus on how problems remain the same (and perhaps will always be that way) rather than how they are different, better or improved from week to week. Focusing on the exceptions, of course, is the beauty and power of the SFT method.

To elicit the exceptions to your problem, ask yourself:

- Between when you first noticed the problem and today, have you noticed any changes in the problem?
- When does the problem not occur?
- When is the problem less noticeable?
- When is the problem a bit more bearable?
- Look at your ORS score. When would you have rated things just one centimeter to the right on any of the scales? When would the total score have been a little better?
- When do you cope a little better?

• Was there ever a time in your life that sticks out when the problem was absent or less intense?

Recall Mark (chapters 2 and 5), his problem of depression and how it interfered with his ability to concentrate and study. When Mark considered whether any of his solution attempts were helpful, he identified an important exception. Namely, he noticed he was able to concentrate a little better when he was with others. This small but notable exception to his concentration problem formed the basis of an entirely new direction in Mark's life. Don't hold back here or get too picky. As Mark's experience will illustrate, any exception can be useful, no matter how small or seemingly insignificant.

If you can't immediately identify exceptions, don't worry. Remember, I told you this is hard and runs against the grain of how we usually think about problems. It may just require a little more scrutiny of your day-to-day life. You may need to do a simple observation task. This is often what happens in therapy: exceptions do not emerge initially, so the therapist asks the client to do a bit of homework. These tasks are designed to capitalize on the constancy of change and encourage you to notice exceptions:

• Between now and next week, note the things in your life (or in another person, or in your relationship, etc.) that you would like to see continue.
• Pay attention to the times you are able to overcome the temptation to drink, eat in front of the TV, yell or whatever the problem is.
• Observe when the problem isn't occurring or is just a little better and how you are able to make it that way.

Consider Maria and Jorge. They were at their wit's end because their thirteen-year-old daughter, Alina, burst into tears and stormed out after an argument about a bad grade on a test. This wasn't the first time. These all-too-familiar scenes, Alina's emotional outbursts in response to almost everything, were the cause of increasing alarm to her parents. Jorge was particularly concerned about the long-term consequences of Alina's inability to control her emotions; he feared that her emotional tirades would hurt her chances in life—that she would be doomed if she kept responding so strongly to life's inevitable ups and downs.

Maria especially liked the idea of looking for exceptions because she thought the atmosphere had just gotten too negative around the house, but she and Jorge were initially unable to identify any times when things went okay with Alina—the situation had gotten that bad. Consequently, they decided to try one of the observation tasks. Jorge and Maria watched Alina closely to note the things they would like to see continue. They told Alina about the task and that they would report their findings back to her.

A couple of weeks later, Maria, Jorge and Alina got together after dinner and discussed what they had seen during the observation period. Despite the previously perceived constancy of the problems, Maria and Jorge were able to share a long list of positive events and attributes. Alina was "caught" being more communicative, more cooperative and able to keep her emotions in check. These exceptions built the foundation for major changes in the family. We will follow this family, as well as Mark, throughout our discussion of the Four-E approach to solution building.

Finally, when fishing for exceptions, it can also be helpful to be curious about *anything* in your life that is helpful to you or going well—*separate from the problem altogether*. This way of thinking seeks to amplify what works in your life as a strategy to minimize what doesn't. Think about this for a moment; it is a simple yet very out of the ordinary idea. Typically when we approach a problem, we want to attack it directly and decrease it or downright destroy it. That's okay, but it is not the only way to make things better. You can also ignore the problem completely and focus instead on increasing those things that are good about your life or that enhance your feelings of competence, confidence or self-esteem. Whether seeking out a trusted friend or family member, working out or taking a walk, purchasing a book or tape, attending church or a mutual-help group, or going to a movie or concert, you might find important clues to gaining relief from your situation by taking a broader perspective beyond just exceptions to the problem. Solving the problem, in other words, could be accomplished by focusing on the aspects of your life completely removed from the problem itself. Increasing your attention on these aspects can turn the tables on a problem, making it shrink to a shadow of its former impact on your life.

For example, Tony was just about climbing out of his skin when he came to see me. After he shared how anxiety attacks tormented his every waking minute and all his frustrated attempts to do something about them (from drugs to therapy to you name it), we talked about exceptions. At first Tony couldn't identify any times without the anxiety. I then asked him what was going well in his life and he immediately responded that his triathlon training was going great. I learned of all the positives that his participation in this rigorous sport brought to him, especially the races themselves—Tony felt invincible during the thrill of competition regardless of how he placed. As the conversation unfolded, Tony intimated that his work only allowed him to participate in a race every three months; his travel schedule conflicted with many of the races. As the discussion concluded, Tony noted that the triathlon contests were huge exceptions to his anxiety and panic attack problem. He just didn't think about it when a race was imminent. Predictably, if you have been following my train of thought, I asked Tony if there was any way he could enter more triathlon events.

And he could. Tony was able to find races in cities where he traveled for business and coordinated his travel schedule to allow him to compete. When he was unable to find enough events to compete at least monthly, Tony joined the triathlon organization that scheduled the races. In short order his enthusiasm and commitment landed him the respect of others, and he was looked upon as the one of the group leaders. The anxiety, while still present, receded into the background. Tony was able to turn the tables on his anxiety; he amplified what was going well to diminish what was not. Some might second-guess Tony's success and suggest that he didn't really deal with the "underlying" problem. But Tony didn't mind.

To search for exceptions to the problem, ask yourself these questions:

- Who or what is helpful or going well in my life?
- What do I seek out for even a small measure of comfort?
- What things are happening that I would like to see continue?

Step Two: Elaborate the Exception

Once you identify the exception, the next step is to *elaborate the exception*—to detail all the related features and circumstances surrounding this remarkable time in which the problem doesn't occur or is somehow less intense or more manageable. Recall from the previous chapter how the MRI approach looks at the problem cycle through a magnifying glass, thoroughly examining the problem and its solutions attempts. The SFT method calls for a similar enlarged and focused look at exceptions. The particulars about the exception form the basis for the solution to the problem. Elaborating the exception asks, "How did it happen?" and requires you to answer "who, what, when, where and why" questions about the noted instance of life without the problem to ferret out all its specifics. For example, a teenager who misbehaves in all classes except math might be asked, "In what ways is your math class/teacher different from other classes/teachers? Where do you sit in math class? How would you rate your interest in math relative to other classes? How is it that things go better in math than in the other classes?" and so forth. A couple complaining of ongoing fights does an observation task and discovers that they do not argue when they go to the movies. Questions about how they miraculously achieve harmony in these circumstances may include: "How do you account for why things go so smoothly at the movies? What do you do or say differently when you are getting along better? What is it about going to the movies that brings out your best? Is there a particular kind of movie that seems to have this effect?" and so on.

Resist the tendency to gloss over successes or any differences in the problem, and instead, doggedly pursue the exception, until all the elaboration is "chewed" out of it. For example, some might diminish the above couple's exception to their fighting because it occurred at the movies where they didn't have to talk to each other. Nothing could be further from the truth. The couple talked on the way to the movies, while parking the car and walking to the theater, at the concession stand, waiting for the movie to start and so on. There were plenty of opportunities for a fight to start, but it didn't. Somehow, something about the couple and the movies mixed together made something good happen, an instance of the problem not occurring. Don't underestimate any exception to the problem! Take exceptions seriously and elaborate on them as much as possible.

Such elaborations paint a vivid picture of the times of liberation from the problem and identify exactly the type of canvas, paint color and brush size you will need to replicate similar pictures in the future. Describing all the details shows you how to repeat and expand your successes.

Spend some time thinking about the exception, or have a good long talk with your change partner about times when the problem doesn't occur.

- What was happening at those times? What do you think you were doing to help that along? What would you need to do (or what would need to happen) for you to experience more of that?
- In what ways is it different, more bearable or less noticeable?
- Who is involved when things are different? Where did the difference happen?
- How do you account for the exception? How do you do that?
- If your friend, family or significant other were here, what would that person say is different about you during times when the problem is not happening?

Keep track of everything that is helpful in any way, even if it appears insignificant.

As previously noted, Mark identified an exception to his concentration problem. It seemed just a wee bit better when he studied with others. Mark had some difficulty elaborating this exception, however, so he used one of the tasks. He observed when the problem wasn't occurring or was a little better and how he was able to make it that way. He discovered a few things: He found that discussing the concepts with his classmates and sharing his ideas and concerns seemed to manage his tendency to browbeat himself; working with others distracted him from his own thoughts and fears. Mark also learned that he actually knew more than his study partners most of the time. This realization really helped him gain confidence. Finally, Mark learned that it was just plain fun to be around people going through the same things that he was; relaxing and laughing with those in the same boat somehow enhanced his ability to concentrate.

Following completion of the "note what you would like to see continue" task, Jorge and Maria shared the positive things they noticed with Alina. Elaborating on those exceptions led to new directions. When detailing these exceptions to Alina's emotional outbursts and what each person did to make them happen, Jorge concluded that his "backing off" and appreciating Alina's strengths seemed to have a big impact on things going better around the house. Everyone agreed. Alina observed that she got what she wanted a lot more often when she had a friendly attitude and made attempts to talk with her parents about everyday stuff rather than only confronting them when she was mad. Finally, Maria observed that when a disagreement did occur, the whole family seemed to take it in stride rather than blowing it up to a huge problem; everyone seemed to be trying just a little bit harder to get along.

Step Three: Expand the Exception

After you identify an exception and flesh out its details, the next step is to make it happen more frequently—to *expand the exception*. Essentially, this step simply encourages you to do more of what is already working. For example, Jo and Jack complained of ongoing conflict. When considering the times they got along better, the couple noted that when they talked about sports, especially tennis and baseball, they didn't tend to argue. To expand this exception, they decided to initiate a discussion about tennis or baseball shortly after arriving home from work each day, before any arguments could occur. They noticed immediate improvement, highlighting the idea that sometimes the best way to solve problems is to amplify what is working already. The couple went even further. They made it a rule to use sports metaphors in any conflict that might arise. For example, communication problems were discussed as missed signals between a third base coach and a batter; disagreements were line disputes between a player and a line judge. Sometimes the metaphors were so silly that the couple forgot what they were arguing about. One success often builds up to another and enhances creativity to resolve problems.

Amplify or do more of what's working by asking these questions:

- How can I do more of what I am doing that is helpful?
- How can I do more of what is going right in my life?

Applying this very simple idea to Mark meant that he needed only to schedule more group study times and that he should organize his schoolwork around getting at least one other person to study with him. In each new class, Mark quickly scoped out a study partner, joined any available study groups and always attended any help sessions the professors offered. Mark made studying with others a critical part of his school experience and ultimately found this was a very positive direction for him to follow.

Maria, Jorge and Alina decided to continue to notice the good things about Alina and expand those items into suggestions for family behavior. The family compiled a list of the things that proved helpful and posted it on the refrigerator.

Step Four: Empower Yourself

The final, crucial step is for you to own the change—*to empower yourself* by taking responsibility for your contribution to any gains that are noted. In effect, the goal is to link the positive change to your efforts, thus highlighting it as an instance of self-healing and perhaps the beginning of an important new chapter in your life. *People who perceive their roles in the change process as active and central are more likely to assume ownership of the desired changes (to experience empowerment) and continue implementing the strategies that are working.*

This is kind of like blaming in reverse or "positive blame."[32] So blame yourself for the solution and any progress you have made. Taking responsibility for your steps in the right direction casts you in your rightful role as the main character in your story and enables you to continue on your path to a better life. Step into the spotlight and take a bow for your creativity, courage and good ideas. Bask in the limelight of what you have accomplished, and you will likely continue to be rewarded for your performances.

One way to showcase your gains as arising from your efforts is to make *before and after* distinctions. The idea is to reflect upon your experiences and distinguish between the way things were before the change and how things are now, after the change. Taking an introspective stance regarding the differences in you before and after the change encourages you to explore the significance of your actions and tell a different story about your life: one of triumph, enlightenment and tenacity. The change itself is a landmark on the landscape of your life—something that you can always point to as the place in your journey where you took a different path. At its best, fleshing out all the nuances of your success with change creates a newfound identity of wisdom and competence gained from the school of hard knocks. Think about and write in your journal or discuss these before and after distinctions with your change partner; these articulations will draft the introduction to a new chapter in your life.

Here are some questions that invite you to reflect on the changes you have made:

- How did you decide that now was the time for action?
- What insights have you gained from your life that you were finally able to put into action?
- What insights have you gained from this change that will help you in the future?
- What does this say about you, the kind of person you are, that you took the bull by the horns at this time?
- Who in your past would not be surprised to see you making these changes?
- How did you do it? How will you maintain the gains you have made?
- How are you different now that you have realized this change? Ponder the difference in your self-image both before you implemented this change and now.

Once you have recognized and owned the differences between the old you and the new you, reward yourself for your changes; do something special to punctuate and celebrate your successes. It doesn't matter what it is; just do something you really like that adds an exclamation point to the fact that you did something very positive for yourself. Revel in your accomplishments; if we don't celebrate our own successes, who will?

Moreover, to further highlight what you have accomplished, do something that symbolizes your change as a turning point in your life—make some kind of a landmark or milestone that will serve as a constant reminder that you took the initiative and did not resign yourself to a less fulfilling existence. This concrete indication, marking the beginning of something new and better, could be anything from growing a beard to getting a puppy, from doing volunteer work to writing poetry. It doesn't matter what it is; it only needs to have meaning to you. Rick and Maggie (the couple with serendipitous change) got a picture of their unexpected visitors, blew it up poster size, wrote the date of the visit on it and hung the photograph in their living room. Janice (the executive who feared flying) made a very funny collage depicting herself before and after she flew to her first regional meeting; on one side were pictures (from horror movies) of people freaking out, mouths wide open screaming in terror, as well as pictures of confinement and prison; on the other side were photos of happy, confident people enjoying themselves on pristine beaches and hiking over breathtaking vistas of mountains, as well as in other exotic travel destinations.

Given Mark's insights about the benefits of working with others, he enlisted a change partner to empower his gains and help him explore the nuances of his discoveries. Mark came to some very powerful realizations as he considered his contributions to his improved concentration, better school performance and now almost nonexistent struggle with depression. Mark took responsibility for his efforts to find study partners, as well as the hard work it took to address the problem in the first place. He noted that he felt a new confidence—not only about attending college, but perhaps more important, about himself. Mark no longer felt like a victim, helpless against a hostile world. Rather, he now believed that he could make a difference in any problem that might arise. This critical before and after distinction allowed Mark to think of his life as entering a new chapter, a chapter in which dormant qualities resurfaced and new strengths emerged. Mark now saw himself as a competent, self-assured person who loved to be around people instead of a loner who seemed to only wait for the next bad thing to happen. He recognized that the problem, his depression, was just what he needed to encourage him to stop and look at his life and make much-needed changes, not only in his approach to school, but far more critical, to his view of himself and his relationship to others. As a symbol of his newfound identity, Mark joined a community project that helped adults learn to read; his confidence in himself and others was contagious. He highlighted that date on his calendar to always remind him of when the change occurred.

Jorge and Maria continued to note the things about Alina that they wanted to see continue and to share their observations with Alina. They kept the task open because both Maria and Jorge attributed the changes in Alina and their overall family harmony to their efforts at backing off from criticizing Alina and appreciating her strengths. But another, more profound change was noted. As Jorge thought about the before and after experiences with Alina, he noticed that at some point he became more concerned about his *relationship* with his daughter, rather than how her emotional storms made her not measure up to her sisters. Upon reflection with Maria, Jorge recognized that he often compared Alina to her more popular and academically successful sisters, and he had not noticed what he had come to deeply respect in Alina. Jorge learned that Alina was not swept away by the urge to be popular, to wear the right clothes or to listen to the right music: she was definitely not the product of the media, and Jorge absolutely loved that. Unlike her sisters, Alina was far more interested in being actively involved in what was going on in the world and invested in making it a better place.

Jorge connected his backing off and appreciating Alina with the important outcome of improving his relationship with his daughter. He looked back at the situation with Alina and the changes he made and concluded that it enabled him to feel better about himself as a parent. Jorge treasured this before and after distinction and highlighted it by scheduling a "political night" with Alina to discuss world events. The spirited debates that ensued forever bonded the father and daughter in ways that neither could have predicted or could ever forget.

CHECKPOINT: The Four-E approach can be reduced to a few questions and actions: "When have I been able to resist giving in to overeating, fear, arguing, drinking too much, depression, etc.?" When those times are noted, next ask: "How was I able to do this at this time?" Take a week and write down each time the problem might have happened but you were able to "hold it at bay," or resist it in some way. Also make note of what you did specifically to accomplish this each time. Think about how to do more of this to continue keeping the problem at arm's length, if not off the radar altogether. Finally, ask yourself, "What does my ability to stand up to, resist, not give in to this problem tell me about who I am as a person and what I am capable of?" "Who else is aware of these traits about me?" "How can I invite others to recognize and celebrate these special attributes I possess?" Give yourself a special treat (party, bubble bath, box of chocolates, movie ticket, fishing trip, day at the beach, etc.) to reward yourself for even small victories over the problem.

Carrie: The Whole Enchilada

The experience gathered from books, though often valuable, is but the nature of learning; whereas the experience gained from actual life is one of the nature of wisdom.

Samuel Smiles

Recall Carrie from chapter 2 and her dieting dilemmas. After she found validation of herself and her dieting disasters, the Four-E model was just the right fit for her.

Step One: Elicit the Exception

Okay, in my situation, eliciting the exception would be identifying when I have been able to be successful with a diet, or successful in losing weight. Actually, I have done that a lot for very short periods of time. The longest time that I consistently was on a diet was for three months; I lost twenty-two pounds. I actually combined the best of three well-known diets.

Also, thinking about what I really enjoy in my life, I really love being outside—that's one reason I live where I do, because of the climate and my ability to be outside for most of the year. I also love doing things with my family, really just about anything.

Step Two: Elaborate the Exception

Okay, now how did I do that? I did a lot of different things:
- *I enrolled in a program that required me to weigh in regularly.*
- *I ate normally, no wild and crazy diets, just good common sense: low-fat, smart carbs, high protein, healthful foods that I bought at the grocery. One of the diets talks about balance and nutrition for life, and I really like that.*
- *I didn't drink.*
- *I didn't prepare food that I couldn't eat.*
- *I did some kind of exercise.*

Things I like to do and would like to do more of:
- *Go on nature walks.*
- *Involve the family in any activity.*

Step Three: Expand the Exception

Okay, I can do all those things more, but one thing that occurs to me in terms of expanding is to involve my family in my diet plan to ensure I stay on it. I can make my diet an activity for the whole family and emphasize the idea of eating for a healthy lifestyle for all of us, not just me. In fact, I will involve them as my change partners. I have never done that part before, and I can kill two birds with one stone.

So here is what I came up with: I enrolled in a diet support group, which included a weekly weigh-in and support session. Together, my family and I purged the house of all items that I can't eat on my diet—the high-carb stuff, mainly. We put all that in a separate cabinet and a very small refrigerator that we bought. My husband installed a lock on both so I wouldn't be tempted. I prepared meals we all could eat, but my husband and the kids prepared the other stuff when they wanted it. They ate those things most often, not always, when I was not around or was busy doing other things. Each family member did one thing a week with me outside, like walking or biking or swimming. Finally, I investigated the area and found several sites to enjoy my neglected hobby of nature walking, and I made it a point to go for a nature walk at least once a week.

Step Four: Empower Yourself

My ORS score increased dramatically! I started out at an eighteen and am now at a thirty-one. More to the point, I've lost twenty-four pounds in four months, which is better than I have ever done before, and there is no indication that I am going to stop until I reach my goal weight. Gradually I have been able to add some "fun" foods into my diet, and I eat the meals that my family prepares about twice a week. I also enjoy a couple glasses of wine one or two times a week. This is my new lifestyle—the new me. I've never felt better.

I guess I was able to do this now because I concluded that I had to accept this as a lifestyle change. Losing weight was my number-one priority, important enough to me that I, for the first time, embraced it as something I would have to do and wanted to do for the rest of my life. Before, I saw it as something I could do for a while and then go back to the old way of eating. Now I know that thinking got me in a lot of trouble and led to continued failures. That's the main difference.

I also finally realized that for me it had to be a family effort. I needed their help to pull it off. My family was key, and the thing I did to make this happen is that I finally enlisted them in my efforts rather than being mad about not being able to eat what they did without gaining weight. I planned the specifics of how they could be helpful and regularly discussed their contributions with them. We had weekly meetings where we went over different dieting books. Our increased awareness at home about nutrition has really helped everyone understand healthful eating a good bit more, and I think it will have long-term positive effects.

The part that is best about this whole thing is that I feel good about me again—I feel like my self-esteem is much better. I was so demoralized by continually failing at a diet. Before, I would start a new diet, do well for a while and then ultimately fail miserably. I thought I was such a loser. Of course now I know that I wasn't a loser; it is just plain tough to lose weight, and it takes all the resources you can muster to be successful at it. Now I feel very confident, partly because I know I look better, and I feel much better, but I think the main reason I feel confident is that I really defeated this weight problem once and for all. Now anything seems possible.

The Glove: Building Solutions

All you need is glove. . . .

Anonymous

Gary was twenty-four and in a lot of trouble. His first love and wife of three years had just left him for another man, and he was devastated. Gary hadn't known anything. The long hours working at the lumberyard didn't leave much time for suspicion, and Gary was the trusting type anyway. But he really wasn't angry at her; Gary blamed himself. He wasn't much into going to therapy, not because he was set against it, but because it just didn't occur to him. Gary spent most of his evenings after work sitting on his front porch drinking beer, listening to old Jackson Browne songs. His beer consumption was steadily on the rise, and socializing with his friends had dwindled to nothing. Occasionally a neighbor would walk by and stop for an evening conversation in the breezy shade on the porch, seeking some refuge and refreshment on the warm summer evenings. A couple of neighbors stopped by more frequently because they were worried about Gary. They knew he was hurting bad—thinking about his wife and their lost dream of restoring their old Victorian house together.

One gloomy night of pallid gray skies and perpetual rain, Gary noticed his neighbor Charles, a sporting goods distributor, running toward him to seek shelter on the porch. Charles had something in his hand. It was a baseball glove. More specifically, it was a softball glove, a George Reach M (for monster) 1000. It was perhaps the premiere softball glove of its era, a real thing of beauty that couldn't help but bring a smile to Gary's face as he slipped it on his left hand, pounding its pocket with his right hand.

Charles and Gary had often talked about baseball, and Charles knew that Gary truly loved the game. Gary had grown up playing baseball on sandlots—games without innings, played from daylight to dark over endless summers. He had played organized baseball through the high school level, and although he was no Barry Bonds, Gary was considered to be quite good. Gary had told Charles on more than one occasion that playing baseball was the most fun he had ever had, that when he was between the lines (baseball talk for playing the game), he felt like a ten-year-old no matter what age he was.

So Charles suggested that Gary buy the glove. Gary balked and said he couldn't afford it, and besides, he didn't play anymore. Charles offered Gary the glove at a discount price and told Gary he could pay him over time. Gary opened the pocket of the glove, lifted it to his nose and absorbed the wonderful smell of the leather—instantly a rush of images of diving catches, clutch hits and playing sandlot baseball flashed through his mind. Gary took the glove into the house.

The next day he bought glove oil and went through the treasured ritual of preparing the glove for play. He oiled it religiously every day after work and wrapped it tightly with rope after placing a softball in the pocket of the glove. Soon thereafter Gary inquired about his lumberyard's softball team and started playing with them.

Oddly enough, Gary noticed that he felt much better. He played more and more softball and then started running to get himself in better shape. He was recruited to play in a more competitive league and loved it. Several other things happened. Gary sold his house, bought a duplex closer to a local university and quit his job to pursue a degree in forestry. In that process, he met many new women.

But he continued to play the game because it had always worked for him. And he always was thankful to the neighbor, Charles, who saw the sparkle in his eyes when he talked about playing baseball. Sometimes, the solution to the problem has nothing to do with the problem . . . at all.

The method of using exceptions to the problem to build solutions and attending to what you like about your life is conceptually simple: find something that works and do more of it. It is the quintessential "what's right with you" approach! However, its application can be challenging because it requires a shift in the way we often tackle problems. This radical shift in perspective, from problems to solutions, is its very strength.

CHAPTER SIX BOTTOM LINE
The Solution Is Already Happening

Exercise Six: Solution Building

1. Elicit the exception.
- Between when you first noticed the problem and today, have you noticed any changes in the problem?
- When does the problem not occur?
- When is the problem less noticeable?
- When is the problem a bit more bearable?
- How have you managed under these circumstances?
- When do you cope a little better?
- What's new or different in your life?

Tasks:
- Between now and next week, note the things in your life (or in another person, or in your relationship, etc.) that you would like to see continue.
- Pay attention to the times you are able to overcome the temptation to drink, eat at bedtime, yell or whatever the problem is.
- Observe when the problem isn't occurring or is just a little better and how you are able to make it that way.

Other questions:
- Who or what is helpful or what is going well in your life?
- What do you seek out for even a small measure of comfort?
- What things are happening that you would like to see continue?

2. Elaborate the exception.
- What was happening at those times? [Give a detailed description.] What do you think you were doing to help that along? What would you need to do (or what would need to happen) for you to experience more of that?
- In what ways is the problem different, more bearable or less noticeable?

- Who is involved when things are different? Where did the difference happen?
- How do you account for the exception? How do you do that?
- If your friend, family or significant other were here, what would he or she say is different about you during times when the problem is not happening?

3. Expand the exception.
- How can you do more of what you are doing that is helpful?
- How can you do more of what is going right in your life?

4. Empower yourself.
- How did you arrive at the conclusion that now was the time for action?
- What insights had you gained from your life that you were finally able to put into action?
- What insights have you gained from this change that will help you in the future?
- What does this say about you, that you took the bull by the horns at this time?
- Who in your past would not be surprised to see you making these changes?
- How did you do it? How will you maintain the gains you have made?
- How are you different now that you have realized this change? Ponder your image of yourself both before you implemented this change and now.

5. Retake the ORS after implementing your harvested solutions.

- If there is an improvement of five points or greater or beyond the cutoff (twenty-five), go to chapter 7 to encourage your change over the long haul. If no improvement is reflected on the ORS, you may need to give it a little more time or try different methods of change. Chapter 7 also discusses what you can do when no change is happening.

7

The Proof of the Pudding

The proof of the pudding is in the eating.
—Miguel de Cervantes

In the late 1970s, the makers of Alka-Seltzer surprised everybody by firing the advertising company that created the slogan "I can't believe I ate the whole thing." The announcement came as a shock because the series of clever commercials had so quickly become part of the national vernacular and garnered much critical acclaim within the industry. Advertising companies all over the world had rushed to produce look-alike commercials. The makers of Alka-Seltzer, however, had one fundamental problem with the commercials—they didn't sell more Alka-Seltzer.

I would like you to adopt the same attitude as the makers of Alka-Seltzer. No matter how clever or compelling, if your change plan isn't producing the results you are looking for, it's time to fire that plan. The proof of the pudding is indeed in the eating. Contrary to popular belief, studies show that change, if it is going to occur, usually happens early on after implementation of a strategy or method. Using this invaluable body of research, this chapter shows you how to monitor the benefits of your plan with the Outcome Rating Scale (ORS), build on your results and, perhaps most important, brainstorm alternatives when change isn't forthcoming.

For those of you working with a change partner, chapter 7 also discusses how to enlist your helper beyond his or her supportive role when change is not happening. Providing you with an insider's view of what mental health professionals do when they are stuck, this chapter shows how to enlist a chorus of supporters—a solution team—to brainstorm different ideas and new directions when you are at an impasse.

Change Happens

The foolish reject what they see, not what they think; the wise reject what they think, not what they see.

Huang Po

Recall our discussion from chapter 2 that *the way change occurs is highly predictable,* with most change occurring earlier rather than later. Recognizing small but meaningful progress in the first few weeks of implementing your change plan predicts whether or not it will work in the long run. And, importantly, an absence of early improvement may substantially decrease the

chances of achieving your goals *with your current methods.*
Consider this: In an investigation of more than two thousand
therapists and thousands of clients, researchers found that when
no improvement occurred by the third visit, progress was not
likely to occur over the entire course of treatment. Moreover,
people who did not indicate that therapy was helping by the
sixth meeting were *very* likely to receive no benefit, despite the
length of the therapy! The diagnosis the person had and the type
of therapy delivered were not as important in predicting success
as knowing whether the treatment being provided was actually
working.[33] Think about that for a moment.

Studies have found that individuals whose therapists got feedback about their clients' lack of progress were, at the conclusion
of therapy, better off than 65 percent of those whose therapists
did not receive any information. Just knowing that their clients
were not benefiting from their therapy allowed these therapists
to modify their approaches and promote change. In truth, clients
whose therapists had access to progress information, like that
provided to you by the ORS, were less likely to get worse with
treatment and were *twice as likely* to achieve a clinically significant change.[34] These are amazing, if not revolutionary, results—
nothing else in the history of psychotherapy has been shown to
increase effectiveness this much!

CHECKPOINT: *Monitoring your progress is essential and
dramatically improves your chances of success.* You don't
really need the perfect approach as much as you need to
know whether your plan is working—and if it is not, how
to quickly adjust your strategy to maximize the possibility
of your improvement.

The Nuts and Bolts of Monitoring Your Progress

*...frothy eloquence neither convinces nor satisfies me...
you're got to show me.*

Willard Duncan Vandiver

Monitoring your progress gives you the best possible chance for success. Start with the graph on the following page. If you have not already done so, record your first ORS score. Plot your subsequent scores based on the number of weeks since that time, the number of meetings with your change partner or simply the number of times that you've monitored your progress with the ORS, whichever you prefer. After ten weeks, or ten meetings or ten times of measuring your progress, use the graph as a follow-up tool.

Remember that the ORS, by design, is a general tool. It offers a bare skeleton of your progress. You must add the flesh and blood of your experiences and breathe life into it with your ideas and perceptions. At the moment you mark the lines on the ORS, you imbue it with meaning—you know what the marks represent in your life—and it becomes a valuable symbol of your progress.

With the first ORS completed, the business of change begins, with your view of your improvement influencing what happens next in your plan. The ORS pinpoints where you are at the time you do the rating and is a basis for comparison thereafter. You become an important observer of your life in progress; your marks in the various life domains become invaluable information for reflection, discussion, clarification and problem solving.[35]

With each subsequent rating, compare the current ORS with the previous one and look for any differences. On your own or with your change partner, you can reflect whether there is an

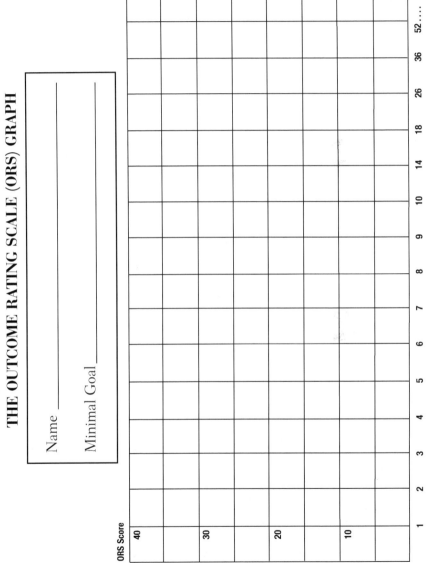

THE OUTCOME RATING SCALE (ORS) GRAPH

Name _____

Minimal Goal _____

ORS Score

40

30

20

10

1 2 3 4 5 6 7 8 9 10 14 18 26 36 52 ....

Weeks, Meetings or Ratings

Directions for Graphing Your ORS Scores

- Make copies of the graph for future use.
- Plot your initial ORS score from chapter 2.
- Plot the rest of your ORS scores since implementing your change plan.
- You may use the ORS graph to plot scores by number of weeks, the number of meetings with your change partner or simply the number of ratings since you began your change plan.
- When you have plotted ten ORS scores (whether by number of weeks, meetings or ratings), begin using the numbers on the bottom of the graph to depict weeks; use the graph for long-term monitoring of your gains.
- Use these graphs to compare your ORS scores and judge whether or not you are on track with your change plan. If you do not notice an increase in your ORS scores, implement the strategies discussed in this chapter.
- When your plotted scores plateau—congratulations!— space out your ratings over longer periods of time even if your scores plateau before ten ratings.

improvement (a move to the right on any line or an increase in score), a slide (a move to the left or a decrease in score) or no change. Don't worry if there are fluctuations of your scores, when your ratings jump up and down a bit. What you want to look at is the trend or pattern of your ratings. Is there an overall upward trend or an overall downward one? The scores serve as a springboard for consideration and discussion about your progress, and more importantly, what should be done differently if there isn't any.

When Your Plan Is Working

Nothing succeeds like success.
Alexander Dumas, the elder

If your ORS score has increased over your previous rating, be sure to implement all the ways to validate your progress and take responsibility for a new chapter in your life. *Please reread the "Empower Yourself" section in chapter 6 (page 165) if your plan is working.* Recall that this is like blaming in reverse, and it is particularly important for you to take ownership of your change so you can specifically identify how you accomplished it and continue the strategies that are working.

Remember too that it is especially helpful to encourage your reflection of *before and after*, the way things were before the change and how things are now, after the change. This helps you incorporate your successes into your changing identity, one that has overcome the problem and recognized your inherent strength.

Finally, at each of your follow-up ratings, continue to note what you are doing that is different and how that contributes to maintaining your gains. The idea here is that you struck it rich, but you are going to keep tapping the gold mine of change for all the nuggets you can find, fattening your bank account for future withdrawals. At each follow-up, continue to monitor what is working, and deposit your findings in the solution bank. Keep track of all the things you are doing to foster your ongoing mastery over the problem, and record these ideas and strategies in your journal.

Now let's take the "Empower Yourself" process a step forward and carry your newfound identity of competence and strength—your new story—into the future. Consider the following questions either alone or with your change partner:

- As you continue to overcome the problem, what will be different in your future?
- How will you see yourself and your prospects differently?
- How will your relationships be different?
- What will others notice about you, this new person without this problem?
- Who is already noticing these changes?
- What will you do instead of worrying about this problem?
- What new vista has opened for your future without the problem?

This step can be greatly enhanced by involving a so-called solution chorus. Here is where the other people you considered for change partners back in chapter 3 can be assembled, either in person or on a conference call, to participate in a celebration of your change and the new you without the problem. Even if you haven't been working with a change partner, this might be a time to consider involving others in your transformation to a better life.

This doesn't have to be a formal thing: you can do the full-fledged solution chorus, or you can simply let people in your life know the good news about how you took charge of the problem. Enlisting others keeps the odds in your favor by providing an audience for this new chapter in the story of your life. Whether you gather your change partners for a solution chorus meeting or simply go out to lunch with a few comrades from work or have coffee with a friend, the idea here is to enable others to hear of your success—to give witness—further solidifying the changes you have made. If you go the more formal route and assemble a solution chorus, it is often useful to videotape these meetings for later review to remind you of all you have accomplished.

Another option is to create an imaginary solution chorus.[36] Some of you may have no interest in sharing your experience with others but might enjoy and benefit from reflecting on what such a chorus might look like, using a cast of players in your life who have been supportive, kind or helpful in any way. These imaginary solution chorus members might include a favorite teacher or coach, an especially kind neighbor or relative, or even a fictional character from a book or a movie.

Here are some questions for the real or imaginary solution chorus:

- When did you first notice his or her tenacity to attack this problem?
- What did you notice that first told you he or she was going to overcome the problem?
- What stories do you know about this person that let you know that his or her success was a foregone conclusion?
- As he or she continues to overcome the problem, what will be different in his or her future?
- How will his or her prospects be different?
- How will his or her relationships be different?

- What will others notice about him or her, this person without this problem?
- What will he or she do instead of worrying about this problem?
- What new vista has opened for his or her future without the problem?

Recall Carrie and her struggle with, and eventual triumph over, her weight problem. Figure 7.1 displays her graph of ORS scores. Carrie's solution chorus included her change partners (husband, Ted; sixteen-year-old daughter, Heather; fourteen-year-old son, Matt) as well as a friend (Jennifer) she met at her weight-loss meetings. To celebrate her changes and further consolidate the meaning of her weight loss, Carrie gathered her choir of supportive voices at week twenty-six. What follows are just a few observations from her team.

Ted: *I never had any doubt that Carrie could overcome this weight problem, although I loved her regardless of her weight. She has dealt with a lot in her life and pulled it off with incredible results—how she took care of her mom when she was sick, while working a high-stress health-care job and managing our lives, was just amazing. Just look at our kids, which she deserves the most credit for.*

Heather: *I can see such a difference in her; she seems so much happier and focused on her future than before. Mom has always wanted to start some kind of business of her own—to get out of the rat race of her job—and now I really see her doing that. I am glad she finally got us involved in her weight plan—she sure has helped all of us with stuff in our lives. I know I couldn't have done nearly as well in school without her.*

Matt: *I remember when I was having trouble with a bully at school. I didn't tell anybody because I was embarrassed and*

FIGURE 7.1 Carrie's, Sarah's, and Anita's ORS Graphs

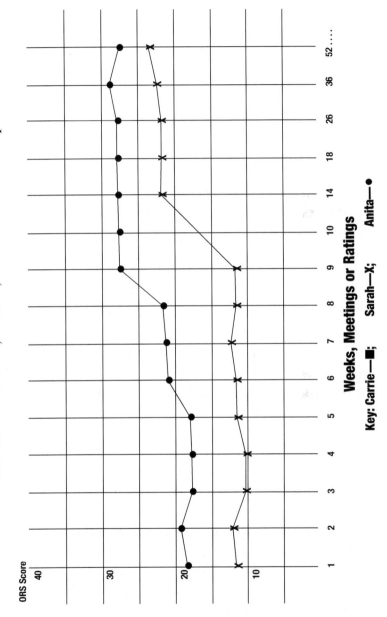

thought I should handle it on my own. I finally told Mom and she really jumped into action. What I really liked is how she took everything I said into consideration and didn't do things I didn't want her to do. She called the principal and got everything straightened out—without nailing the kid or anything. She really helped me see that I don't have to continue dealing with stuff alone, and she didn't betray me along the way. So I guess I knew she could do anything she set out to do, if she got the right help from us along the way.

Jennifer: *I can see Carrie's confidence and success with her change plan having reverberations throughout her life. She just seems to "carry" herself differently! I know she tortured herself before, and now she walks around like a big load has been taken off her shoulders. Now the sky is the limit for her. We've been talking about going into business for ourselves, with one of the diets that we really like and their line of nutritional products.*

A final step to consider in securing your change is to offer your experience of overcoming life challenges to others. As twelve-step programs have taught us, helping others, giving back to the community, serves many important functions, not the least of which is forever establishing your identity without the problem—as someone who has been there and survived to tell the story as a conquering hero. With her reestablished confidence, Carrie volunteered to speak to community groups and schools about her weight loss—not about the latest dieting craze but rather how validating herself and recruiting relational support helped her unleash her natural strengths to overcome her weight problem. Once again, this need not be a formal event, but rather a sincere attempt to help someone else who might benefit from your successful experience. You may want to volunteer to be a change partner for someone important in your life.

The Web site *www.whatsrightwithyou.com* offers another venue for you to celebrate your success and give back to others.

If your plan has been successful, that's great! Congratulations. Your graph, then, like Carrie's, shows a nice upward slope until at some point it starts to flatten out or plateau. This means that you have probably achieved *most* of the benefit that you will during this encounter with change. As Carrie's graph illustrates, the amount of change that occurs after the plateau will likely be slower, with longer periods of time having to pass for any more change to occur. When your graph flattens, it is a good time to start spacing your ratings out over longer periods of time. If this happens before ten weeks or ten rating times, as it will most often, space out your measurements to every four weeks, then eight weeks and so on. Recall Sarah, who struggled with addiction and HIV, and Anita, who was troubled by depression. Both achieved rapid benefit following the validation of their struggles and strengths and subsequent efforts of their own. Figure 7.1 illustrates their progress and the subsequent spacing of their ratings over longer periods of time after the slope of their change began to flatten.

When Your Plan Needs Adjusting

I haven't failed. I've found ten thousand ways that won't work.

Benjamin Franklin

If no change has occurred, the scores also invite a discussion, perhaps an even more important one. Here is the basic conversation that needs to happen, either internally or with your change partner:

*Okay, so things haven't changed since the last rating. How
do I make sense of that? Should I be doing something different here, or should I continue on course, steady as she goes? If
I am going to stay on the same track, how long do I think I
should go before getting worried? When will I know when to
say "when"?*

In your deliberations, it is useful to distinguish between when
your change plan is not working versus when you are having a bad
time because of unexpected stressors—stuff that just happens
(kids get sick, new boss, fender bender, etc). Sometimes such
events can keep your score on the ORS down temporarily. Your
change plan could be going very well, but some transient factors
may have slowed your progress. You wouldn't want to abandon
your change plan—a potentially successful path out of your problem—because you hit a pothole in the road, regardless of the
temporary discomfort inflicted by the hole.

The idea is to think about the lack of progress, make sense of
it and then decide what to do next. This process is repeated at
each rating, but later ratings gain increasing significance and
warrant additional action. These later ratings, for dramatic
emphasis, are called *checkpoint reflections* (or *conversations* if
working with a change partner) or *last-chance deliberations* (or
discussions). In a typical therapy setting, checkpoint conversations are usually conducted by the third session and last-chance
discussions are initiated in the sixth meeting. This is simply saying that by the third session, clients who receive benefit from the
services of a given agency are showing at least some progress;
and if change is not noted by session six, then the client is at a
significant risk for not being helped *if things remain the same.*

The precise number of ratings or weeks with no change that
trigger extra attention or increased discussion is totally dependent on what *you* think is reasonable for you. Just as a guideline,

I suggest a range of three to six weeks of no change to warrant a checkpoint reflection, and a range of seven to ten weeks of no progress for the last-chance deliberation. The additional attention paid at these two junctures enables you to switch directions to avoid continuing on a path that is leading nowhere. The main purpose is to consider other options and ideas to help you meet your goals. Your judgment is what counts here; these are not rigid rules. Trust your instincts.

Checkpoint Reflection

A lack of progress at the checkpoint stage is a clear indication that you should at least *consider* something different—even a small tweak could be useful. This can take as many forms as there are people. The idea is to brainstorm options: take a different approach; involve other people to bounce around ideas (e.g., a spouse or significant other); consult a religious adviser or another change partner (or get a change partner); or attend a self-help group—whatever seems to be of value and worthy of consideration. The checkpoint reflection is the time to thoroughly examine the approach you have chosen. Review chapter 4, and make sure your chosen method is a good match with your ideas about change. Could another approach be a better fit for you? If you tried something based on your theory of change and are not getting anywhere, think about the options in chapters 5 and 6. Go over the different approaches and ideas in the appendices. Implement any ideas that surface, including doing what you are doing for a while longer. Some plans just take a little bit longer. *Don't be afraid to stick with your plan if you feel it is right and just needs a little more time.*

The idea here is to open yourself up a bit so you can gain some perspective on your situation and what you can do about it. Having other people involved is the easiest way to achieve the needed distance from the problem and entertain alternative directions, but you can also go it alone if you prefer. You can gain this perspective by taking yourself outside the problem, allowing your mind to run free in a variety of ways: take a hike or connect with nature in some way; soak in a bubble bath or stimulate your senses, especially touch, in some form; go to a movie or indulge in a selfish pleasure of some sort; imagine yourself having a conversation with and getting advice from a wise elderly person (see appendix A). Such simple activities allow access to "nonordinary parts" of ourselves—places in our own minds where we normally do not travel. Pay attention to what emerges from these various "altered" states. Sometimes our internal wisdom is beckoned by experiences that differ from our usual thinking processes.

When we struggle with a problem, we are often so close to it and analyze it so much that we cannot see the forest for the trees. Our vantage point can be severely restricted by our conscious problem-solving side. This is the part of us that lists pros and cons and attempts to solve troubling situations through logic. This type of problem solving is, of course, very useful, but there is much more to our minds than that. Many people believe that our rational problem-solving abilities only scratch the surface of our inner wisdom and that a larger reservoir of resources exists at a subconscious level—a place we do not normally access. When we set aside our usual conscious deliberations about problems and engage our senses, we connect to this other place and other ideas occur to us.

For example, Tanya was feeling pretty low and didn't really want to discuss her situation with anyone. Who could blame her? Her history of abuse painted an ugly picture. But here it was, nine weeks after she implemented her plan—her theory of change—to explore and experience her traumatic past so she could put it behind her. Tanya had surveyed self-help materials and found a highly recommended approach to guide her through her abusive history. But after six weeks of diligently following the program, nothing changed, not even a tiny bit to give her encouragement. Despite that, she continued another three weeks because she truly believed the approach was right on the money—but now it was time to face the music. Unfortunately, no other approach seemed to have the same appeal. So Tanya went for a hike and tried her best to just appreciate the sensual experience of connecting with nature. As she was taking in the majesty of the view, the fresh cool air, the smell of pine and the sound of rushing water from the nearby creek, Tanya felt different than she had for several weeks. Then a funny thing happened.

Although she didn't even notice thinking about the problems she was having with her troubled roommate, it suddenly occurred to her that she needed to find a different apartment. The more she thought of that idea, the better she seemed to feel. The pressure of living with a roommate who was struggling with drug abuse and had a party lifestyle had taken a greater toll than Tanya had realized. The idea of finding an apartment gained momentum until ultimately Tanya moved out, which markedly improved her ORS score. Gaining some much-needed perspective, she also found a different approach to address her abusive past. Sometimes the best way home is not always the most direct or the most logical. Try the long way home for a change.

If you are working with a change partner and your plan is not working by the checkpoint conversation, it may also be useful to think about the Relationship Rating Scale (RRS). The idea is to simply take the temperature of how things are going and make adjustments if needed. Please review the information about the alliance in chapter 3. Alliance problems, or not quite a good fit with your change partner, could be a contributor to a lack of progress. Going through the RRS can help you get a better sense of what may or may not be working. A simple conversation could also suffice. This is the perfect time to iron out any issues that may not be optimal for your growth endeavor. Of course, this need not be formal or heavy-handed in any way.

Let's see what a checkpoint conversation would look like by considering Dave and his change plan. Figure 7.2 depicts his efforts at change. Dave, a twenty-seven-year-old computer engineer, was very distressed about his marriage. His wife, Fariha, had recently begun coming home late from work and going out for long periods of time at night to work on an election campaign. Several telephone calls in which theother party hung up after Dave answered resulted in a suspicion that Fariha was having an affair.

Dave began restricting trips out of the home because he wanted to "be there" for Fariha when she returned home. He brought up the possibility of an affair with Fariha, but she denied it and accused him of attempting to control her. Thereafter, Dave held a vigil at home each night, waiting anxiously for his wife. With increasing frequency, he accused Fariha of having an affair, and she became more vehement about her right to go where she pleased.

Dave's theory of change was that open communication would solve the problem. He searched for information about affairs and what he could do about it on the Internet and at a bookstore. After some research, Dave decided he would try various communication approaches, as well as become a detective, to get the goods on his wife. Dave thought that if Fariha would open up and come clean about the affair, he could forgive her and things could go back to the way they were. Dave also believed, as some sources had advised, that if he found incontrovertible evidence, Fariha would finally admit the affair.

So Dave implemented his change plan and arranged a time for the couple to do communication exercises. Fariha agreed to one sitting but quickly became frustrated when the conversation migrated to accusations about the affair. Thereafter she refused

FIGURE 7.2 Dave's and Anna's ORS Graphs

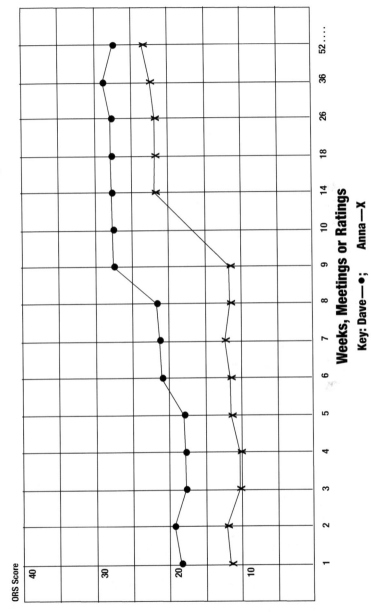

any more offers to talk about their marriage. Simultaneously, Dave began tracking her comings and goings, checking credit card bills, calling her at work and at other times on her cell phone, checking the mileage on the car and using other intrusive strategies to catch Fariha in the affair. This only infuriated her, and she responded by turning off her cell phone and staying out more.

Dave called for a meeting with his change partner, his sister Teresa. Here is a much shortened version of their conversation about the RRS and trying different options:

Dave: *Well, my situation has gone from bad to worse. My ORS score started at an eighteen, then went to nineteen, but now is down to thirteen, mainly because Fariha is less communicative and home even less. Can we talk about how you have been helping me, using this RRS form to guide us?*

Teresa: *Sure, let me see that. Wow, am I going to get a grade on that thing?*

Dave: *No, no. It is only a way for us to make sure that I am being clear about what I need from you to support my efforts. . . . Okay, you have been validating through and through. You helped me know I wasn't crazy for worrying about what was going on—that anyone would be concerned under these circumstances. Most important, you didn't tell me I was a fool for wanting to forgive Fariha and take her back if I discovered she was having an affair. You have been great! You know, as I am thinking about it, it would be helpful if you helped me sort out some ideas about what to do next. I read chapter 5 from the book and think it could be helpful. I know it's a lot to ask, but do you think you could read that chapter too?*

Teresa: *I can't really get to it until next week. Will that be okay?*

Dave: *Sure, that's fine.* [In the next conversation] *I was wondering about that "solution is the problem" thing, because it seems like the more I have tried to approach Fariha about not coming home after work and staying out at night, the more she has done it.*

Teresa: *That makes sense to me too. Okay, let's go through the exercise in that chapter.*

Dave and Teresa agreed that Dave had been "trying to solve a relationship problem by persuasion, argument and contention." They thought about the problem cycle and Dave's solution attempts: (1) what can Dave do to stop waiting on Fariha and his accusations? and (2) what can he do that would run counter to these attempts?

Dave decided he would "go with the flow" and make himself less available to Fariha—giving her plenty of space to do as she pleased—by pursuing his own neglected interests. This entailed making trips out of the house to do things with his friends or for himself, particularly when Fariha was home or about to arrive. This strategy would also require him to completely back off from any accusations or pressure for conversation and wait for his wife to initiate any discussion. These ideas are in the spirit of flying in the face of his previous solutions and to accept and support (go with the flow of) Fariha's desires to come and go as she saw fit.

Dave reinvested himself in his passion for fiction and got involved in a John Irving reading group at the local bookstore. His wife? Well, Fariha started spending more time at home and told Dave she feared they were growing apart; she even joined the book club to spend more time with Dave. The affair was no longer discussed. Over time Dave ultimately concluded that perhaps he had become a little too reliant on his wife and continued to engage in more outside social activity. He also realized that the affair was no longer an issue and probably never was.

Last-Chance Deliberation

If you have brainstormed and implemented different possibilities, or have continued the same strategy for a longer period and still have not experienced change, it is time for the last-chance deliberation (or discussion). Last-chance deliberations occur after seven to ten weeks of no progress since you have implemented a change plan. As the name implies, there is some urgency to look for something different, because people usually start achieving change by this time if the chosen method is going to work. It's like you are driving into a vast desert and running on empty, and a sign on the road says "Last chance for gas." The metaphor depicts the necessity of stopping and considering the implications of continuing a plan without reaching a desired change. To be sure, this doesn't mean it is the "last chance" for you but rather the last chance of a given change plan. There is no last chance for you!

This is the time when a different path should be thoroughly considered. Rarely is there justification for continuing to work with a plan that is not producing results. Rarely, though, is not never. *Keep in mind that you should still use your own judgment and trust your instincts.* The ORS ratings and last-chance deliberations are not meant to be followed robotically. Rather, they are intended to stimulate your reflection of whether your plan is beneficial or if you should do something different. If you feel that you just need to stay the course with your plan, then do so! But do consider when it will be appropriate to abandon the plan and do something else. *Know when to say when.*

When you continue using ineffective strategies, you actually become the main obstacle to reaching your desired destination. Think about this: research shows there is no connection between one unsuccessful effort to change and the likelihood of success in the next attempt. Not receiving benefit from a plan, then, only says something about the current methods—nothing about you or your potential for change! *So even if you have to go through a few renditions of your plan, the lack of progress does not mean that you won't be completely successful in the next attempt.* Monitoring your plan and having last-chance deliberations or discussions helps you get out of your own way and opens new possibilities for transformation.

To begin your last-chance deliberation, repeat the suggestions given under the checkpoint reflection section. Although new directions usually appear from those methods, if nothing emerges there are still many options. If you are working alone and want to (or have to) continue to do so, consider the following task to loosen up your creative process and get you going. First, though, make a pact with yourself that you will follow through with this task no matter what you think of it when you read it—no matter how difficult, inconvenient or unreasonable it might seem. It is nothing immoral or illegal or harmful.[37] The worst outcome would be that it won't be helpful, although it is very likely to get you on track.

Here is the task: Go to appendix A and sincerely try any and all ideas that address your circumstances, whether you think they fit or not. You can start by closing your eyes and picking one at random, or you can begin at the top of the page and implement the first one that lists your problem or situation as its purpose.

For example neither James nor Sharon had a clue what to do about Kevin, sixteen, and Melissa, fifteen. The teens were staying out until 2 A.M., swearing when asked to do a chore, trashing the house and eating every scrap of available food in the refrigerator. The parents had tried everything—grounding, taking away privileges, even bribery—nothing worked. Then they tried searching for exceptions, but that didn't get them anywhere either. Nothing else made much sense to them. They were too embarrassed to involve anyone else. Although they thought it a shot in the dark, Sharon fanned the pages of appendix A and looked for ideas until she picked one that addressed parenting— the Invariant Prescription. Crazy idea, they thought, but no more crazy than their present lives.

This task required a commitment that was as strong willed as their two willful offspring. It suggests that instead of the teens, the parents would be out of the home without a clear explanation of their whereabouts. All the teens would find would be a note saying the parents would be away for two hours. Two hours couldn't cause any more damage than already occurred when both siblings were home alone after school. Sharon and James did not tell the children what they were doing or where they went. They faithfully followed the crazy idea for two weeks, with six total "disappearances." After their daughter found the first note, she shrugged it off. The second note instigated a discussion between the siblings and some off-the-cuff comments about their parents' strange behavior. By the third note, both teens confronted their parents together, demanding to "have a talk." But by this time, the parents were getting the hang of it and simply got busy with other things. The second week was a little strange. The children went from having mini-tantrums to strange bouts of politeness. They eyed their parents suspiciously. The daughter helped do the dishes while the son mentioned to his dad that they had not gone fishing in a while. Clearly the parents noticed that a dynamic in the home had changed. While there was much to be done, James and Sharon felt they had reclaimed some part of their authority *and* their relationships with their son and daughter.

They simply did something different. Sometimes randomly selecting something to do—with a predetermined commitment to do it no matter what—is just what we need to get our juices flowing. It is akin to the process of experiencing a writing block. Staring at the computer screen or blank page often results in more of the same: no fresh ideas and continued frustration. Writing something, however mundane, ill defined or unrefined, stimulates our thinking and creative processes and gets us moving.

Another way to open things up when your plan is not working by the last-chance discussion is to enlist a solution team.

The Solution Team

When mental health professionals get stuck, they consult others in so-called case conferences, or they assemble colleagues for a treatment team meeting. A case conference is simply a presentation of the "case" by the primary therapist, then other therapists make suggestions and give opinions about what to do. These ideas are then brought back to the client for discussion. The treatment team is an exciting alternative that brings together a group of therapists for a conversation about the problem and options with the client. This usually happens through a one-way mirror, but some teams do this with everyone in the same room. Whatever the format, the result is often a wonderfully creative mix of ideas and possible paths to follow.

You can accomplish the same thing with your change partners or a few of your friends or colleagues. The solution team meeting can run the full gamut from a totally informal chat to a formal, mediated discussion with similar guidelines that therapists follow. Feel free to make you own rules based on whatever you feel comfortable asking your team to do. You might just encourage a free-floating exchange of suggestions and thoughts and ask your team to do no more than bring themselves and their experiences to the meeting. Or you might prefer a more structured discussion and request that your team explore the Internet or read a chapter in this book or other self-help materials before the meeting. It doesn't really matter as long as the opportunity exists for sharing experiences and generating possibilities. You might also choose to exercise the imaginary-team option, in which you create the best possible solution-team of people who you feel would stand up for you. The idea here is simply that two (or more) heads are better than one.

If you want to go a more formal route, to approximate what therapists do, first make sure your change partners are on board. A more formal solution team places rather high demands on your change partners, so this avenue is definitely not for everyone. If you think it is asking too much, feel free to take a more informal route. You can still benefit greatly from the ideas that emerge from a "coffee talk" format.

If your team of change partners is willing to participate on a formal team, here are some guidelines: Each person is given an assignment to prepare for the solution team meeting. All should read chapter 2, especially the section about validation. One person should read chapter 4 and come prepared to discuss the problem from the vantage point of your view of change. Another should read chapter 5 and be ready to discuss your situation from the perspective that the solution is the problem. Still another should read chapter 6 and be primed to listen to your story for exceptions. The last person should become familiar with the approaches surveyed in the appendices. All team members, of course, bring their own ideas and experiences with overcoming problems and making important changes. Plan on a two-hour meeting. Make sure everyone knows that the purpose of the meeting is to generate new ideas and directions; there is no pressure for anyone to fix anything or come up with any miracle cures!

Your primary change partner should moderate the meeting, note any ideas that have currency and keep things on track. There are three steps to the meeting: First you should present your situation—your goals and your view about how and why you are stuck—and any ideas you have about changing your approach to the problem. Next each member of your solution team is given time to ask about the situation, especially questions that come from the materials they read before the meeting. Finally, the remainder of the time, at least an hour, should be reserved for brainstorming any and all ideas. Before any suggestions are brought forth, however, each change partner should preface his or her thoughts with a heavy dose of validation—regarding both your struggles and your inherent resources and coping abilities. What follows is a "best-case scenario" example of a solution-team meeting. Remember that your meeting need not be as formal or demand as much from your team.

Anna was depressed and struggling. Her initial ORS rating was a very low twelve. She had tried therapy but felt her therapist had given her "the big brush-off." Her doctor had also prescribed a popular antidepressant, but that didn't help either because Anna didn't like the way she felt taking the drug. Anna really liked the idea of looking for exceptions to her depression, so she applied the steps in chapter 6. Unfortunately, although she and Paul, her change partner (a long-term mentor), found a few exceptions and attempted to expand them, it just didn't pan out—it didn't produce any meaningful changes in the way Anna felt. The checkpoint conversation revealed that Anna and Paul were in sync and that Anna believed more time was needed to implement the ideas they had come up with. Several weeks later, however, Anna still felt crummy.

At the last-chance discussion, Anna and Paul decided to form a solution team. Anna called her other potential change partners and recruited them for a meeting. The team included her friend Steve (a colleague from work), her sister Elizabeth and her partner, Chris. Anna explained what the meeting would entail and gave each of them an assignment. Anna had skipped the chapter on her view of change so she and Paul agreed to read chapter 4 in preparation for the solution team meeting; Steve was asked to read chapter 5; Elizabeth and Chris were assigned the appendices for possible brainstorming of different options. All were asked to read the validation section of chapter 2.

Building on what she read in chapter 4 about her view of change, Anna presented her ideas. She described multiple rejections by parents, siblings, teachers, lovers, coworkers and professional helpers. Anna became emotional and cried during this discussion. She concluded by saying that although she knew she had many strengths, something about her past kept her from moving forward—all those rejections were providing some kind of obstacle. Anna truly believed that she needed to address this root cause if any progress was to occur.

After the team members asked Anna questions about her situation from the vantage point of the chapters they represented, each validated Anna and told stories that highlighted her perseverance. Here is a much shortened description of the solution team discussion:

Steve: *Something that strikes me about this, from my chapter, is that it seems as if you have been sort of trying to help your feelings of depression by avoiding it a bit—that you think a lot of it is because of all the crap you experienced in your life and that you have been avoiding dealing with that. I don't know if that makes any sense.*

Chris: *Well it does to me. It's like the depression is a message saying that maybe you should take a look at some of your beliefs about yourself based in all those rejections you are carrying around with you. I really believe it is a big obstacle that somehow you carry around this idea that you are basically a broken person that nobody could love.*

Elizabeth: *That sounds right to me, that no matter how people love you, you don't really believe you are lovable. I don't know; I don't want to sound too psychological or anything, but I think it would be good to look at some of those ideas.*

Paul: *Okay, so it sounds like a couple of ideas are percolating here. One is to look at those rejections a bit closer, to experience them and then examine some of the beliefs that may be getting in your way.*

Anna: *This is good.*

Elizabeth: *Anna, I also think that your rejection stuff started with never really getting Dad's approval. I don't know; I just wanted to throw that in.*

Chris: *So I was thinking that looking at what was called a cognitive approach may be good thing because it looks at your beliefs and negative self-talk and teaches you how to change them. The Web site listed a bunch of books that help you do that.*

Elizabeth: *Yeah, that's a good idea.*

Steve: *And I was thinking that some kind of self-help group might be good.*

Elizabeth: *Like maybe that would help you talk through some of the things that happened in our family and those experiences you think are obstacles—especially how you weren't accepted by our father.*

The solution team bandied about several possibilities. Anna investigated a cognitive approach and also started attending a self-help group that looked at her family of origin and other past experiences. She found a book about changing self-defeating beliefs and discussed what she read with Paul. These different actions led to a marked change in Anna's ORS scores—her rating increased to a twenty-one after just five weeks. Figure 7.2 (page 199) also shows Anna's journey with change.

The previous lack of progress that Anna experienced had nothing to do with her or the initial change plan. It was simply not the right fit: it looked great on the rack and even in the dressing room, but when she got it home, it just wasn't right. It is important to note that although her previous attempts at change were unsuccessful, they had no impact on her subsequent growth when she implemented a different plan. Anna's earlier lack of change did not make her any more likely to fail at a subsequent attempt.

The Death of George Washington

To exchange one orthodoxy for another is not necessarily an advance. The enemy is the gramophone mind, whether or not one agrees with the record that is being played at the moment.

George Orwell

On a cold, blustery December day in 1799, the sixty-seven-year-old former president of the United States, George Washington, returned to his mansion from his usual morning ride on the grounds of his Mount Vernon estate.[38] The day continued in normal fashion. The former president and first lady read newspapers together in the parlor while the household staff performed the usual duties. As the day wore on, however, a minor sore throat the president had experienced since his morning ride worsened. By early the next morning, his condition was so grave that a doctor was summoned.

The doctor—along with two other physicians who eventually made it through the snowy weather to Mount Vernon—skillfully administered the accepted therapy of the day. When no results were observed, the three agreed that more of the same treatment was indicated. Several hours and two additional treatments later, the president was dead. The cause of death? Whatever course the disease might have taken, historians agree that the treatment Washington received in his weakened state likely hastened his demise. The treatment, of course, was the accepted "standard of care" for late eighteenth-century medicine—bloodletting.

While it might be tempting to believe that we have evolved beyond such primitive practices, the very same forces that led Washington's physicians to administer (and then readminister) an ineffective (and ultimately lethal) treatment continue to guide not only the practice of therapy but also many attempts at self-change. People get hung up on the apparent rightness of the solution *instead* of its success. Conventional wisdom suggests that using the "right" method will resolve the problem. As the death of George Washington illustrates, however, the apparent "rightness" of a method is no guarantee of effectiveness no matter how competently it is administered. *What is considered "right" is nothing more than the prevailing wisdom of the day.* More important perhaps, the story shows that having no way to monitor the benefit of an approach—whether or not it is producing the results you want—may encourage you to continue a method that is not working. Not having a way to measure progress encourages persistence in a plan that ultimately will, as in the case of Washington, drain the life right out of you.

CHAPTER SEVEN BOTTOM LINE
Monitor, Adjust, Celebrate

Exercise Seven: Tracking Your Progress

1. **When Your Plan Is Working:**
   - **Plot your ratings. Space out ratings when the graph starts to flatten.**
   - **Empower yourself: Blaming in reverse; before and after distinctions; monitor and journal your ideas and methods to create a solution bank.**
   - **Take your gains into the future. Consider these questions:**
     - As you continue to overcome the problem, what will be different in your future? How will you see yourself and your prospects differently?
     - How will your relationships be different?
     - What will others notice about you, this person without this problem?
     - What will you do instead of worrying about this problem?
     - What new vista has opened for your future without the problem?
   - **Assemble a solution chorus or informally chat with friends. Have them consider these questions:**
     - When did you first notice his or her tenacity to attack this problem?
     - What did you notice that first told you he or she was going to overcome the problem?
     - What stories do you know about this person that let you know that his or her success was a foregone conclusion?
     - As he or she continues to overcome the problem, what will be different in his or her future?
     - How will his or her prospects be different?
     - How will his or her relationships be different?
     - What will others notice about this person without this problem?

- What will he or she do instead of worrying about this problem?
- What new vista has opened for his or her future without the problem?

- **Build on your accomplishments; share the benefits of your experiences.**

2. **When Your Plan Needs Adjustment:**

- **Plot your ratings. Compare each subsequent rating on the ORS with the previous one. Have this conversation with yourself or your change partner:**

Okay, so things haven't changed since the last rating. How do I make sense of that? Should I be doing something different here, or should I continue on course, steady as she goes? If I am going to stay on the same track, how long do I think I should go before getting worried? When will I know when to say "when"?

- **Checkpoint Reflection/Conversation:**

Consider options including: staying the course, changing plans and bringing in other people. Look at your view of change and make sure your plan is a good fit. Do activities to free your mind to gain perspective and distance. If using a change partner, take the temperature of the change potential of the relationship. Consider other alternatives from the book or elsewhere.

- **Last-Chance Deliberation/Discussion: Repeat above process. If nothing new emerges, then try the "pact" if working alone or assemble an informal or formal solution team.**

Let your instincts guide the type of team that fits for you. Different perspectives are what you want—two heads are better than one. If you want a more formal structure: (1) Have each team member read the validation section of chapter 2 and give each a chapter or appendix to bring to the table for discussion; (2) present your concerns, goals and any new ideas that you have about how to address your situation; (3) the team asks questions from the vantage point of the materials they read in preparation for the meeting; (4) each member of the team validates you; (5) the team shares any ideas that have emerged from their readings and the discussion; (6) your change partner moderates the meeting and notes any ideas that seem to make the most sense to everyone, especially you.

- **Implement the ideas and continue to track your progress on the ORS.**

Epilogue

*That so few dare to be eccentric
marks the chief danger of the time.*

John Stuart Mill

Ruby Slippers

Some might say that this book is Pollyannaish—that the ideas and methods presented here are overly optimistic and the examples are too good to be true. People with *real* problems cannot *really* rally their resources to overcome life struggles and certainly not with *real* "disorders." I couldn't disagree more. This criticism is one I often hear from mental health professionals mired in the Killer Ds—even when they see videotaped examples! The results *are* real. With over seventeen thousand hours of face-to-face work, plus countless hours of phone coaching with people in all levels of distress, problems big and small, I can assure you that people, like you, do change—quickly and dramatically, and research emphatically bears this out. That doesn't mean, of course, that change is easy. But it does mean that it is more common and possible than many would have you believe.

I hope you have discovered that you already had the power to get back to Kansas and have used the ruby slippers of your inner strengths and inherent resiliency to get you where you wanted to go. Throughout this book, you've read a lot about how to tap in to your innate resources, recruit relational support and implement a change strategy that is not only a good fit but also informed by feedback about its benefit. This final chapter distills that information into a sort of pocket guidebook or quick reference.

If you have not made any progress after reading this book, please do not despair! It means nothing other than that this was not the right path for you to take to make a change in your life. Please continue to monitor your progress in any other routes you may travel in your journey toward change. Therapy may be an option to consider (see appendix C for tips about finding a therapist and deriving the most benefit from it). There are many other sound options as well. Please don't be afraid, as the epigraph suggests, to be eccentric when considering your options.

Six Steps to C*H*A*N*G*E

"Who are you?" said the Caterpillar. Alice replied rather shyly, "I—I hardly know sir, just at present—at least I knew who I was when I got up this morning, but I must have changed several times since then."

Lewis Carroll

C—Challenge the Killer Ds: Debunk Dysfunction and Ditch the D Detector

Recall the discussion from chapter 1 about the Killer Ds—

disease, deficits, disorders, dysfunction, disabilities and so on. In recent years there has been a deluge of diagnoses. (See appendix C for a critique of psychiatric diagnosis.) New ones appear almost daily. However impressive they might sound, please do not think that naming a problem or explaining it with a diagnosis has anything to do with solving it. Unfortunately, describing the struggles of living in this way gives people the message that there is something wrong with them. This mind-set is *the first freeway to failure* in trying to make personal changes. Whether simply saying that you are dysfunctional or receiving a formal diagnosis, once set in motion, creates an expectancy of hard going and, if left unchecked, becomes a forgone conclusion. The Killer Ds erode your ability to confirm and affirm your strengths and natural capabilities to help yourself. They are a product of the D Industry with all its self-serving interests. Discard this way of looking at yourself—ditch the D Detector—and discover what's right with you! Replace the Killer Ds with the Kinder Ds: not disease, dysfunction or disorder, but rather distress, discomfort or dilemma. Think of problems, not pathology.

Consider Carol, who had been through the mill and felt miserable. She struggled with depression and regularly pummeled herself with thoughts of worthlessness. She spent the greater part of three sessions telling me what was wrong with her: as she described it, she was from an abusive, dysfunctional family, was codependent and suffered from obsessive compulsive disorder and post-traumatic stress—she thought she might have borderline personality disorder to boot. In short, her D Detector was not just set on stun; it was on full Killer D mode. Tragically, Carol had been sexually abused as a child. But what struck me, transcending the Killer D–dominated story, was a footnote she shared in one of her stories of abuse. Carol told the tale of a ten-year-old girl who said "no" to an abusive uncle, despite his obvious superior strength and size, when he pushed her into the

backseat of his car. Although he overpowered her, this coura-
geous kid maintained her spirit and sense of self throughout the
horrific event. As it turned out, there were many instances of
heroism in Carol's life. Over time, Carol started telling different
tales about her life and who she was. In our last meeting she
said, "You know, Barry, there were horrible people in my life who
gave me problems that a child should never have to deal with.
But, in retrospect, I am now convinced that the only thing wrong
with me was my idea that there was something wrong with me!"

H—Honor Your Heroic Self: Validate Your Struggles and Your Strengths

Frankly, I have never seen anyone make a change based on
blaming and berating himself or herself for a problem or troubling
situation. I guess it's possible, but I have never heard anyone say,
"Barry, I am having these problems because I am a worthless
human being with the worst of intentions, and consequently I am
now going to make meaningful changes in my life." As I said in
chapter 2, self-blame and self-loathing are just not precursors of
action for most people. The entrance ramp to *the second highway
to hell* is invalidation. Sure you have your part in the problem, but
there are a lot of factors that have contributed to the situation,
and maybe, just maybe, you were doing the best you could under
those strenuous and tumultuous circumstances. *Validating your
struggles, or understanding your troubling situation as the confluence of many factors, legitimizes your actions and feelings (without
absolving you of responsibility for change) and is a critical step
toward meaningful growth.* You have to give yourself a break.

Further, recognizing that your problem has meaning beyond
its distress allows you to see the current crisis as an opportunity,
an important juncture in your life that could open new possibilities and perhaps even a new sense of yourself.

I am also hard-pressed to remember anyone changing by putting his or her faults under a magnifying glass. Sure, we all have weaknesses, and recognizing one's shortcomings allows a person to work on them and improve—but a little of that goes a long way! The story about what is wrong with us is greatly over-told and oversold. It is simply not what it's cracked up to be in terms of helping you take important steps to change your life. Making permanent changes in your life requires an appreciation of your strengths, the more heroic aspects of who you are. Consequential growth is achieved by marshaling your inherent resources against the obstacles before you.

Consider Harold, who began suspecting his wife of having an affair after he discovered unidentified footprints in the snow. Other bits of evidence resulted in Harold beginning to check the bedsheets for signs of semen, which would provide ironclad evidence of her unfaithfulness. Throughout Harold's growing mistrust, his wife emphatically denied the affair, told him he was crazy and filed for divorce. Harold continued checking the bedsheets until he found stains. He took the sheet to a laboratory that confirmed the presence of semen. His wife insisted the semen was his. She began telling friends and family, including their own children, that Harold was paranoid and sick.

Harold told me that he was obtaining a DNA profile of the semen to see if it matched his own. Harold nervously asked if I thought he was crazy for spending the money for the very expensive test. I simply replied that peace of mind is cheap at any price. Harold wept when I said that. It seemed his company doctor and the first therapist he was referred to had told him he was imagining things, needed drugs and the DNA test was a waste of money—a very heavy dose of invalidation, to say the least.

With the foundation of validation, Harold tapped into his resources—his deep love for his children, close relationship with his parents and outstanding work history. Since divorce seemed imminent, Harold decided he would stop acting "crazy" (trying to persuade everyone of his wife's affair), go back to work, move out of the house and arrange for immediate visitation with the children. The DNA test? Well, despite the company doctor's and previous therapist's belief that Harold was mentally ill, the test revealed that the semen was not Harold's.

A—Add a Helper: Recruit a Change Partner

Relationships are the essence of humanity. We are social creatures who thrive in connection with others. A supportive and caring relationship sustains us in tough times and encourages us to bring out our best. Life is just plain easier when we have help. So is change.

I well remember Al, who only left his house to come to our sessions. When he was a long-haired, nineteen-year-old college student, Al had been arrested in an auto-wrecking yard trying to steal parts for his broken-down Toyota. In the local county jail, he was repeatedly raped and beaten, setting in motion a chain of events that led to a term in state prison and a stay in a state psychiatric hospital. He'd been deeply afraid of leaving his house ever since and was the veteran of numerous unsuccessful psychiatric treatments.

In our first session, Al made only a few brief references to this history. Most of our conversation was devoted to shooting the breeze about hockey—the Stanley Cup play-offs were in full force, and both of us were fans. Al became very animated as we discussed the various teams, coaches and players, and I enjoyed his insight into the sport and his company.

In each session, we spent more and more time talking about hockey and less and less about the "agoraphobia." Halfway through meeting four, partly because I thought we ought to be doing something, I asked Al to write down some goals, ranking them from the most difficult to the least difficult. His three most difficult contemplated actions were going to the bank, going to the dentist and going to the mall. At the beginning of the fifth session, he opened the list, handed it to me and told me he'd accomplished all three! I was dumbfounded and curious, but Al wanted to return to talking about the Stanley Cup finals. So in the interstices of our hockey conversation, I asked him what the achievement of these goals meant to him, where he thought these changes might lead and what might keep them going.

We kept talking mainly about things we both enjoyed—hockey, politics and the wilderness. On the margins of these talks, Al told me he wanted to exercise and to contribute financially to his family, which depended on his wife's modest income as a laboratory technician while he took care of their young son. Such discussions took no more than ten minutes of every session. By the eighth and final meeting, Al had begun a jewelry business in his garage, regularly ran errands in town and had taken up biking.

In that last session, we looked back and talked about all the times we'd shot the breeze. He told me I was the only therapist who had really understood him. The others, he said, had cut off his attempts at conversation to focus on his problems. Interestingly then, change had nothing to do with my professional degree or expertise—it was the relationship that counted, that provided the magic. I was a change partner to Al, a supportive and friendly companion who cared about what happened to him. While it is possible to be the "Lone Changer," it is a lot easier to have a faithful companion in our ride into the sunset of transformation.

N—Never Underestimate Your Own Ideas: Value Your View of Change

The resonance of your ideas with any change plan you select is critically important. Recall the "impossible" case project I mentioned in chapter 4. The major reason for unsuccessful therapy, regardless of the severity of the problem or how long it had been around, was that the client's own ideas were ignored. So *the third pathway to impossibility* is paved by neglecting your motivations, perceptions and ideas. When you ignore or dismiss your ideas about change, the plan may not inspire the necessary hope to encourage action.

Consider Nora, a delightful seven-year-old girl, who was soiling herself when she was at school. After talking to Nora about the problem and validating what it was like to deal with such an embarrassing situation, we explored her view of change and what she thought would be helpful. Nora told me about this very mean third-period math teacher she had, Mr. Miller, who wouldn't let her go to the bathroom. Nora said she repeatedly raised her hand to be excused but he ignored her and that was why she soiled her pants. I asked Nora what she thought could be done to set this guy straight, and Nora responded by telling me she needed for her mother to write Mr. Miller a note that scolded him and told him he had better let Nora go to the bathroom. Nora and I discussed her ideas with her mom, and she wrote the note with the appropriate tone that Nora had wanted. Nora approved it and took it to school.

Nora never soiled her pants again. But there's more: After Nora and I shared her plan with her mother, Nora's mother asked to speak to me alone. Chuckling, she told me that Nora's math class was actually her fifth period and that her teacher was a woman, and finally there was no teacher by the name of Mr. Miller! Nora's mother and I decided to implement the plan anyway because there is something about following through with a person's ideas that stimulates positive movement.

One can speculate many reasons why Nora suddenly took control of her soiling problem, but the fact remains that she eliminated the problem when her own ideas were solicited and enacted. Don't underestimate the power and wisdom of your ideas. Follow your own ideas about change to their logical conclusion and see what happens.

G—Give Yourself a Chance: Do Something— Implement a Plan

Several avenues were discussed for using your view of change as a guide to design and implement a plan of attack. Chapter 4 suggest ways for you to *just do it* and how *to find a fit* with your ideas. Chapters 5 and 6 present two very different problem-solving models, and the appendices and Web site, *www.whatsright withyou.com,* provide more directions to consider, as well as other places to find information. The common thread that unites the wide range of possible ideas is the formulation of a strategy that *competes* in some way with your current experience of your concern—any plan encourages a live experiment, a competition, with your usual way of being or acting. In the actual presence of the problem, the various methods ask you to do, think or feel something that is unlike business as usual. This is very important because when we do something different—anything different—it not only encourages altered responses in ourselves and others but also sets the stage for new understandings.

Consider twenty-five-year-old Gwen, who described her problem as low self-esteem; she just didn't seem to like herself much these days. Gwen wasn't really sure what to do, so she decided to try The Rate and Predict Exercise (see appendix A). Each night before retiring, she would predict her level of self-esteem for the following day. She would then compare the predicted level versus the actual the next night. If there were any discrepancies between the two ratings (her predicted rating was either better or worse than what she actually experienced), her task was to make sense of it given the events of that day. Upon reflecting about her self-esteem ratings, Gwen realized that her marriage was the biggest contributor to her lack of self-esteem. She realized this when her husband went on a fishing trip; when Gwen compared her ratings, she was astonished to find that her low self-esteem was miraculously cured while he was gone.

Gwen then knew she needed to address the problems in her marriage. And she did. The key is to do *something* about your problem and not continue to let it to do damage in the same way day after day. Doing something creates the possibility of new insights and new directions. As long as the plan makes sense to you and enlists your natural strengths, it will likely get you to a better place. Doing *anything* rallies your resources and creates an opportunity for good things to happen. Any approach to address your problem is like a magnifying glass on a sunny day—it brings together, focuses and concentrates your strengths, resources and ideas, narrows them to a point in space and time, and causes them to ignite into action.

In any given situation there are many possibilities that could result in problem improvement, many different outfits that you would look good wearing. Please always know there is something else you can do about your situation! *The fourth road to ruin* is traveled by giving up on yourself and doing nothing. Implementing one idea, even though it may not help your immediate concern, may lead to a solution that will.

Change can be a scary place to go, an undiscovered country that holds its own risks and pitfalls. As Hamlet says, though, we cannot let this undiscovered country make "us rather bear those ills we have than fly to others that we know not of."

E—Empower Yourself: Monitor, Adjust and Celebrate

You are the engine of change. If you are going to arrive at your destination, you have to know if the engine is on the right track, or you may experience the old "you can't get there from here." As discussed in chapters 6 and 7, if you are on the right track, you need to keep the engine fueled: take responsibility for the change, identify your successful strategies, envision the future, celebrate the new you without the problem and perhaps give something back to others. If you are not on the right track—the change you desire is not happening—then it is time to consider switching tracks. Checkpoint conversations and last-chance discussions help you monitor and make sense of your ORS scores when they are not reflecting any benefits from your plan. Enlisting a real or imaginary solution team and tapping in to your subconscious problem-solving abilities—your "nonordinary" talents—can infuse your change endeavor with new ideas.

The failure of a plan says nothing about you or the plan. *All approaches or ideas are helpful some of the time with some people.* The lack of benefit from a particular plan says nothing about the likelihood of success with your next plan. A lack of change only says it's time to do some soul searching about your chosen strategy. One gem of an idea that the Mental Research Institute (chapter 5) taught us is *the fifth thoroughfare to trouble*—continuing to do the same thing despite evidence that the solution is not working.

Let me tell you about fifteen-year-old Erin. Each morning, she would say good-bye to her mom, Rhonda, and walk toward the bus stop near her home. But instead of getting on the bus, she'd walk to a friend's house, where she would spend the day, returning home just as the afternoon bus drove down the street. If not for the notices the school eventually mailed home, her family might never have learned what was going on. When confronted, Erin said she had panic attacks when she tried to go to school. Rhonda took her to the doctor who prescribed an antidepressant and recommended psychotherapy. Erin didn't like the therapist much, so she did everything she could to not go to the sessions.

At the same time, she was fighting more with her parents and seemed increasingly aggressive. When informed about an

incident in which Erin threw a glass against the wall, the
alarmed therapist admitted Erin to the hospital. Her medication
was changed to two different antidepressants and an antianxiety
drug to help with the agitation often caused by the antidepressants. After three nights, Erin was sent home with orders to take
her meds, see the therapist regularly and come back to the hospital psychiatrist on a monthly basis.

Soon thereafter Erin ran out of the house in a panic in an
attempt to still the tumult inside her. This outburst led to hospitalization. At the hospital her doctor diagnosed her with bipolar
disorder and added an anticonvulsant to her medication regi-
men. Fortunately for her, Erin's story doesn't end here, but let's
pause to contemplate the mental health care she received—care
dominated by Killer D thinking, a mistrust in human resilience
and *especially* a penchant for doing the same thing over and over.
By the way, Erin's capabilities and perspective on her problems
were never enlisted in her treatment. No one ever really asked
her what she wanted or formed a personal connection with her.

Rhonda decided to try something else and made an appointment with me. I gave both Erin and Rhonda the PRS and asked
them to rate where they were when the problem first started. Erin
rated herself a seventeen when the problem of the panic attacks
first started and an eight currently. Rhonda's rating was a twenty-
four when the problem started and an eleven now. Both had actually gotten worse with treatment! Holy George Washington!

Please don't take this story to be an indictment against medication (although a diet of multiple medications has zero research
support and none of the drugs Erin was prescribed had FDA
approval for adolescents). Medication can be helpful for some.
But this story is a strong indictment against continuing to do the
same thing despite no change or a worsening of the problem.

With her family's help, I got a more complete portrait of Erin,
not just the one painted by the Killer Ds. I learned about her

judo class, her love of pets and volunteer work at the animal shelter, and her passion for the drums. Erin and I hit it off, and she and her family worked hard. They began a homeschooling program, which took off some of the pressure, and after three months, with the help of her family doctor, Erin decreased her medication to just one antidepressant. After six months, she argued less, worked on her anxiety attacks and decided to go back to school. It was no picnic, but she did it.

Last Call for Your Innate Abilities

If you have built castles in the air, your work need not be lost; that is where they should be. Now put the foundations under them.

Henry David Thoreau

I started this book by telling you about all the people I have seen in therapy who have overcome serious, often debilitating struggles. And I told you that you could too.

When I was a young man, coming out of a very rough period of drug abuse, a life-threatening accidental overdose, the loss of my best friend in a car accident and a subsequent failure at college, I was trying to get things on the right track. I had a job interview I was very nervous about and decided to talk to my dad about it. Dad, who never gave up on me (nor did my mom), first delivered his standard-issue pep talk about how everyone puts their pants on one leg at a time—that no one possessed anything I didn't. Then in a quiet voice he told me that he knew I had been through some rocky times but that who I was as a person was separate from all that. He asked me if I remembered the day when the elderly widow, Mrs. Hickman, had called him about me. I had not thought of her for years; Mrs. Hickman had been my favorite person on my paper route. She always came to the door to receive the evening newspaper and oftentimes greeted me with hot chocolate or cookies, but unfailingly with kindness and a warm smile. There was one particular day she didn't come to the door. Concerned, I let myself in to check on her and found her sick in bed. I brought her some tea and discovered that her wood-burning stove was nearly empty. The stove was her only source of heat and the temperature outside was below zero, so I brought in an ample supply of wood, loaded the stove and made sure she was okay. She called Dad the next day to tell him. Dad said that the pride he felt after that call still made him glow to this day; more important, he said, anybody who would do that at eleven years old must be made of the best stuff possible. After a pause Dad added that I never have to continue being someone I am not happy with. He said that, starting that day, I could define myself in any way I could dream of. And he was right. And I did. And so can you.

❧ EPILOGUE BOTTOM LINE ❧
Ask Not What's Wrong
but Rather What's Right with You

Six Steps to C*H*A*N*G*E

C: Challenge the Killer Ds: Debunk dysfunction and ditch the D Detector.

H: Honor Your Heroic Self: Validate your struggles and your strengths.

A: Add a Helper: Recruit a change partner.

N: Never Underestimate Your Own Ideas: Value your view of change.

G: Give Yourself a Chance: Do something—implement a plan.

E: Empower Yourself: Monitor, adjust and celebrate.

Appendix A

Nothing is as dangerous as an idea when it is the only one you have.

Emile Chartier

A Smorgasbord of Ideas

There are many possibilities for change out there—many versions of "the truth"; all provide a structure for focusing your efforts to do something different about your circumstance. Think of your choices as offerings at a smorgasbord restaurant. Feel free to taste any and all that look or smell tempting, knowing you can always go back to the table and make another selection if your choice doesn't turn out to please your palate. There are many different dishes to try. Some you will like and some you won't. I have selected those that you are less likely to run across elsewhere to encourage you to think outside the box. Sample more at *www.whatsrightwithyou.com*.

My Favorites

Tapping Your Internal Wisdom: Advice from an Elder

Purpose: This task can be useful for any situation in which you are seeking guidance.

Source: Unknown

Description: Find a quiet, comfortable place and relax as much as possible, away from the hassles of everyday life. Embellish this story in any and all ways possible—employ all the senses to construct the most sensually compelling images that fit your ideas of a relaxing, beautiful, serene setting. Imagine you are riding in your car with the windows down on a warm, clear blue day, feeling the sun on your arm, smelling the freshness of the air and appreciating the rhythmic bump of the wheels on the road as you go farther and farther away from the city, until you decide to park and follow a path that beckons you to hike into the forest. You feel the crunch of twigs and leaves under your feet, and you take in the smell of the pines and songs of the birds as you walk through the sunlight dancing through the tree limbs high above. You continue until you see a clearing: a meadow of wildflowers, an explosion of purples and yellows and a rush of sweet fragrance that compels you to close your eyes and take a deep, satisfying breath. When you open your eyes, you see the figure of a person across the meadow, but you feel no fear and begin walking closer until you can see that the person is an elderly person with whom you feel an instant familiarity—like you have known him or her your entire life. As you walk closer and closer, you feel more and more taken with the warmth and wisdom you find in the lines of the elder's face. The elder welcomes you, and you sit together and share a cool drink while swapping stories and observations about life. Finally, encouraged by the connection you feel to this kindly sage, you say that you have something on your mind, that you want to ask a question. The elder nods and smiles and you ask the question. As the elder speaks, you allow the words to wash over you, feeling their truth cover every part of you like sliding into a comfortably warm bath. After a while of silence and contemplation, you notice that the sun is low on the horizon and that you must leave. You thank the wise old man or woman and start across the colorful meadow. As you are just about to enter the forest, you turn, and the elder waves, and you notice that you have not felt quite so resolved in some time. You continue through the forest back to your car and drive back to the city, full of peace, enjoying the rhythmic sound of the road and knowing you are ready again to face life and do what needs to be done. . . . There are three parts to this exercise: (1) Create a sensually compelling, serene surrounding to meet your elder self in the place you feel most comfortable; (2) create the image of the wisest, kindest elder person you can imagine; and (3) ask your most burning question, and pay attention to your inner wisdom's response.

The Odd/Even Day Ritual

Purpose: Useful for parents whose disagreement about a course of action may be preventing a child's problem from being resolved. Combine with tasks to find exceptions (chapter 6). This technique is also useful in making a tough decision.

Source: Matteo Selvini, *The Work of Mara Selvini-Palazzoli* (Northvale, NJ: Aronson, 1988); Joseph Rock and Barry Duncan, *Let's Face It—Men Are @$$#%\¢$* (Deerfield Beach, FL: HCI, 1998).

Description: For a child problem, the odd/even day ritual suggests that one parent handle the problem in any way he or she sees fit on odd days (day 1, 3, etc.) without interference from the other; and on even days (days 2, 4, etc.) the other parent pursues the course he or she deems best. The child is asked to note any infractions, and all observe the problem and note when it is better. This strategy reduces conflict over the "right" way to do things and allows different realizations and directions. It also creates a team atmosphere to combat problems.

Regarding decisions, the odd/even day ritual allows you to compare the emotional consequences of both sides of a decision before you actually make it. This can be particularly helpful if your rational decision-making has reached an impasse or the pros and cons of both (or many) sides seem pretty equal. On odd days you live your life as though you have made the decision in one way. On even days, you go through your daily activities as if you have chosen another path. The idea is to fully experience your decision on an emotional level by carrying out the behavioral routine it implies. What feelings does each scenario bring up? Compare your daily levels of energy, satisfaction and self-esteem. Paying attention to the emotional consequences of a decision ahead of time can save you from making a big mistake.

The Rate and Predict Exercise

Purpose: For any personal problem, depression, self-esteem, etc. This exercise encourages the noting of exceptions (see chapter 6), as well as the connection between what you do—how you live your life—and the problem.

Source: Steve de Shazer, et al. "Four Useful Interventions," *Family Process* (1986).

Description: Before going to bed, predict your rate of (depression, anxiety, self-esteem, etc.) on a scale of one to ten (one is very bad, ten is very good) for the following day. The next night and thereafter, record your actual rate for the day, and then compare your actual versus predicted rate. Note any differences and consider what the differences are about. This technique provides the opportunity for insightful connections and promotes helpful actions to address the problem at hand. An example can be seen in the epilogue.

The Write, Read and Burn Ritual

Purpose: To deal with bad experiences, lost relationships, past traumas, affairs, abuse, etc. This ritual can be useful for any situation you would like to put to rest in your mind. It also helps turn down the volume of troubling feelings.

Source: Adapted from Steve de Shazer, *Keys to Solution in Brief Therapy* (New York: Norton, 1985).

Description: The first step involves recording in minute detail the event or situation that is troubling you, including your emotional experience of it— the pain, suffering and anger. This may take several attempts until you have really captured the experience in a way that truly does justice to the way you feel. This is a tough process, so it is wise to include your change partner or a friend for support. Once you have written a nuanced account of the circumstances that continue to haunt you, read what you have written out loud to your change partner, friend or others who might benefit from knowing. For example, if you are completing this exercise to help you work through an affair, you may read it to the person who had the affair. This however, is not a requirement. The final step is to find a safe place (fireplace, old metal wastebasket, etc.) and burn what you have written. As you watch it burn, pay keen attention to the flame and its total consumption of the paper, turning the event and experience to ashes to be discarded in any way you see fit. This exercise won't "cure" anything, but it does help put some closure on the pain or situation.

Advertise Instead of Conceal

Purpose: For a wide range of problems whose common denominator is embarrassment or a feeling of social inhibition—usually evolving from some perceived imperfection or belief that you don't quite measure up for one reason or other. This strategy tends to take the heat off and promote different experiences that challenge the problem's dominance in your life.

Source: Adapted from Paul Watzlawick, John Weakland and Richard Fisch, *Change* (New York: Norton, 1974).

Description: This technique simply requires you to embrace the very problem you strive most to conceal and openly advertise it to others. The idea is that the more you attempt to conceal the perceived imperfection, the more exaggerated it becomes. The person who is afraid of public speaking might openly announce his or her anxieties and try to mimic the nervousness (trembling hands, cracking voice, etc.); the individual inhibited by stuttering might bring it up before it happens and intentionally stutter; the person who goes way out of the way to be perfect or hide mistakes might make intentional mistakes and announce them to the world. The individual worried about his or her appearance might intentionally mismatch socks or lipstick. Advertising instead of concealing tends to teach us that life goes on and that we pay a heck of a lot more attention to our faults and frailties than others do. There is something about advertising our foibles that changes our beliefs about them.

The Ordeal Technique

Purpose: For any problem that seems resistant to change. This technique encourages you to act rather than think about the problem. One must really want to get over the problem to try this!

Source: Jay Haley, *Ordeal Therapy* (San Francisco: Jossey-Bass, 1984).

Description: This approach entails attaching a negative or distasteful, but productive, consequence to a problem and only to the problem. The idea here is to impose an ordeal more severe than the problem itself—it must cause distress at least equal to, but preferably greater than, that caused by the concern. For example, in the evening following the occurrence of the problem, set the alarm for 2:00 A.M. and get up to mop and wax the kitchen floor or to go for a long walk. The ordeal must be beneficial but extremely difficult—sounds nuts, but it sometimes encourages people to address the problem in ways they hadn't before. Chapter 5 provides an example of this technique.

The Pretend Identity Technique

Purpose: For any situation that you feel you do not have the wherewithal to face (first date, big meeting, etc.). This technique encourages new experiences of competence and mastery.

Source: Coale, "Costume and Pretend Identities," *Journal of Strategic and Systemic Therapies* (1992).

Description: Select a person, living or dead, who you believe could handle the situation you need to face. Imagine yourself playing the role of that person and create a detailed idea of what his or her performance at the upcoming event might look like. Pay attention to how it feels to play the role and how things go. A variation is the magic sword technique. Many people believe that others have something they don't to face tough situations, a magic sword of sorts to slay the dragons of fear and anxiety. This technique simply suggests that you find a magic sword at the toy store and carry it with you in your purse or briefcase as you face the situation with which you are uncomfortable—no one knows of your special sword but you. Both of these techniques "arm" you with the little extra that can get you over the hump in tough situations, building confidence in your ability for the next encounter. Chapter 4 provides an example.

Externalizing the Problem

Purpose: For depression or any problem in which the problem seems to dominate your life. This technique separates you from the problem to elimi-nate recrimination, blame and judgment. Or in other words, you are not the problem; the problem is the problem.

Source: Michael White and David Epston, *Narrative Means to Therapeutic Ends* (New York: Norton, 1990).

Description: First *personify the problem*. Attribute oppressive intentions and tactics to it. Refer to the problem by name: "the depression," "crappy atti-tude" or "the fear monster." Talk of the problem as if it were a person, a very bad person. Make the problem an alive, dastardly villain.

- How long has the Problem been lying to you?
- How long has the Problem been hanging out with you?
- When Mr. Problem whispers in your ear, do you always listen?
- How does the Problem bully you around?

Next *build a case against the problem*. Investigate how the problem has been disrupting, dominating, discouraging and ruining your life. Discuss the hurtful feelings that have resulted from its influence, tactics it has used to discourage and unhelpful habits the problem has invited.

- What kinds of tricks does the Problem use to alienate you from those you love?
- What kind of lies has the Problem been telling you about your self-worth?
- How has the Problem deceived you into behaviors you now regret?

Then *search the past for the real you*. Look to your past to facilitate a rewrite—a new story that proves you have not been oppressed by the problem all the time or completely. Find times when you haven't been dominated or influenced by the problem. This is a similar process to eliciting exceptions, but with a twist.

- What's the longest time you stood up to the Problem?
- When was the last time you didn't listen to the Problem's lies?
- What is it about you that you were able to go on strike against the Problem?
- How do you explain that you are the kind of person who would lodge a complaint against the Problem?

As you remember stories of standing up to the Problem, you are rewriting your identity. Gather details to tell a different story and accumulate more evidence for this new identity.

- What can others tell you about your past that would help you understand how you are now able to take these steps to stand up to the Problem so well?
- Who knew you as a child who wouldn't be surprised that you've been able to reject the Problem as the dominant force in your life?

Now that a new story has been written, it is time to *look toward the future* and envision how the real you will act from now on.

- As you continue to stand up to the Problem, how will your future be different from what the Problem had planned for you?
- As you continue to disbelieve the lies the Problem tells you, how do you think that will affect your relationships?
- What do other people think your stance against the Problem has shown you?
- Who needs to know that you've made a commitment to keep Mr. Problem from hanging around?
- Who would benefit from knowing about your overthrow of the Problem government?

Constructive Payback

Purpose: Discharges anger in a harmless and constructive way and creates the conditions for different insights or directions to emerge. This strategy is useful for adolescents or others who persist in grossly inconsiderate behavior despite multiple requests for change. It is also fun and tends to loosen things up.

Source: Richard Fisch, John Weakland and Lynn Segal, *Tactics of Change* (San Francisco: Jossey-Bass, 1982); Barry Duncan and Joseph Rock, *The Lone Changer* (Fort Lauderdale, FL: WRWY Press, 2005); *www.whats rightwithyou.com*.

Description: The idea here is to attach a negative but absolutely harmless consequence to the chronically irritating behavior of another person. This could include acts of incompetence, lateness, forgetfulness or anything else that makes the person pay in ways that you don't have to take ownership for. When confronted about the instance of payback, your response must be apologetic, passive and self-deprecating (e.g., "I am so sorry;" "I must be losing my mind") and not angry or sarcastic. This technique is a confusion strategy that often results in the other person focusing more on the effects of his or her behavior on you and less on his or her selfish concerns. When done without vindictiveness, it can also be quite entertaining, thereby changing the "feeling tone" of the problem and allowing more creative solutions. Chapter 4 provided an example.

My Favorite Therapists' Favorites:
Dr. Joseph Rock

The Dangers of Change

Purpose: This can be used with virtually any problem in which there is ambivalence about change, but it is especially useful for situations in which change has been tried and found difficult to achieve. There are always drawbacks to change. An old joke tells of a man who thought he was a chicken. His sister, with whom he lived, got him some good therapeutic help, and his beliefs changed. When the therapist asked her how her brother was doing, she replied, "Great, for the most part." The therapist requested that she elaborate. "Well, there is no nest in the living room, he doesn't scratch at the rug and make clucking noises, and I'm not embarrassed to invite friends over." The therapist wondered, "What did you mean 'for the most part'?" She said, "We miss the eggs." When a person changes, there are always some "eggs"— aspects of the old way of being that are missed.

Source: Richard Fisch, John Weakland and Lynn Segal, *Tactics of Change* (San Francisco: Jossey-Bass, 1982); Barry Duncan and Joseph Rock,

The Lone Changer (Fort Lauderdale, FL: WRWY Press, 2005); *www.whats rightwithyou.com*

Description: This technique entails a concerted effort to acknowledge the dangers associated with improvement, thereby exploring your natural ambivalence about changing. The idea is to set time aside, say an hour, and list all the potential downsides of making a change. Pull out all the stops, and list anything and everything, regardless of how wacky it sounds. There is always something gained from the problem, no matter how bad it hurts or interferes with your life. Addressing the pitfalls to change serves several purposes. One, it can remove pressure and provide a better perspective on the situation. Sometimes just recognizing there are some negatives that go along with the change allows us to see that life with the problem may not be as bad as we think it is. This awareness may also allow us to relax our efforts to change, which sometimes is the greatest enemy, giving new perspectives and opening up new paths. Two, it may provide some insight into why change has not been forthcoming, allowing you to address the aspects that may be slowing you down. For example, a young woman was depressed and never left her apartment after work. Considering the advantages of her depression, she realized it prevented her from being hurt in another relationship—that staying in her apartment protected her from the pain of another breakup. Her realization that the depression was sort of like the lesser of two evils, as well as a protective device, enabled this young woman to take action to get out of her apartment more.

Slowing the Pace

Purpose: To deal with our self-imposed pressure to change. When you are hurting, the tendency is to want to end the pain as quickly as possible, naturally. If you are lonely, you *have* to meet someone soon. If you hate your job, you *have* to find another. Feeling this kind of urgency can lead you to act before you've had time to really evaluate all the options. Pressure rarely helps performance.

Source: Richard Fisch, John Weakland and Lynn Segal, *Tactics of Change* (San Francisco: Jossey-Bass, 1982); Barry Duncan and Joseph Rock, *The Lone Changer* (Fort Lauderdale, FL: WRWY Press, 2005); *www.whats rightwithyou.com*

Description: There are two ways to slow the pace of change. One is to stop your change efforts altogether for a while. Giving in to a sense of urgency about change gives you the message that the pain you feel (i.e., loneliness, fear) is intolerable. Allowing yourself to sit with your discomfort sends you the message that it is endurable. It also gives you the opportunity to see if the pain decreases or goes away on its own. Knowing discomfort is time and intensity limited frees you up to act when you're ready. A second strategy is to deliberately pace yourself. When you rush, you tend to try to do several things at once and send your mind racing in many different directions. Focusing on the activity at hand by talking yourself through it step by step keeps you grounded in the present and focused on things over which you have immediate control or influence. A very simple pacing strategy my clients have found helpful is to focus on slowing down obvious things you do quickly when pressured—walking, talking, thinking, writing. Most important, pacing yourself gives you the tacit message that you are in control of yourself and your situation. Sometimes the rush to get over a problem sabotages our best efforts at change. Go slowly.

Scheduling Time to Worry

Purpose: For problems that you drive yourself nuts worrying about. If you have ever tried not to think about something (a trip to the dentist, a deadline at work), you know what a futile endeavor that can be. When confronted with an unpleasant thought process (worry, guilt, obsession with another person), we often try to put it out of our minds altogether.

Source: Barry Duncan and Joseph Rock, *The Lone Changer* (Fort Lauderdale, FL: WRWY Press, 2005); *www.whatsrightwithyou.com*

Description: There is another way to control something that is unwanted or uncomfortable: you can work on deciding when, where and for how long it occurs. In other words, you can try to contain your discomfort instead of getting rid of it. As it relates to unwelcome thoughts, the strategy involves *scheduling time to worry* (or grieve or obsess). For example, if a woman is trying to stop thinking about a man with whom she just broke up, she can decide to *make* herself think about him from 7:00 to 7:30 P.M. each night. During that time, she will try to think of nothing else, and she will welcome all painful thoughts, regrets and sadness. If she begins to think about him outside of that time frame, she will encourage herself to postpone her obsessing until 7:00 P.M. (and reassure herself she will give those thoughts time and attention then). The idea is that a part of us wants to worry, grieve or obsess, and that part rebels if we refuse to do so. Scheduling time to think those thoughts reassures us that the subject will be given our full attention daily and reduces the internal "think/don't think" conflict.

Strive to Be Average

Purpose: For those people who pummel themselves with perfectionism. We don't want to be perfect; we just want to do things the "right" way—whatever that is. Pressure to do our best in every situation can lead to performance anxiety, procrastination and "completion issues" (where a person can't seem to finish things).

Source: Barry Duncan and Joseph Rock, *The Lone Changer* (Fort Lauderdale, FL: WRWY Press, 2005); *www.whatsrightwithyou.com*

Description: I often suggest to people who fall into this trap that they *strive to be average*. Since no one knows what "average" is, it is hard to put pressure on oneself. Making *no* mistakes is clearly above average, so you can't do that. Basically, by trying to be average, you confuse yourself, remove pressure and allow yourself to go with the flow. There are a number of positive outcomes that can result from this strategy. One is that performance can actually improve once the pressure to be perfect is gone. A second is that your performance will be average, and you will discover it isn't the end of the world. A third possibility is that things will get done that might not have otherwise. Some people refuse to do things unless they have the time, energy and resources to do them the right way. Striving to do them in *acceptable* ways makes it easier to proceed even if conditions aren't ideal.

Self-Control

Purpose: For those situations in which willpower is the main strategy. Willpower and self-control are often confused. People usually try to exert willpower when trying to start a new behavior (exercise) or change a current one (smoking, diet). Using willpower to produce change involves making yourself change by exercising the strength of your will ("Starting tomorrow, I'm going to the gym every day"). This works for relatively few people. Your life tends to be set up to maintain current behavior patterns, and even if you can change at first, it is very easy to revert to old habits.

Source: Barry Duncan and Joseph Rock, *The Lone Changer* (Fort Lauderdale, FL: WRWY Press, 2005); *www.whatsrightwithyou.com*

Description: *Self-control* involves altering your environment to make it easier to do things you want to and harder to do things you don't. For example, if you want to begin exercising more, it might be easier to put on athletic shoes and walk briskly around your neighborhood than to drive to a gym, change clothes, exercise, shower and drive back home. For other people, going to a separate location makes it easier to exercise because the environment (others doing the same thing) encourages them. Attend to what is easier for *you*, and do what you can to set up your environment to accommodate yourself. Overeating, smoking and not exercising are notoriously difficult to change. People start out with a lot of motivation and the best intentions, only to quickly get off track and fall back into their old habits. In addition, aspects of a person's environment can trigger old habits. A cup of coffee can signal the need for a cigarette. A break at work might serve as a cue to visit the candy machine. A soft reclining chair can beckon its owner to take a nap. People like to think they have free will and independently decide what they will do. The reality, however, is that many factors, including physical and emotional needs and aspects of our surroundings, exert some control over our behavior. Consider dieting: Whatever new diet you choose, do what you can to make it easy to follow. Keep foods you don't want to eat out of the house, particularly ones that take no preparation (potato chips) or can be microwaved quickly. Stay away from restaurants that have few dishes that fit with your diet or that have foods you love but don't want to eat. Using willpower to overcome temptation is a poor strategy compared to removing the temptation. These examples are very simplistic and obvious, but people don't follow the main concept. Make it hard to do what you have decided you don't want and easy to do what you do. Allowing oneself to eat only in one room of the house, not doing anything else while eating (watching television, reading), chewing each bit of food a minimum of ten times, and eating with the nondominant hand only are but a few possibilities for making overeating more difficult. Similarly, many people who try to stop smoking have been helped by using techniques to make smoking harder and less pleasant. Those include buying one pack at a time, keeping a record of how much is smoked by marking a card prior to lighting up, only smoking outdoors, changing brands after each pack is finished or sitting in nonsmoking sections in restaurants—all of which make it more difficult to smoke. The bottom line to *self-control* is to organize your life and your environment in a way that allows success to be a possibility, not a fantasy based on willpower.

Shifting the Focus

Purpose: The strategy of shifting the focus applies to any persistent unpleasant emotion, worry or physical pain. An anxious person might think, "I feel a little queasy today. What if I go shopping and get sick in the store in front of everybody?" That thought creates some anxiety, which in turn motivates the person to think more about the potential problem (which hasn't even occurred yet). The next thought might be, "I had better just stay home. But if I keep doing that, I'll never get anything done, my wife will think I'm going crazy and my whole life will fall apart." More anxiety ensues, and the negative cycle continues (negative thought, anxiety, more negative thoughts, greater anxiety, etc.). It is easier to think anxiety-provoking thoughts when you are anxious and to get anxious while thinking anxiety-provoking thoughts. The same concept holds true for depression, anger and other unpleasant emotions.

Source: Barry Duncan and Joseph Rock, *The Lone Changer* (Fort Lauderdale, FL: WRWY Press, 2005); *www.whatsrightwithyou.com*

Description: Thinking is instrumental in creating and maintaining unpleasant feelings. Yet the tendency is to keep thinking about how to resolve the problem. The focus remains internal (in one's own mind) and future- or past-oriented. People seldom, if ever, think about the present while feeling really bad. They think about the future (what they have to do, what might happen) or the past (mistakes they made, how much better it used to be, something unfair someone else did). The strategy of shifting the focus involves moving one's attention to external reality and to the present. To better understand this concept, take time out to try a brief experiment. For a few minutes close your eyes and think about all the things you have to do in the next week and when you will get them all done. After a few minutes notice how you feel, then open your eyes and describe in detail to yourself everything you see, hear, feel (sense of touch, not emotion) or smell at that moment. After a couple of minutes, note how you feel emotionally. Most people notice a couple of things about the time they have their eyes closed and are thinking. They tend to be unaware of what's going on around them (they are in their own little worlds), and they feel uncomfortable emotionally. Conversely, when they are describing what their senses are picking up, they are very aware of their surroundings and feel more relaxed and calm. *Shifting the focus* is based on this kind of experience. This strategy involves three steps. The first is to recognize the problem (anxiety, anger, worry). The second step is interrupting the problem by slow, timed breathing, relaxing one's muscles or just getting up and moving around a little. This step may seem inconsequential, but it is very important since it is difficult to shift one's attention to something new until the old focus is stopped. In the final step, attention is focused outside of oneself and into the present. There are many ways to do this, but a couple are simple and widely applicable. The first is "sensory focus": one describes what one's senses (sight, smell, hearing, touch and even taste) are picking up at the present moment. A second method for accomplishing this shift is "activity focus" in which one describes to oneself in detail everything he or she does moment by moment ("I am picking up a plate, scraping all the food, running it under hot water, putting it in the dishwasher, etc."). Both methods achieve a shift of focus from inside one's head to outside (one's immediate surroundings) and from thinking of the past or future to thinking of the present. The *shifting of focus* strategy works for a number of reasons. Bringing one back to the present refocuses attention in a place where one can deal with reality and have an immediate impact on one's surroundings (impossible in the future or past). It also breaks the chain of "negative thought, unpleasant emotion, more negative thought" described earlier. Anxieties, fears and worries are often nothing but bridges to the past or future; when we stay in the present and do not cross those bridges, we find that our unpleasant emotions diminish.

My Favorite Therapists' Favorites: Dr. Jacqueline Sparks

Don't Ask, Don't Tell

Purpose: Shifts attention in family or couple from hostility and blame to goodwill and effort. This strategy also helps to give hope for the future.

Source: Jay Haley, *Strategies of Psychotherapy* (Rockville, MD: Triangle, 1990).

Description: Have a conversation with the person you are having difficulty with in a close relationship. Ask the person what he or she would like to see you do differently that would help the relationship improve. Let the person know what you would like him or her to do differently. Next agree that, over the following week, each will do the specific thing identified by the other as being helpful (a minimum of two times during the week). However, each person should *not* advertise when he or she is doing the special thing, and the other person should *not* ask (or guess out loud) when it is being done. In fact, *do not discuss* the exercise at all during the week. However, each person will privately look for and guess when the other person is doing the requested acts. These guesses can be written down, with specifics about what was noticed and when it occurred. Finally, at the end of the week, get together and share with each other what you noticed and your guesses about when the other person was attempting the requested behavior. Some guesses may be accurate, and others may just be spontaneous noticing of the other's attempts to help things go better. Spend some time talking about the difference it makes when each is attempting to meet the other's wishes as well as what it says about his or her commitment to the relationship. Talk about how the week went overall. Discuss doing the exercise another week or simply doing more of those things that made the most difference.

Letter from the Future

Purpose: Loosens the hold of a traumatic past event over a person's present life and helps to envision and create a better future.

Source: Yvonne Dolan, *A Path with a Heart* (New York: Brunner Mazel, 1985).

Description: Imagine a time in the future when you are living a satisfying life. The problem you are dealing with right now is solved. Pick a date in the future when this is happening. Write a letter (to a real person) from that point in time and that point in your life. Explain how things are going. Tell the person about your daily life, your relationships, your dreams. Describe how you got to this place. Whatever you think is important to put in the letter, put it in. When you are done, keep it in a special place so you can take it out from time to time. It is a portrait of you, even if it isn't perfect. It is also a map to a future not clouded by the oppression of the past.

Miracle Question

Purpose: Identifies small, concrete changes, not necessarily directly related to the main problem, that can assist in resolving the main problem. This strategy creates the possibility of problem resolution by imagining a future when the problem is gone.

Source: Steve de Shazer, *Keys to Solutions in Brief Therapy* (New York: Norton, 1985).

Description: First sit comfortably in a quiet place where you are not likely to be distracted. Start by carefully and thoughtfully imagining the following:

> *Imagine that [now here you have to suspend your disbelief—just for the moment, forget your reservations about what can and can't happen and go into pure imagination] . . . after you have gone to bed tonight . . . you are in your bed and sound asleep . . . and while you are sleeping . . . a very miraculous and strange thing happens. While you are asleep, a miracle*

happens! And here is the miracle: the problem that is most distressing you, right now in your life . . . IS GONE! But here's the thing: YOU DON'T KNOW THIS HAS HAPPENED [because you're sound asleep, remember]. In the morning, when you wake up as usual, you haven't got a clue that this miracle happened overnight while you were sleeping. However, it doesn't take long before you notice that SOMETHING SEEMS DIFFERENT! "What could have happened while I was sleeping?" Now think hard; you're in bed and just getting up, WHAT IS THE FIRST SMALL THING YOU NOTICE THAT TELLS YOU THIS DAY IS DIFFERENT—THINGS ARE NOT THE SAME? Keep in mind, we're not talking winning the lottery here, but the first small thing that would alert you to the fact that a miracle occurred overnight while you slept. This is the basic Miracle Question exercise. When you have identified what you will first notice that is different after the miracle has happened, ask yourself what the next sign will be and the next. Ask yourself if others in your immediate family or social circle will notice something different. If so, what will they notice? What might they notice different about you? What might you notice (we're talking small here) different about yourself? What will they be doing differently? Keep on with these kinds of question until you've pretty much gone through your post-miracle day. Then it is not a difficult step to either (1) see if any part of the post-miracle day might already be happening in your life that you can amplify or expand to happen more frequently, or (2) purposefully build some of the small miracle differences into your life. The small, everyday events you tease out of this exercise can change your life.

Changing Places

Purpose: Creates an opportunity for people stuck in predictable routines to experiment with less familiar behaviors. In so doing, they can break out of repetitive patterns that promote problems. Because it is an experiment, people do not have to give up old patterns, just try new ones. This makes change more comfortable and more under the control of all involved.

Source: Jay Haley, *Strategies of Psychotherapy* (Rockville, MD: Triangle, 1990).

Description: It is not uncommon for a person in a close relationship to play one role while the other person in the relationship plays a complementary or opposite role. For example, in partner relationships one person may be more the organizer while the other waits to be told what needs to be done. In a parenting relationship one parent might have all the fun with the child while the other consistently plays "the heavy," meting out chores and discipline. Sometimes one person can be the optimist while the other is the constant skeptic or pessimist. These contrasting roles often work just fine. However, sometimes the roles become rigid and can be part of chronic relationship problems. If you are experiencing a problem in a relationship—spouse, partner, parenting, child, etc.—see if you recognize this type of predictable role patterning. If so, there's a relatively painless way to loosen up patterns and, at the same time, loosen up problems. First sit down with the person you believe predictably responds in a way that contrasts with your own when dealing with a specific problem. After discussing this pattern, decide together to each take a vacation from the usual and to experiment with a less familiar response to the problem. One way to do this is, on even days of the week, everyone does the usual; on odd days, each plays the role of the other, at least as far as the problem is concerned. For example, if you are always grounding your daughter, but the other parent is always taking her out for ice cream, you swap your tough role with the other parent's fun role every other day. This gives each of you a chance to expand your skills as parents and gives your daughter a chance to know another side of her parents, enriching these relationships. You can do this for one or two weeks, then get back together to discuss the experiment. What was it like playing the other role? How did it affect your daughter? How did it affect your relationship with each other? What parts of this experiment worked, and what parts would you like to build into your everyday lives? The same strategy can be applied to other kinds of relational problems. It gives both parties a chance to develop a different side of themselves, sometimes in only one or two weeks of serious experimentation with "the other side."

Invariant Prescription

Purpose: For parents who have tried everything and are as predictable to their children as the sun coming up in the morning. This strategy provides a dramatic opportunity for parents dealing with a tough problem with an adolescent to reverse typical parental attempts to correct behavior.

Source: Matteo Selvini, *The Work of Mara Selvini-Palazzoli* (Northvale, NJ: Aronson, 1988).

Description: Parents join together in a pact of secrecy involving their disappearance from the home for several hours (to be used only for older teens). They keep their whereabouts and the purpose of their outings a secret, shifting themselves out of their usual roles of monitoring the adolescent's behavior. This task requires the parents to be out of the home without a clear explanation of their whereabouts. All the problem teen finds is a note saying the parents will be away for two hours (for example). You absolutely must not tell the teen about the "pact" or where you go (strictly the parents' business), nor should you discuss or entertain interrogation about the little absences. If badgered, you might simply change the subject or give a nonsensical answer ("We went to the moon"). After faithfully following the pact for at least two weeks and five "disappearances," something should start to happen. The troubled teen will want to know what is going on and want to talk more. Continue to be mysterious and watch your parental authority return and an improved relationship result. This technique reconnects parents in a coalition that helps clarify and strengthen the family. It reestablishes proper parental authority without demanding it. Chapter 7 provides an example.

Appendix B

Specialized meaninglessness has come to be regarded, in certain circles, as a kind of hallmark of true science.

Aldous Huxley

Approches To Therapy

What follows are descriptions of the *major* approaches to individual and family therapy—emphasizing how they conceptualize problems and how they see those problems being resolved. Reducing these models of therapy to their essence allows you to check the fit with your own ideas. If any of these approaches resonate with your theory of change, pursue more information on the Internet or at your local bookstore. Please be aware that there are many, many other approaches, too numerous to list.

Individual Psychotherapy Approaches: by Joseph Rock, Psy.D.

Cognitive Therapy

How problems develop: Cognitive therapy might currently be the most popular of the individual therapeutic approaches. Cognitive therapies, such as Ellis's rational-emotive therapy and Beck's cognitive therapy alter the thoughts that are believed to underlie emotional problems. Ellis believes that problems like depression and anxiety are caused by internal sentences which people repeat to themselves, and these self-statements reflect unspoken assumptions—irrational beliefs—about what is necessary to lead a good life. Beck holds that problems like depression are caused by negative beliefs that individuals have about themselves, the world and the future. These negative beliefs, called "schemas" (e.g., I am inept; problems are insurmountable), are maintained by thinking plagued with "overgeneralization" ("I didn't do well on this test means I will never do well on any test") or other errors in logic. Here is a simple translation of cognitive therapy: In response to internal events such as thoughts and memories, and external events like a fight with a spouse (A), we perceive or think about them in certain ways (B), which lead to certain feelings, behaviors and physical responses (C). Problems occur when distorted, irrational perceptions at B lead to painful feelings or counterproductive behaviors at C.

How problems are resolved: By becoming aware of distortions or irrational perceptions in response to certain events or "triggers," people can consciously change how they interpret those events and thereby produce different, less upsetting responses. Ellis's aim is to eliminate self-defeating beliefs through a rational examination of them; instead of looking toward the past, Ellis suggests that focus on these beliefs in the present is where the action is. Beck's approach similarly seeks to provide clients with experiences that alter the negative "schemas" that guide their lives. Therapists who practice this model tend to be very active and directive.

Example: Jimmy sunk deeper and deeper into depression after his nine-year marriage ended in divorce. He saw a cognitive therapist who followed an Ellis rendition of cognitive therapy. The therapist persuaded Jimmy that his depression would benefit from the rational examination of his thoughts and beliefs and gave Jimmy a homework task to monitor and record his thoughts and beliefs when he noticed himself feeling particularly bad using the ABC format mentioned above. Jimmy returned with the following notes: (A) Memory of my wife leaving me and the thought of the end of our marriage. (B) I think, "What if I never meet anyone else? That would be terrible." My belief, "I am a worthless jerk; no one else will want me." (C) I feel hopeless and depressed. Through teasing, cajoling and lively dialogue (other cognitive approaches are a bit "kinder and gentler"), the Ellis-style therapist prods and confronts Jimmy until he is aware of his unhelpful thoughts at B, so he can change how he looks at A. The therapist teaches Jimmy to replace irrational self-statements with an internal dialogue meant to ease the emotional turmoil. ("It's normal to feel hurt. There are other people I will meet, but I might not be ready right now.") Through continued examination of his beliefs and self-statements and dogged experimentation in his everyday life, Jimmy is able to substitute appropriate sadness for depression as a response to the breakup of his marriage. He learns to challenge his irrational beliefs about himself in general, manage unpleasant emotions and live a far more fulfilling life.

Signature idea for change: By being aware, in real time, of counterproductive thoughts and perceptions of events, one can change those thoughts and produce a different emotional and behavioral outcome.

Behavior Therapy

How problems develop: Behavior therapy remains popular with both adults and children, largely for dealing with specific problems such as phobias, child behavior problems and sexual difficulties. One way problems develop is that a particular situation (such as public speaking) becomes associated with anxiety; the person learns that the two events occur together. This is called conditioning, which is a form of learning. The person then tends to either perform poorly in the situation or tries to avoid it altogether, which makes it worse, and the person further learns that anxiety (or fear) necessarily goes with the situation in question. Another way problems develop is that certain behaviors (a child's acting out) is followed by a consequence (attention) that reinforces (increases the strength of) the problematic behavior. The problem behavior, therefore, is learned because of the contingencies (reward/punishment) that surround it.

How problems are resolved: If problems are learned through conditioning and reward, they can be "unlearned" the same way. A person can be trained (learn) to produce a more helpful emotional response (relaxation) in a situation (public speaking) that previously provoked anxiety. The coping response (relaxation) then *competes* with a previously learned ineffective response (anxiety) to a challenging situation. Most often, once the relaxation is learned, it is gradually associated with images of increasingly more difficult levels of the anxiety-filled event; the person struggling with public speaking may start with implementing the relaxation technique while visualizing preparing for the speech, followed by several stages of the problem leading to images of giving the speech. Then the individual, armed with a coping response now associated with public speaking, can go through the same process in real life (preparing, practicing, etc.) until the speech is finally given. In the acting-out behavior situation, a behavior receives consequences that discourage rather than encourage its recurrence. A child can be exposed to a different consequence (being ignored, punishment) in response to acting-out behavior and learn different ways of behaving or can be rewarded for appropriate behavior so those behaviors are strengthened. This is often referred to as behavior modification and is very familiar to most of us. Behavior therapy, however, is very systematic in its approach and implements solutions with far more rigor than we might. Behavior therapists tend to be active and directive.

Example: Charlie, a middle-aged construction worker, sought help because he was experiencing panic attacks after a series of unfortunate events including the breakup of his marriage, an on-the-job accident that prevented him from working for six months and the resulting serious financial problems. Charlie was starting to get quite depressed because he couldn't go through with the interview required for him to go back to work. He hadn't been to an interview in twenty years, and he remembered them as nightmares of nervousness—he always felt judged and that he didn't quite measure up. Whenever Charlie scheduled an interview to go back to work, a profound feeling of dread and foreboding came over him. Sometimes, as a result, Charlie just stayed in bed. One time when he tried to force himself, his heart pounded so hard that he thought he was having a heart attack, which resulted in an emergency room visit. The doctor arranged for a consultation with a behavior therapist, and Charlie started therapy. The therapist and Charlie broke down the interview into its component parts and created a list that was ordered according to the least anxiety-provoking to the most anxiety-provoking aspects of attending an interview. Then the therapist taught Charlie progressive muscle relaxation. Charlie liked it and reported that he noticed a big difference in how he felt each time he did it. Now the therapist went through each item on the list, starting with the easiest (making the phone call to schedule the interview) to the hardest (answering questions about his accident and readiness for work) and instructed Charlie to relax while the therapist described each item in full detail. Charlie practiced the exercise at home until he was ready to try the real thing. The therapist went through a dry run with Charlie and coached him through the entire interview situation. Charlie got a handle on his panic and successfully attended the interview and returned to work.

Signature idea for change: Behavior, both adaptive and maladaptive, is learned and therefore can be unlearned by either changing the learned associations (e.g., anxiety and public speaking) or the contingencies occurring after the unwanted behavior.

Psychodynamic or Analytic Therapy

How problems develop: This type of therapy, also know as Freudian, is much less common than it was several decades ago. Relatively few people enter true psychoanalysis, which involves several sessions per week. Most therapists who adopt this general approach use a modified version with less frequent sessions; there are many derivatives of this model. Problems are seen as a result of conflicts between different aspects of a person's personality (id, ego, superego; child, adult, parent) that develop in response to early experiences in one's life. These conflicts are repressed (pushed out of awareness), and therefore the past holds all the keys to understanding current problems. Symptoms reflect the ways the subconscious mind protects the conscious mind from having to deal with the real problem: the conflicts from childhood. Problems occur because of these repressed conflicts—when people do not understand what motivates them.

How problems are resolved: Problems are resolved when people discover the true reasons for their actions or emotions. In essence, this approach believes that the truth (the real reasons for your motivations and drives) will set you free (of the symptom and other problems). The greater awareness of these internal motivations yields better control over one's life, and subsequently, the person no longer needs the symptom. The insight gained, in more modern applications, is also used to develop coping strategies that effectively address the current expressions of the conflict. At the heart of therapy is the attempt to remove the repression preventing the individual from growing into a healthy adult. When this happens, more choice becomes available to the individual. The focus in therapy is not on the presenting problem but rather on the subconscious conflict buried in the mind since childhood. Only by lifting the repression can the person confront the underlying problem and reevaluate it from a mature adult perspective. Psychodynamic therapists tend to be less active, less directive and more interpretive.

Example: Pat, a fifty-year-old vice president of a bank, couldn't feel confident and competent no matter what she did. She decided to see a therapist to gain insight to these seemingly inexplicable problems. Through several sessions of exploring Pat's past, the therapist began to suspect that Pat's feelings

of failure stemmed from her childhood experiences with an extremely punitive and critical father—a man even more successful than Pat and a person
who seemed never to be satisfied with his daughter's efforts. A recurring
theme of the sessions was Pat's sullen and somewhat surly attitude at times
in therapy. Over time, the therapist interpreted Pat's somewhat angry remarks
as really reflecting Pat's resentment toward her father. The therapist believed
that Pat's anger had been "transferred" from her father to the therapist—that
the anger was not really about how she felt toward therapy or the therapist
but rather an expression of her real feelings about her father and his chronic
disapproval of her. As time passed and more examples from Pat's past were
discovered that illustrated her father's lack of approval, Pat came to understand that her feelings of failure arose from those childhood experiences of
her father's cold, critical and often punishing interactions with her. Pat began
to apply this insight in her life and was able to look at herself and her accomplishments from a more mature perspective, which included no longer berating herself or feeling inept in the face of an otherwise successful life.

   Signature idea for change: Insight into internal conflicts, motivations
and fears eliminates the need for the symptom and opens up more realistic
choices for behavior.

Humanistic Therapy

   How problems develop: This type of therapy focuses on personal meaning and self-actualization, often looking at what has been called "human potential." People usually enter humanistic therapy for purposes of personal growth
as opposed to looking for relief from emotional symptoms or particular problems, but not always. There are a wide variety of humanistic therapies. One is
called "existential" therapy, which arose primarily from European existential
philosophy. Humanistic therapists regard people as having the innate ability to
realize their potential and believe that people have the freedom to decide at
any given moment to become different. Probably the best known approach
from the humanistic camp, however, is the person-centered therapy of Carl
Rogers. Rogers trusted the basic goodness of the individual and believed that
problems arise when there is incongruence between the ideal self and the
authentic self. The ideal self is the person one feels he or she needs to be or
strives to be. The authentic self is who the person really is.

   How problems are resolved: Rogers believed that people can be understood only from the vantage point of the individual, and a Rogerian approach
seeks to help people understand their own worlds in a deep and satisfying

way—healthy people are aware. Through empathy and unconditional positive regard for their clients, Rogerian therapists help people view themselves more accurately, which guides them toward their own instincts for self-actualization. The solution to life problems always lies within the self. Via "active listening" in which the therapist empathically feeds back to the client the emotional meanings of the client's expressions, the client develops a deeper understanding of his or her authentic self. Through this process, over time, the individual acquires a profound understanding of his or her inner world and moves on to an authentic existence—self-actualization. Rogerian therapists tend to be passive and nondirective, seeing therapist direction as manipulative and getting in the way of the client's own self-healing capacities.

Example: On her first trip home since starting at the local university, Batina had her new boyfriend, Scott, follow her home for dinner and to meet her parents. The dinner seemed okay, but her parents were more quiet than usual. After Scott left, the fireworks started. Batina's parents couldn't seem to say anything good about him—he was the wrong religion, he was undecided about his future and he had funny hair. Batina listened quietly, then just told her parents she disagreed; the rest of the weekend passed without incident. When she returned to college, her blood began to boil. She became furious about her parents' criticism of Scott and decided to see a counselor at the school clinic. The therapist listened intently and empathically to Batina's story and reflected back to her the feelings and meanings connected to her expressions. Although the emotion first expressed was anger, the therapist, over time, came to believe that Batina was really fearful of her parents' disapproval—that this fear was underneath her anger and the real meaning for it. After the therapist explored what was implied but not expressed, Batina realized that she had always arranged her social life, and picked her boyfriends, to please her parents. Her new recognition of the fear of disapproval became the focus after the therapist helped Batina see beyond her anger. Batina, now aware of her fear of disapproval, worked with the therapist to become more authentic with her parents and more in charge of her own personal affairs.

Signature idea for change: Wisdom is within the client, and the challenge for the therapist is to assist the client in his or her search for knowledge about the self without the therapist's interjecting his or her ideas, opinions, analyses or biases.

Family Therapy Approaches:
by Jacqueline Sparks, Ph.D.

Structural

How problems develop: Structural family therapy understands problems as products of human relationships, especially intimate family relationships. It is most interested in the structure of the family, including the boundaries between people in the family and the alignment of those boundaries along a hierarchy. The theory maintains that in so-called healthy families, people interact with not too much closeness and not too much distance, and the adult members of the family are "in charge." If family members get too close, they are said to be "enmeshed"; if they are too distant, they are "disengaged." When children "run the show" in a family, then the hierarchy has been reversed, leading to child behavioral problems and psychological distress for one or more family members.

How problems are resolved: Problems are resolved in structural family therapy through a realignment of family boundaries, correcting overinvolvement (enmeshment) or underinvolvement (disengagement) and by placing adult family members in their presumed rightful positions as heads of the household. Structural family therapists tend to be active and directive in asking family members to engage in different interactions while keeping these goals in mind. Structural therapists can be provocative and challenging, hoping to shake up typical patterns of interacting and reconstruct more functional boundary alignments.

Example: Carla, a structural family therapist, was assigned to work with Tanya and Ron and their six-year-old child, Raymond. Raymond was repeatedly having temper tantrums just as his mother was about to take him to school. Tanya frequently could not get him in the car, so he ended up staying home all day watching TV. During her first meeting with the family, Carla noticed that whenever Tanya cajoled and demanded (unsuccessfully) that Raymond sit still and answer questions, Ron would eventually pick the child up and start playing with him, then put him down to wander about the room. Carla assessed the family as having an overinvolved mother, a largely disengaged father and a hierarchy headed by Raymond, thanks to the father's help. In the session, Carla asked that Tanya sit on the far side of the room and remain quiet. She then asked Ron to insist that Raymond pick up the mess of toys he had made in the room and to follow through on this command.

After much directing and interrupting to create this new pattern, Carla was able to guide the parents in a new way of interacting with their son, who finally, after many shed tears, picked up the toys and sat obediently on the couch. Next Carla asked that Raymond go to the waiting room with the staff assistant. She then negotiated a new morning routine with both parents in which Ron would arrange to leave for work later so he could be responsible for taking Raymond to school. Tanya agreed to go to her sister's house until they had left. Further family therapy meetings ensured that these changes stayed in place, and Raymond soon after abandoned his tantrums and resumed his school activities.

Signature idea for change: A change in the structure of a system—boundaries, emotional distance and hierarchy—changes behaviors, interactions and relationships of individuals in the system.

Strategic

How problems develop: Like structural family therapy, strategic family therapy is based on viewing problems as products of problematic patterns of interactions, particularly in close family relationships. The emphasis here is on the belief that power and hierarchy are inherent in all relationships. When the hierarchy is unclear, the result is a "power struggle" and, frequently, symptoms or symptomatic behavior. A confused hierarchy may occur when a member of one generation crosses the generational boundary to form a coalition with someone in a different generation. A cross-generational coalition plays out in predictable and observable patterns within the family. These sequences begin to define the family and individuals within the family. People tend to resist change and cling to familiar ways of behaving, even when they know them to be counterproductive. Consequently, problem sequences often become "stuck" and very difficult to change. A variation of this approach sees symptoms or problems as metaphors for problems in relationships. For example, a child's asthma attack could be viewed as a metaphorical expression of one of the parents feeling suffocated in the marriage.

How problems are resolved: Strategic therapy differs from a structural approach in that not all family members need to be present for change to happen—one person doing one thing different will change the whole family. Additionally, strategic therapists, aware of the tendency of families to resist change, often work indirectly. For example, when family members fail to follow through on tasks assigned directly, the therapist might suggest "paradoxical" tasks, such as deliberately scheduling or increasing the problem and observing the results. Paradoxical tasks may also include ordeals where the therapist asks clients to engage in activities more uncomfortable and more extreme than the problem. In this way, the problem becomes less a focus than the ordeal, and predictable patterns surrounding it break up. The goal of all strategic therapy is the realignment of family organization based on repetitive and sequenced communications and interactions.

Example: Miguel and Anna, married six years, sought marriage counseling due to increasing cycles of conflict. The therapist asked the couple to describe the "before, during and after" events that surrounded their disputes; she then was able to identify consistent, repetitive sequences of how the arguments played out. The therapist explained to Miguel and Anna that their marriage was proceeding through a pivotal developmental stage that could result in either the demise or maturing of the relationship. The therapist asserted that arguing is one way couples decide which path the relationship will take. However, their arguments were not getting the most of this potential benefit and, instead, were proving nonproductive and even destructive. Therefore, the therapist instructed Anna and Miguel to be more disciplined about their arguing in order to maximize the benefits. Instead of just "letting loose," they should build it systematically into their week, just like a job. They should schedule their arguments, dutifully and faithfully, to occur every other day, at the same time, and for one hour. This will, the therapist assured them, turn their unproductive fights into ones that "get somewhere." The couple and therapist spent the rest of the session deciding which days were "fight days" and which were "peace days." Anna and Miguel returned one week later expressing their dismay that they had failed the task: they had been unable to fight even one day of the week and, instead, much to their chagrin (but guilty glee) had taken a weekend excursion to a local motel for a "honeymoon getaway!" The therapist scolded them on being remiss in accomplishing the task, though much of the session was spent listening to their descriptions of the getaway. Urging them to try again, the therapist sent the couple away smiling. Anna called a week later, canceling their appointment, with the message to the therapist that they had decided to schedule a getaway once a month and that, if they felt the urge to fight, they would be sure to implement the fight days/peace days plan. The therapist saw this rapid problem resolution as an example of simple interruption of repetitive sequences, allowing the emergence of new and more helpful patterns of interaction.

Signature idea for change: Clarifying confusing hierarchies or disrupting problematic behavioral sequences changes the behaviors and relationships in systems.

Intergenerational

How problems develop: Intergenerational therapies view problems as the product of a multigenerational process. According to this theory, families are similar to biological organisms. Like cells, they must gradually permit the differentiation of individual members away from the family of origin to form new, autonomous selves and new, separate families. This process is called differentiation of self. Differentiation for humans, however, means that individuals are appropriately separate from yet, at the same time, connected to their families of origin. When the process of differentiation goes awry, individuals become "fused" in the family's emotional system. This happens not only when individuals are highly reactive to and dependent upon other family members, but also when they are "cut off" from the family; both forms of emotional fusion result in various kinds of symptomatic behavior. Sometimes a third person is "triangulated" to defuse the emotional intensity in a fused family. When this occurs, the triangulated person typically experiences significant distress and symptomatic impairment. The process of emotional fusion is transmitted to later generations and, the theory maintains, can eventually culminate in the more pronounced forms of "mental illness" or in the demise of the family altogether.

How problems are resolved: Behavioral or emotional problems require attention to and assistance with the process of self-differentiation from one's family of origin. If a person is emotionally fused in a dependent and reactive way with his or her family, the individual must create distance and a more autonomous self. If the person is cut off, he or she must reconnect with the family of origin in ways that do not threaten, but foster, an autonomous yet connected self. These tasks are often quite arduous and lengthy, requiring the person to revisit members from his or her extended family over time and experiment with new ways to be with, and apart from, significant family members. A therapist assisting with this process must have an authentic degree of individuation from his or her family of origin in order to model appropriate distance and connection within the therapy process itself.

Example: While he had excelled in his junior and senior years in high school, Josh now found his college freshman standing in grave jeopardy. After two months of classes, Josh discovered that whenever he would get ready to go to his first class, he spiraled into a nightmare of sweating, rapid heart rate and pounding headache. At the same time, he felt overcome by an unexplained fear that something very bad would happen. Consequently, he remained in his room, a virtual prisoner of his own irrational emotions. Josh's roommate encouraged him to make an appointment at the college counseling center. Initially Josh's counselor requested that they do a "genogram" of Josh's family, where they mapped Josh's family tree back three generations, including diagrams of close, distant and conflicted relationships. In the process, Josh began to explore his history and how he felt co-opted by his father's covert demand for family respectability at the expense of his own emotional growth. He learned that this was not unlike his father's relationship to his own father, requiring a strict subservience to the family's drive to rise beyond its immigrant roots and gain position in a new land. In essence, Josh lived for others, not for himself. All of this put his own panic into perspective—for him not to succeed would, in essence, mean the end of the only self he knew, a self bound in the requirements of family survival. Josh's counselor assigned him the task to go home and speak with his mother, then visit his grandfather in New York and, finally, to confront his father's expectations of perfection. Josh survived his father's initial rejection after this conversation. In fact, it was like a weight had been lifted off him: he found that facing the challenges of his college life no longer overwhelmed him with dread. At the successful completion of his freshman year, Josh took a year off to explore Europe on his bike, finding new experiences and forging a new self along the way. Change happened for Josh because he broke away from the family's emotional stranglehold. At the same time, he reconnected with family members as a more mature, independent person, capable of expressing and following his own dreams and desires.

Signature idea for change: Change happens when individuals in an emotional system successfully differentiate from that family, becoming autonomous yet still connected.

Narrative

How problems develop: Narrative therapists base their work on the premise that we can only know and make sense of ourselves and the world through language. In other words, there is no direct access to reality, only the stories we tell about it. These stories not only reflect reality, they shape our experience of it. We all have our own "biography" that defines who we are and what we can be—both a definition of the present and a blueprint for the future. Families, too, each have unique biographies that, in turn, are situated within the narratives of the local community and culture. According to narrative theory, some stories are better at allowing flexible and productive lives, while others are "impoverished," casting long shadows of hopelessness and despair. "Problem-saturated" stories limit possibilities for flexible and creative adaptation to life circumstances. Without alternative narratives, solutions and change are invisible and inaccessible. As a result, problems, including problem identities, appear intractable.

How problems are resolved: Problems change when the narratives that produce and sustain them change. Sometimes people simply imagine new ways of viewing and explaining problems in their lives. Instead of being the villains, they are the heroes, fighting formidable odds with great courage. This viewpoint shifts their relationship to their distress, giving new resources for fighting it and new hope for prevailing against it. Instead of being a "loser" or a "borderline," people place the events of their past into a framework of problems overcome by unique resourcefulness to life events. Tales of victory replace tales of defeat, offering an array of options and resources, not the least of which are optimism and hope, to combat even the most daunting life challenge. Often the shift from failure to success in a life narrative is triggered by a special relationship that mirrors for the person previously forgotten or unseen aspects of his or her past or present—those attributes that are the shining moments of a person's personality and life. Narrative therapists play this role with their clients. As they listen to impoverished life histories, narrative therapists attempt to tease out the nuggets of heroism and resiliency each life holds, offering it back to the client and fashioning, in the process, more resources—rich narratives. Old stories and the problems that inhabit them simply fade away, replaced by new tales of creative and daring accomplishment.

Example: Lisa was on her third hospitalization. She had lost twenty-three pounds in five weeks, down from her high of 119, three months after her last stay. Lisa managed to sip her milk shake and agreed to see the new therapist, though she doubted it would make much difference. Her new therapist, Jan, didn't spend much time discussing eating or her relationships with family. Instead she was a friendly presence with a good ear for listening. During their third meeting, Lisa realized she had been talking away about home and her friends. Jan asked only one question: how had she managed to be so successful against anorexia the last time and to put it in its place by showing it she was the boss and could weigh any damn thing she wanted!? The question tantalized Lisa, and she ventured a guess: "I just felt it was time to do something for myself instead of for everyone else." Jan's look of amazement grew, and she followed with more questions about how Lisa had come to that decision; did this reflect a glimmer of a "new Lisa," or was this simply the "old

Lisa" that anorexia had kept in the shadows all this time? This strange dialogue continued for some time, with Jan leaving with the musing, "I wonder if this was just a prelude to a bigger fight with anorexia—maybe you have a plan to 'up the ante' next go-round?" Jan had begun to speak with Lisa in a way that allowed her to retell her story about her identity and about her relationship with her problem. Jan's questions suggested that Lisa was, instead of a defeated and desperately ill person, on a path to reclaim her life from the clutches of a force that sought to subjugate her. Their future conversations dealt with this theme and Lisa's history of resistance to a culture that worshipped thin women. Lisa began to relish each pound gained, viewing it as a concrete symbol of her powerful self. She now had the resources to not only live but to live with a sense of herself as a feisty, creative and beautiful young woman.

Signature idea for change: Change happens when people, families or communities create stories to replace those that limit change; these new stories offer resources for growth, adaptation to life circumstances, and redefinition of identities and relationships.

Other Family Therapy Approaches

In recent years, a number of new approaches have emerged in the field of family therapy. Like the ones just described, all share an interest in the patterns of relationships in human systems. However, these have combined additional theories and strategies to address particular kinds of problems. A brief summary of these approaches and links to learn more follows:

Emotionally Focused Therapy: Emotionally focused therapy (EFT) is most often used with couples, though it can be effective with families as well. EFT draws from systems and attachment theory and emphasizes the emotions that underlie words, stressing these rather than "communication skills" per se. EFT proponents provide relatively short-term therapy to deal with "attachment injuries" to rebuild security and trust in relationships. *www.eft.ca/*

Functional Family Therapy: Functional family therapy (FFT) is an approach designed to work specifically with at-risk youths age eleven to eighteen. Services can be provided in outpatient clinic settings or in the home and can range from eight to thirty sessions. Treatment for the youth and his or her family moves through specific stages, from engagement to behavior change to generalization, with set tasks and goals for each phase. *www.fftinc.com/*

Multisystemic Therapy: Multisystemic therapy (MST) serves the families of juveniles age twelve to seventeen who are at risk of placement out-side their homes. MST believes that the behavior of individuals are nested in family and community networks. Therefore, the approach crosses multiple systems, including individual, family and extrafamilial (school, neighborhood, peer). MST therapists have low caseloads, enabling intensive and crisis responsive intervention to preserve the family and assist the youth to reorient his or her life in a positive direction. Services are home and community based, empowering parents and youths by fostering positive social networks. While length of treatment is generally four months, services can adjust to the needs and goals of the family. *www.colorado.edu/cspv/blueprints/model/ programs/MST.html*

Appendix C

Where there is no vision, the people perish.
Proverbs 29:18

A Guide to Seeking Mental Health Services

If you decide to seek therapy, I want it to work for you—and not for the D Industry. So I am encouraging you to be an informed consumer and perhaps a little skeptical of mental health services. Let me begin by saying that therapy works! In fact, fifty years of research have unequivocally demonstrated that those in treatment are better off than 80 percent of the people in the comparison groups that receive no treatment. So seeking a therapist to assist you in your efforts can be exactly what you need to inspire the changes you wish to make. But a key factor is finding a therapist who is a good fit—not all therapists are created equal nor are all therapeutic approaches a good enough match with your theory of change.

Finding a Therapist

Experience is not what happens to a man. It is what a man does
with what happens to him.

Aldous Huxley

The best way to start is to call prospective therapists and interview them
by phone. It doesn't really matter what professional degree the person holds
(social worker, counselor, psychologist, marital and family therapist) or whether
he or she has a master's or a doctorate, unless of course you have a real pref-
erence or believe that such distinctions are important for you; it is much more
critical that you find a person you can work with—who is good fit for you. Get
the nuts and bolts questions regarding fees, insurance and location out of the
way with the receptionist or office manager if there is one. Tell him or her that
you are interviewing prospective therapists and would like to schedule a ten-
minute phone call with the therapist or counselor. An unwillingness to give
you ten minutes to ensure a good fit should be all the information you need
to cross this one off your list. Respect the therapist's time and keep to the ten
minutes. Ask these questions or others you think relevant:

- What is your philosophy or orientation of therapy? How do you think
  change happens?
- What do you think of diagnoses?
- How important do you consider collaboration and client participation?
- How many sessions do you average per client?
- Do you keep outcome data? Tell me about it.
- [If they don't monitor progress.] Do you mind if I monitor my progress?
  How are you at taking feedback from clients about the direction of
  therapy?

Listen for answers that reflect faith in client resources, strengths and
capabilities as the cornerstone of any change. Listen also for an emphasis on
having a good relationship and the importance of your participation. Compare
the answers with your own views of how change occurs. If the therapist identifies with a particular orientation, reflect about whether it fits your theory of
change. If it is different but you still think it has some merit, try it out. Recall
that change principally results from your input and participation—you are the
star of the therapeutic drama. Research shows the following:

- Change depends on your resources and abilities. Effective therapy utilizes your strengths to create solution possibilities.
- Change depends on your perceptions of the therapist and the relationship formed in therapy. Effective therapy is based on a strong alliance.
- Change depends upon addressing what you want and fitting your views of change and inspiring the hope necessary for action. Effective therapy matches your theory of change.

The Mythology of Mental Health

The greatest enemy of the truth is not the lie—deliberate, contrived, and dishonest—but the myth—persistent, pervasive, and unrealistic.

John F. Kennedy

Please don't take my criticisms that follow to mean that therapy is not helpful. I believe in therapy. If I didn't, I would be like a priest who didn't believe in God! I only intend to caution you about the pitfalls in seeking services. There is no doubt in my mind there are good therapists and good services out there. It is my hope that your understanding of mental health mythology helps your informed use of therapy services.

The Myth of Psychiatric Diagnosis

A word carries far—very far—deals destruction through time as the bullets go flying through space.

Joseph Conrad

Sigmund Freud once said, "I have found little that is good about human beings. In my experience, most of them are trash." Surprising commentary from the founding parent of psychotherapy! But the field still finds little that is good about human beings. The only difference is that "trash" has been cataloged into hundreds of specific disorders in the professional digest of human disasters, the *Diagnostic and Statistical Manual of Mental Disoders (DSM)* of the American Psychiatric Association. Diagnosis—while providing comfort for some who are relieved to have a name for a problem—is not a factor in successful therapy and is neither reliable nor valid. *Reliability* means therapists can agree about what diagnosis a person has. Unfortunately, mental health diagnoses, unlike medical ones, are not reliable: agreement under the best conditions for general categories is about 66 percent; on specific categories, it is as low as 26 percent! So how useful can it be if agreement among professionals only happens one in four times? *Validity,* or the ability of diagnosis to do what it purports to do—namely, to distinguish normal from abnormal behavior and between types of abnormal behavior so the proper treatment is selected—simply doesn't exist. All people do the things listed in the diagnostic manual at one time or another, so there is no way to distinguish the behavior of an individual under stressful circumstances from someone who has a "disorder." There is no biological marker—no blood test or x-ray— to show the presence or absence of the "illness." Further, because all approaches work for some people some of the time, a diagnosis provides little help in selecting the right approach. Remember the TDCRP. Knowing a person's diagnosis tells nothing about whether or not a person will benefit—there is no correlation between a person's diagnosis and the likelihood of success in therapy. Naming a problem has very little to do with solving it. So in other words, diagnosis is worthless! In addition, diagnosis can cause harmful attributions by the labeled individual, his or her family and helping professionals. Most therapists dislike it, actively lie to protect clients from its implications and report that it does not inform their day-to-day work. They only do it because it is required for payment purposes. Finally, diagnosis is culturally biased and incredibly subjective; diagnoses differentially point the finger at women and minorities—the more the person is different from his or her doctor, the more likely the person is to receive more serious diagnoses and more serious drugs. Don't be fooled by the myth of psychiatric diagnosis. Diagnosing mental "disorders" has multiplied like weeds. They choke and smother alternative, hopeful ways of understanding and encouraging change and are based more on political and economic factors than science.

Resources: Stuart Kirk and Herb Kutchins, *The Selling of DSM* (New York: Aldine, 1992); Herb Kutchins and Stuart Kirk, *Making Us Crazy* (New York: The Free Press, 1997); William Glasser, *Warning: Psychiatry Can Be Hazardous to Your Mental Health* (New York: HarperCollins, 2003); Bruce Levine, *Commonsense Rebellion* (New York: Continuum International, 2003).

The Myth of the Guru Therapist and Silver-Bullet Cure

The savage bows down to idols of wood and stone: the civilized man
to idols of flesh and blood.

George Bernard Shaw

Research has led to an unarguable conclusion that is good news for both mental health professionals and clients alike: psychotherapy is effective in helping human problems. The good news of therapy's usefulness, however, has led to the impression that therapy operates with technological precision. The illusion is that the all-knowing therapist assigns the proper diagnosis and then selects the right treatment for the particular disorder at hand. The therapist sizes up the demon that plagues the hapless client, loads the silver bullet into the psychotherapy revolver and shoots the psychic werewolf terrorizing the client. The truth is that the therapist will offer the approach he or she was trained in or is most comfortable in delivering, regardless of the problem or your preferences about how it should be handled.

Over the years, new schools of therapy have propagated like rabbits and arrive with the regularity of the Book-of-the-Month Club's main selection— now comprising four hundred models and techniques. Most profess to have captured the true essence of psychological dysfunction, as well as the best remedies; most claim to be the true silver-bullet cure for whatever ails you. However, such claims and counterclaims that one approach is better than the rest have no basis in reality. In the hopes of proving their pet approaches superior, a generation of investigators ushered in the age of comparative clinical trials. Winners and losers were to be had. Thus, behavior, psychoanalytic, client-centered or humanistic, rational-emotive, cognitive, time-limited, time-unlimited and other therapies were pitted against each other in a great battle of the brands. All this sound and fury produced an unexpected bonfire of the vanities. The underlying premise of the comparative studies, that one (or more) therapies would prove superior to others, received virtually no support. Despite the herculean efforts of legions of model worshippers, no one succeeded in declaring any religion to be the best. These findings have been creatively summarized by quoting the dodo bird from *Alice's Adventures in Wonderland,* who said, "Everybody has won and all must have prizes," first articulated back in 1936 by the amazing Saul Rosenzweig.[39] The so-called dodo bird verdict has proven to be the most replicated finding in the therapy literature. The dodo verdict means that because all approaches appear equal in effectiveness, there must be factors that overshadow any perceived differences among approaches. If therapies work, but it has nothing to do with their bells and whistles, what are the common factors of change? Our recent bestselling book for professionals, *The Heart and Soul of Change*, answers that question. We assembled the leading researchers in the world to review five decades of investigation and reveal its implications for practice. Chapter 1 talked about these factors that do make a difference—your resources, a supportive relationship and a plan of action that fits your ideas and engenders hope. Don't be beguiled by the myth of the guru therapist and the silver-bullet cure. There are endless possibilities for ideas and techniques that could prove useful to your change endeavor. There is no single silver-bullet approach. Change is far more about you and the alliance you form with the therapist than his or her flashy brilliance or the brand of therapy he or she practices; tapping into your strengths and wisdom is the only silver-bullet cure.

Resources: Robert Fancher, *Health and Suffering in America* (New Brunswick, NJ: Transaction Publishers/Rutgers, 2003); The ambitious reader may try Barry Duncan, Scott Miller and Jacqueline Sparks, *The Heroic Client* (San Francisco: Jossey-Bass, 2004).

The Myth of the Magic Pill and the Chemical Imbalance

He's the best physician who knows the worthlessness of most medicines.

Benjamin Franklin

Like therapy and all approaches to human problems, medication can be useful. Some people are helped by medication and freely choose drugs as a first line of defense. In truth, I am not antidrug; rather, I object to marketing and corporate influence holding sway over public and professional opinion when both the explanation for and success of drug treatment is, at best, unconvincing—especially for children. The use of psychiatric drugs for human suffering has become our culture's conventional wisdom despite the fact that they have not been confirmed by the latest discoveries of neuroscience, nor are they strongly supported by research. Mass-market advertising has succeeded in its intention to make taking antidepressants, for example, seem as normal and pervasive as swallowing aspirin. Perhaps the most impressive job of public awareness and product identification has been accomplished by Zoloft's cute, little oval-shaped guy—who initially mopes and frowns while we are told about chemical imbalances and then starts bouncing around, cheerfully smiling, presumably after taking Zoloft. "Chemical imbalance" is now an irrepressible part of the American vernacular. Paradoxically, while research has fervently pursued the illusive biological marker that will unlock the mysteries of mental illness, it has never been found! In truth there is no chemical imbalance that has been identified by science—any medical text will tell you that. There are theories about chemical imbalances, but that's it. Furthermore, little information about the long-term neurological consequences of drug therapies have surfaced; as neuroscientist Elliot Valenstein points out in his book *Blaming the Brain*, the arguments supporting chemical imbalances are not only unconvincing, but ignore the possibility that drugs create, not cure, biochemical problems because of the brain's plasticity and rapid adaptation to pharmaceuticals. Although medications like antidepressants are helpful for some, they are not helpful for others, and still others cannot tolerate the side effects. Studies often find they are barely better than sugar pills in alleviating depression! This doesn't make them worthless, but rather not the panacea for human problems that they are cracked up to be. It means one should take them only after considering the possible risks and with knowledge that there are many equally or more helpful options available to consider. Nevertheless, we are left with the darling little Zoloft guy's words of wisdom. Despite the paucity of evidence, conventional belief now is that depression and other human problems are not a bundle of miseries shaped by many forces, but rather are chemical imbalances—not requiring one to get meaningful support from others or change anything. There is only one solution needed: the passive consumption of a magic pill. Of course this doesn't mean there is anything wrong with trying drugs if you feel it is the right choice for you. Just don't buy the "chemical imbalance" tagline, monitor your results and stop taking them, under medical care, if they don't produce a noticeable benefit. The biggest pitfall of the myth of the magic pill is that it tends to obscure other choices for addressing human suffering and the challenges of life. Finally, realizing that psychiatric drug therapy is a profit-driven industry, built on a flimsy science, may be the bad-tasting medicine we've needed to debunk the myth of the magic pill.

Resources: Peter Breggin and David Cohen, *Your Drug May Be Your Problem* (Cambridge, MA: Perseus, 1999); Robert Whitaker, *Mad in America* (Cambridge, MA: Perseus, 2002); Elliot Valenstein, *Blaming the Brain* (Cambridge, MA: Free Press, 1998); Marcia Angell, *The Truth About the Drug Companies* (New York: Random House, 2004).

Seven Tips for Therapy

The way out is through the door. Why is it that no one will use this exit?

Confucius

1. **If you don't like your therapist, find another one.**

   Don't be shy. No therapist can be all things to all people. Trust your gut. If you get a bad feeling or vibe from your therapist, don't waste your time trying to figure it out. Just go see someone else. Follow Paul Simon's advice: just slip out the back Jack, make a new plan Stan, no need to be coy Roy, just get yourself free![40]

2. **If you think that your therapist doesn't like you, understand you or appreciate your point of view, find another therapist.**

   It is essential that you believe your therapist is on your side and that you don't have to worry about his or her evaluation of you. If you are worried about it, this likely is not the therapist for you. Discuss this problem with your therapist and carefully attend to his or her reaction. If he or she doesn't change, hit the road Jack! This is one of three key elements of the alliance. Problems here usually result in no change.

3. **If you don't agree with the goals of the therapist, or do not think they are your goals, find another therapist.**

   If your therapist is telling you that you can't get there from here, then you probably won't. Stick to your guns about your goals. Recall that your goals represent all your motivations and desires and will encourage you to work hard. Agreement on goals is the second aspect of a strong alliance, so if your therapist does not accept your preferred port of destination, abandon ship.

4. **If you do not agree with the opinions or suggestions of your therapist, or if you are asking for something and not getting it, and your feedback does not alter his or her approach, find another therapist.**

   If you want to give the therapist's approach a shot, then do it. But if you don't, tell your therapist that you disagree with the approach and give him or her a chance to adjust to your feedback. But leave if he or she persists in an approach that does not seem relevant or does not fit for you. Agreement about the approach represents the third piece of the alliance. Get off at the next stop before this train derails.

5. **If you think your therapist sees your problem or situation as hopeless or unchangeable, or that it will require years to change, find another therapist.**

   Nothing is permanent, especially problems, and besides, who needs a pessimistic therapist? Hope is critical to the change process. Without it, this plane is going down; parachute out before it crashes.

6. **If you don't get something positive going within three to six sessions, talk to your therapist. If no progress is made, find another therapist.**

   Recall that change, if it is going to happen, usually happens relatively quickly. This doesn't mean you will be "cured" of all difficulties in six sessions; it only means that you will begin to notice some inroad to your concerns, and you will know that you are on the right track. Remember George Washington. Ironically, old George even requested the blood-letting to be done the third time. Don't make the same mistake when you have evidence (on the ORS) that you are not making any progress. Just hop on the bus, Gus.[41]

7. **If the therapist (or your doctor) recommends psychiatric medication, and you have not asked for it or have any doubt whatsoever, find another therapist (or doctor). If anyone tells you that you have a chemical imbalance, discuss what that really means. If you believe that medication is the right choice for you, then try it.**

   Please keep in mind that just like bloodletting in George Washington's era, treatments today are just prevailing wisdoms of this day and time. They are driven by market pressures and economics. Drug companies spend far more money on advertising than on research and development, about $10,000 per physician per year. It is hard for any doctor to resist such a barrage of marketing; they just don't have the time to research drug company claims about their products. Drugs are the prevailing wisdom of the day. If that fits for you, as it does for many, then go for it; if it doesn't, please feel free to just say "no" to drugs. You don't need to discuss much . . . just drop off the key Lee, and get yourself free.[42]

Notes

1. From perhaps the first known self-help book, aptly entitled *Self-Help* and published in 1882 (London: John Murray).

2. All of the discussion of the factors that contribute to success in therapy draws heavily on the work of Michael Lambert. See Ted Assay and Michael Lambert, "The Empirical Case for the Common Factors in Therapy: Quantitative Findings," in *The Heart and Soul of Change: What Works in Therapy,* eds. Mark Hubble, Barry Duncan and Scott Miller (Washington, DC: American Psychological Association, 1999).

3. This section relies on Scott Miller, Barry Duncan and Mark Hubble, *Escape from Babel* (New York: Norton, 1997). Two caveats here: one, not everyone agrees that all approaches are created equal; and two, while medication has been found to be about as effective as psychotherapy in the short run, longer term follow-up studies give the clear edge to therapy over medication. (See also note 6.)

4. The work of Art Bohart and Karen Tallman heavily influenced this discussion about clients. See Bohart and Tallman, *What Clients Do to Make Therapy Work* (Washington, DC: American Psychological Association, 1999); and Tallman and Bohart, "The Client as a Common Factor: Clients as Self-Healers," in *The Heart and Soul of Change: What Works in Therapy,* eds. Mark Hubble, Barry Duncan and Scott Miller (Washington, DC: American Psychological Association, 1999).

5. Meta-analytic research by Bruce Wampold suggests that these figures may even underestimate the centrality of client and relationship factors. See Wampold, *The Great Psychotherapy Debate: Models, Methods, and Findings* (Mahwah, NJ: Erlbaum, 2001).

6. The pitfalls and pratfalls of the mental health field—as well as solutions to the noted problems—are detailed in Barry Duncan, Scott Miller and Jacqueline Sparks, *The Heroic Client: A Revolutionary Way to Improve Effectiveness* (San Francisco: Jossey-Bass, 2004).

7. This section and others of this chapter are adapted from Mark Hubble and Barry Duncan, *The Great Mental Health Rip Off*, unpublished manuscript, 1996.

8. This interpretation of the story is adapted from Gregory Rusk, "Wizards, Humbugs, or Witches," in *Heroic Clients, Heroic Agencies: Partners for Change*, eds. Barry Duncan and Jacqueline Sparks (ISTC Press, 2002).

9. "Tin Man" by America (written by Dewey Dunnell) from the album *Holiday*, Warner Bros. Records, 1974.

10. The research of this section is reviewed in Barry Duncan, Scott Miller and Jacqueline Sparks, *The Heroic Client: A Revolutionary Way to Improve Effectiveness* (San Francisco: Jossey Bass, 2004) and relies on the pioneering work of Ken Howard in Howard et al., "The Dose-Effect Relationship in Psychotherapy," *American Psychologist*, 41.2 (1986): 159–64; and Michael Lambert, in Lambert "The Effects of Providing Therapists with Feedback on Patient Progress During Psychotherapy: Are Outcomes Enhanced?" *Psychotherapy Research*, 11.1 (2001):49–68; as well as the work of my colleagues and myself, in Scott Miller, "Using Outcome to Inform and Improve Treatment Outcomes," *Journal of Brief Therapy* (2005).

11. Scott Miller, et al. The Outcome Rating Scale: A Preliminary Study of Reliability, Validity, and Feasibility of a Brief Visual Analogue Measure. *Journal of Brief Therapy* 2. (2003): 91–100.

12. Elie Wiesel, *The Gates of the Forest* (New York: Schocken Books, 1966), i–iv.

13. The validation discussion is adapted from Barry Duncan, Andrew Solovey and Gregory Rusk, *Changing the Rules: A Client-Directed Approach to Therapy* (New York, NY: Guilford, 1992), which was our first attempt to translate research about the importance of "affirmation" to the therapy process.

14. This section is adapted from Barry Duncan, Scott Miller and Jacqueline Sparks, *The Heroic Client* (San Francisco: Jossey-Bass, 2004). It also builds on the inspiring work of Michael White and David Epston, *Narrative Means to Therapeutic Ends* (New York: Norton, 1990).

15. Christopher Peterson and Martin Seligman, *Character Strengths and Virtues* (Washington, DC: American Psychological Association, 2004).

16. This story is adapted from John Wilford, *The Riddle of the Dinosaur* (New York: Knopf, 1985).

17. This section about the relationship and the alliance is largely based on Bachelor and Horvath, "The Therapeutic Relationship," in *The Heart and Soul of Change: What Works in Therapy,* eds. Mark Hubble, Barry Duncan and Scott Miller (Washington, DC: American Psychological Association, 1999) and John Norcross, *Psychotherapy Relationships That Work* (New York Oxford Univ. Press, 2003).

18. Irene Elkin, et al. National Institute of Mental Health Treatment of Depression Collaborative Research Program: General Effectiveness of Treatments. *Archives of General Psychiatry* 46. (1989): 971–82.

19. Although the preponderance of the evidence supports this statement, there are exceptions, and not everyone agrees with the conclusion I reach here.

20. Gerard Connors, et al. The Therapeutic Alliance and Its Relationship to Alcoholism Treatment Participation and Outcome." *Journal of Consulting and Clinical Psychology.* 65.4 (1997): 588–98.

21. Barry Duncan, et al. Miller, Sparks, Claud, Reynolds, Brown and Johnson. The Session Rating Scale: Preliminary Psychometric Properties of a 'Working' Alliance Measure. *Journal of Brief Therapy* 3. (2004): 3–12.

22. Don Lederer and William Jackson, *The Mirages of Marriage* (New York: Norton, 1968).

23. Irene Elkin, et al. 'Patient-Treatment Fit' and Early Engagement in Therapy. *Psychotherapy Research* 9. (1999): 437–51.

24. Reid Hester, et al., *Effectiveness of a Community Reinforcement Approach.* Paper presented at the twenty-fourth annual meeting of the Association for the Advancement of Behavior Therapy, San Francisco, 1990.

25. We first articulated the idea of the client's theory of change in Barry Duncan, Andrew Solovey and Gregory Rusk, *Changing the Rules: A Client-Directed Approach* (New York: Guilford, 1992).

26. Barry Duncan, Mark Hubble and Scott Miller, *Psychotherapy with "Impossible" Cases: The Efficient Treatment of Therapy Veterans* (New York: Norton, 1997).

27. This discussion is adapted from Barry Duncan and Jacqueline Sparks, eds. *Heroic Clients, Heroic Agencies: Partners for Change* (Ft. Lauderdale, FL: ISTC Press, 2002).

28. Barry Duncan, Scott Miller and Jacqueline Sparks, "Exposing the mythmakers," *Psychotherapy Networker* (March/April 2000): 24–33, 52–53.

29. This entire chapter is adapted from and dedicated to the creative clinicians and researchers at the MRI: John Weakland, Paul Watzlawick, Richard Fisch and Lynn Segal. See Fisch, Weakland and Segal, *The Tactics of Change: Doing Therapy Briefly* (San Francisco: Jossey-Bass, 1982), and Watzlawick, Weakland and Fisch, *Change: Problem Formation and Problem Resolution* (New York: Norton, 1974). Their work represented one of the first challenges to the Killer Ds and consequently formed a central foundation to all my subsequent publications.

30. This chapter is adapted from several solution-focused authors, but most notably Steve de Shazer: de Shazer, *Words Were Originally Magic* (New York: Norton, 1994); de Shazer, *Keys to Solutions in Brief Therapy* (New York: Norton,1985); Insoo Kim Berg and Scott Miller: Berg and Miller, *Working with the Problem Drinker* (New York: Norton, 1992); and the solution-oriented approach of Michele Weiner-Davis: Weiner-Davis, *Divorce Busting* (New York: Simon and Schuster, 1993); William O'Hanlon and Michele Weiner-Davis, *In Search of Solutions* (New York: Norton, 2003).

31. The Four-E Method of Solution Building is adapted from my good friend John Murphy's work: John Murphy and Barry Duncan, *Brief Intervention for School Problems: Collaborating for Practical Solutions* (New York: Guilford, 1997).

32. Ron Kral, "Indirect Therapy in the Schools," in *Indirect Approaches in Therapy,* eds. Steve de Shazer and Kral (Rockville, MD: Aspen, 1986), 56–63.

33. Jeb Brown, Sandra Dreis and David Nace, "What Really Makes a Difference in Psychotherapy Outcome? Why Does Managed Care Want to Know?" in *The Heart and Soul of Change: What Works in Therapy,* eds. Mark Hubble, Barry Duncan and Scott Miller (Washington, D.C.: American Psychological Association, 1999). All of the discussion in this chapter owes tribute to the late Ken Howard, a psychologist whose pioneering work inspired a generation of research about the prediction and management of change.

34. Jason Whipple, et al. Improving the Effects of Psychotherapy: The Use of Early Identification of Treatment and Problem-Solving Strategies in Routine Practice. *Journal of Counseling Psychology* 50. (2003): 59–68.

35. The entire discussion of the use of the ORS to monitor benefit and make adjustments is adapted from Barry Duncan, Scott Miller and Jacqueline Sparks, *The Heroic Client: A Revolutionary Way to Improve Effectiveness* (San Francisco: Jossey-Bass, 2004).

36. Thanks to Nick Drury for this creative idea from his work with folks without access to others.

37. Paul Watzlawick, John Weakland and Richard Fisch, *Change: Principles of Problem Formation and Problem Resolution* (New York: Norton, 1974).

38. This story is adapted from James Flexner, *Washington: The Indispensable Man* (Boston: Little, Brown and Company, 1974).

39. All of psychotherapy owes a great deal to Saul Rosensweig, who first said, way back in 1936, that all therapies were equally effective because of the factors, discussed in chapter 1, common to all approaches. His prophetic words ring true today more than ever. Sadly, this icon of American psychology just passed away, but the impact of his work remains timeless.

40. "50 Ways to Leave your Lover" by Paul Simon (written by Paul Simon) from the album *Still Crazy After All These Years*, Warner Bros. Records, 1987.

41. Ibid.

42. Ibid.

About the Author

Barry L. Duncan, Psy.D., is a therapist, trainer, and researcher with over 17,000 hours of clinical experience. He is director of the Heart and Soul of Change Project (www.heartandsoulofchange.com), a practice-driven training and research initiative that focuses on what works in therapy, and more importantly, how to deliver it on the front lines via consumer feedback about the benefit and fit of services or what is called the Partners for Change Outcome Management System. Barry has over one hundred publications, including fifteen books. His latest books include the 2nd edition of the *Heart and Soul of Change: Delivering What Works* (American Psychological Association, 2010) and *On Becoming a Better Therapist* (American Psychological Association, 2010). He co-developed the ORS/SRS family of measures designed to give clients the voice they deserve as well as provide clients, clinicians, administrators, and payers with feedback about the client's response to services, thus enabling more effective care tailored to client preferences. He is the developer of the clinical process of using the measures. Because of his self-help books, he has appeared on *Oprah, The View,* and several other national TV programs. He can be reached at barrylduncan@comcast.net and www.heartandsoulofchange.com.